Public Administration

A Critical Perspective

Robert D. Miewald
Department of Political Science
University of Nebraska—Lincoln

McGraw-Hill Book Company

New York St. Louis San Francisco Auckland Bogotá Düsseldorf
Johannesburg London Madrid Mexico Montreal New Delhi
Panama Paris São Paulo Singapore Sydney Tokyo Toronto

PUBLIC ADMINISTRATION: A Critical Perspective

1234567890 DODO 783210987

This book was set in Times Roman by National ShareGraphic, Inc.
The editors were Lyle Linder and Laura D. Warner;
the cover was designed by Joseph Gillians;
the production supervisor was Charles Hess.
R. R. Donnelley & Sons Company was printer and binder.

Library of Congress Cataloging in Publication Data

Miewald, Robert D
Public administration.

Includes index.
1. Public administration. I. Title.
JF1351.M53 350 77-24337
ISBN 0-07-041908-6

ACKNOWLEDGMENTS

Quotations in the text are reprinted from the following sources:
page 19: From *Decadence* by Jim Hougan. Copyright © 1975; reprinted by permission of William Morrow and Company, New York.
page 99: From *Gravity's Rainbow* by Thomas Pynchon. Copyright © 1974; reprinted by permission of Viking Press, New York.
page 49: From *The Sunlight Dialogues* by JohnGardner. Copyright © 1972; reprinted by permission of Alfred A. Knopf, Inc., New York.
page 122: From *The Bureaucrat*, vol. 5, no. 1 (April 1976). Copyright © 1976; reprinted by permission of Sage Publications, Inc., Beverly Hills, Calif.
page 181: From *The Case of Sergeant Grischa* by Arnold Zweig. Copyright © 1927; reprinted by permission of Viking Press, New York.

Contents

Preface

Ralph Waldo Emerson once wrote, "There are some subjects which have a kind of prescriptive right to dull treatment." Public administration has always been one of those subjects. This is so because textbooks in the field tend to reflect two questionable premises: (1) the reader is going to become an administrator, and (2) the reader will learn scientifically valid methods for making things work well. The time is ripe for a book with a more realistic basis, namely, the reader is or will become an "administratee," and things seldom work at all, let alone well.

However, this book is not meant to be one more disjointed and cranky screed on the evils of the administrative state or the organization man. Instead, it takes the unifying concept of the study and practice of administration and presents its reverse side in order to develop a coherent way of understanding the field. Administration is nothing if not the implementation of a tightly structured rationality; by using the tension between that rationality and the "everything else" which is thereby excluded—and which will be defined as "irrationality"—one can begin to make sense out of a number of current problems.

To act rationally, a person must possess a certain body of knowledge and be motivated by certain values. This book raises a question often ignored by most writers: What if the knowledge of the administrators is defective or at least severely limited? Further, what if that knowledge promotes values which are repugnant to other members of society? In short, how can administration, based as it must be on a stable body of knowledge, function in a universe of divergent ways of knowing and a multitude of values? The rationality-irrationality theme opens up a new and valuable perspective on problems at both the societal and the individual levels.

Public administration is the heart of modern politics, largely because the nature of reality is not an abstract question for the bureaucracy; the formal rules describe what is and what is not. But if politics is a way in which citizens can change the definition of social reality, how do we accomplish that today? Furthermore, at the individual level, within the organizations where we will spend most of our lives, each of us is a unit of potential irrationality. Each of us has the capacity to foul up the best-laid plans. It is from the various devices used to ensure a rational discipline extending to all members of the organization that the traditional study of administration, public or private, draws its substance. Organizations are not evil because they require predictability, which is the only basis for any accomplishment, but the pressure for compliance does place a burden on the individual.

Although the tension between rationality and irrationality is a useful way of investigating public administration, it must be admitted that this tension does not automatically lead to any brilliant conclusions about the resolution of the disharmony. There is no endorsement here of any of the presently popular nostrums—not transcendental meditation, nor primal therapy, nor sensitivity training, nor behavior mod, nor biofeedback, nor organic cooking, nor communal living, nor revolution, nor consciousness expansion by mescaline or muscatel. The whole point is that the tension is more than ever a part of the human condition. To resolve the conflict would be to make us all less than human—either beasts or machines. For the impatient reader, there is only the consolation that that's the way it is, and it is up to each individual to make a separate peace with the situation.

So this is no time for a dull book in public administration. There is rather a need for a rowdy, contentious book. We are done for if administration is regarded as a science which must be presented in a solemn and reverent fashion. The subject is fascinating because it is so large a part of our existence, and therefore every aspect of it ought to be subject to the liveliest discussion. Administration is too important to be left to the administrators, and society cannot afford to relegate the subject to professional training schools. If we are not to go gentle into a totally administered society, administration must be a substantial part of a liberal education.

The word "perspective" in the title is an admission that the book is not a codification of all the world's wisdom about public administration. Only a single view is presented, and thus there is an inevitable degree of distortion. None of the conclusions, however, is the product of a feverish imagination. Even the most extreme statement is connected to the basic premises about the direction in which our society is moving. Decent people, sensitive people, people of goodwill and right reason may say, "Yes, but surely we will never actually go that far." Perhaps not, or so one devoutly hopes. But the defenses against the encroachment of administration into inappropriate territory will be more secure when we stop to think about where and how to draw the line. If some of the assertions in this book aid in such reflection, than it shall have succeeded.

The production of a book, I found, requires a whole lot of "cooperative human effort," and the other participants, whether willing or not, have my sincere thanks. Peter Shocket deserves a special note of appreciation; in his fashion, he stimulated me to start and finish the book. Kenneth Dolbeare, Peter Kobrak, Joe Cayer, and Ron Schmidt read all or part of the manuscript and generously provided many helpful comments. The people at McGraw-Hill gave the lie to my contention that big organizations do not work well. In particular, Lyle Linder's advice and encouragement were always welcome. Laura Warner and others on the editing staff were invariably helpful. But there is not a jury in the land which would hold any of those good people responsible for what follows. That is mine, all mine.

Robert D. Miewald

Public Administration

Part One

Administration and Society

Chapter 1

Administration and its Limits

It was done through official channels, and halfheartedly. What they're short of is imagination. Officialdom can never cope with something really catastrophic. And the remedial measures they think up are hardly adequate for a common cold. If we let them carry on like this they'll soon be dead, and so shall we.

Albert Camus
The Plague

Our sermonette will be based on the graffiti: "Reality is a crutch." For so it is. In our various ways, we have given up on trying to comprehend the world. We latch on to some oversimplified formula and proclaim, "This is the truth! This is my reality!" And if we are able, we proceed to flail away at the universe with our pitiful little weapon.

Happily, most of us are too impotent to cause much immediate damage with our private fantasies. But not so the administrators, who are just as convinced of their official perception of reality. And their whole reason for being is the implementation of this perception. Since we are all clerks, things do not seem to be too bad. Sure, we suffer the frustration of a

Yossarian as we listen to the explanations about Catch-22. But we are content because tomorrow we will be the ones to tell other sorry devils, "There, there." No wonder the motto of the twentieth century is: "Don't get involved." Don't kick out the other person's crutch or that person might get yours on the way down.

But there is not much kicking because at the technical level, where we go about carrying out the functions we assume society has assigned to us, nothing much is out of kilter. In fact, in every day in every way, science tells us more about our little crutch. Our being is becoming more isolated on a lonely dot in a vast archipelago of functional islands.

This has meant the end of politics. Perhaps it is easy to become hopelessly romantic about politics; perhaps there never was a time when politics worked as it should. But today the vision of politics as an area of human behavior in which people try to figure out their collective future is outdated. Politics now seems a systematic series of failures.

Our society might survive in such a state of stupor, but history indicates that we are fated to be knocked about by swells of discontent. One-eyed people constantly emerge to shock the inhabitants of the kingdom of the blind, and in particular the young, because they have not yet found their crutches, ask embarrassing questions. Most of all, our senses are not yet so dull that we are prevented from seeing that several individual crutches cannot support a habitable world. We feel impending doom, we scream and moan, as we did in the 1960s, and then we sink back in exhaustion. And we will repeat the whole ordeal in a few years, since nothing has been resolved.

The thesis of this book, to be developed in sufficient detail, is that there is a problem called administration. It is a problem because, while it is self-evident that we cannot live without it, it is becoming increasingly clear that we cannot live with it. I cannot solve this riddle, and so I will not offer here a blueprint for the "new, improved, carefree administration." The only answer to the riddle is another riddle. Administration will be less of a threat the more we realize what a threat it is. To that end, this critical perspective is dedicated.

ADMINISTRATION AND ENVIRONMENT

The study of administration is not helped much by the fact that there is little agreement about the meaning of the word. One recent study identified fifteen different English uses of "administration," not an encouraging sign for a reader seeking definitional purity.[1] The aim of Chapter 1 is to avoid semantical pitfalls by stating a single working definition.

One point about the following definition must be kept in mind. We are concerned with administration in a state of uncertainty. Administration within a completely inert environment, where the consequences of every act can be predicted, is of no significance, other than to say that if such a condition ever existed then a true science of administration might be possible. Since the world is still full of surprises, even for the best prepared administrator, we must confront directly the element of uncertainty.

What, then, is administration—in a sense useful for further analysis and as something to which we can later attach the adjective "public"? It is best to start at the simplest level, that is, with the nature of the social universe we all share. Here the key word is "environment"—the people and things, characterized by some order and some chaos, with which we must cope if we are to survive. Those of us outside asylums have learned, to some degree, to relate to the environment so that we do not even notice its problematical nature. We might appreciate the dangers it poses if we could regain the eyes of an infant and see it as a "blooming, buzzing confusion" where little makes much sense. An individual cannot survive by responding to this confusion on a random basis, and we learn patterns of dealing with the environment in order to satisfy our needs. Most of us adapt so well that we presume ourselves to be in control of our environment. And what is true of the individual is also true for the group when people join together for even greater control.

THE ORGANIZATION

Just as an ability to deal successfully with the environment is a sign of maturity in individuals, so organized responses are signs of civilization. The ability to organize is a prerequisite for anything but the crudest sort of social arrangements. However, we should never forget that the organization is costly for the individual, and after several thousand years we are not close to answering the great ethical questions about organized life. As the historian Carl Becker remarked of the paradox of organization, "the power of man has been extended by limiting the freedom of men."[2] Self-imprisonment through enduring relations with others makes us free in the sense of having a wider range of choices among alternatives. To achieve a variety of goals, we have to cooperate with others, and cooperation usually requires subordination on the part of someone. Even the superiors, however, lose some independence of action since they must now take into account the behavior of others in the group.

ADMINISTRATION

Anarchists insist that the cooperation needed for organized activity could be a natural, spontaneous human act. If that were so, we would need to go no further, for such a happy world would not require administration. But here it must be emphasized that organizations do not *do* anything. Individuals do things together in certain patterns, and that is what we call an organization. However, there is no magic way to ensure that each individual will do something in exactly the way necessary for the achievement of collective goals. Most organizations require some system of control, and it is this system which can be called, in the most general sense, "administration." It is no doubt true that all human endeavor involves administration. But such a broad definition does not tell us enough about administration or, more importantly, about what is not administration. And you will recall that the title of the chapter is administration *and its limits.*

GOALS

We come closer to the essence of administration when we concentrate on goals. Administrators are not in charge of random behavior; administrators do not run an organization so that members can do whatever they please. Thus, the study of administration is concerned with the "formal organization," that is, with a group of individuals who have been brought together for the attainment of more or less explicit goals. In actuality, the line between the formal and informal organization is often very vague, but we generally recognize that some cooperative human effort does not require all the paraphernalia of administration. The family has traditionally been one sanctuary from the administrator, although the proliferation of by-the-number manuals on how to enjoy sex or rear children is an ominous sign.

RATIONALITY

Our definition now reads: Administration is the means by which formal goals are achieved through cooperative human effort. It is still necessary to incorporate into that definition the most complex component: a high degree of rationality. This concept continues to be the intellectual quicksand into which the student of administration easily disappears. After all, rationality is the key to all human action, inside or outside the organization.

In his analysis of the concept of rationality in political science, Edward Friedland provides a good summary of the high-powered theorizing about the term. Most important, he does not overlook the marshmallow core of all the theories: "At their best, theories of rationality are logically consistent presentations built upon a set of necessarily unprovable beliefs about the way in which choices should be made." He also reminds us of the paradox of our faith in reason. Rationality, as a function of independent thought, permits us to engage in social criticism, even though "the standards of our consciousness, the way in which we think about what is reasonable, and what accords with reason and what does not" are products of specific social institutions.[3] What, then, does this tenuous concept mean in the real world of administration?

A rational act is one designed to accomplish certain goals. Well and good, but how do we determine what is rational action in any specific situation? Theorists would tell us that individual rationality is almost impossible to assess, except through hindsight. If we observe a person to evaluate his or her rationality, we must know the following:

1 *The person's goals.* Beyond a certain point, most people do not have their lives plotted out in terms of goals and subgoals.
2 *The information available at the time of decision.* Most people engage in very limited search activity, which is probably wise since a lifetime is not enough to acquire every bit of relevant data.
3 *The person's belief disposition or value system.* How does one attach weights or assign priorities to the various alternatives?
4 *Complete exposure of all alternatives.* Every possible choice must be identified and compared with all others, and the best one selected.

And so, after our rational actor has spent three days making a decision about getting out of bed, the next problem is which shoe to put on first.

There are other caveats about rationality to be noted.

Rationality is not an absolute. It is defined according to specific values and information. If somebody is convinced that he is Napoleon, is he irrational in planning for the invasion of Russia? Recently, a couple in California were informed by their religious beliefs that their son had been cured of diabetes, and he died when they withheld his insulin. Many were shocked by what appeared to be an act of cruel madness, but we are wrong in calling it irrational behavior because we do not share their view of the world.

Rationality is not a "good" thing. Simply put, one can rationally carry out evil acts. The student who, a decade ago, killed several people at the University of Texas demonstrated a high degree of rationality in conducting the slaughter. It would have been far better had he irrationally selected a BB gun instead of a rifle for his bloody work.

Most important for our purposes, there are levels of rationality. Although many writers have made the same point, Karl Mannheim offered one of the most concise discussions of the differences. He identified first "substantive rationality," defined as "an act of thought which reveals intelligent insight into the interrelations of events in a given situation." It is the ability to place one's acts within the context of a bigger picture. Substantive rationality is not easy to define further except in contrast to Mannheim's second type, namely, "functional rationality." That is based on the ability to use predetermined techniques in the attainment of specific goals. The most grotesque example of such rationality was provided by the Nazis in their solution of the "Jewish problem" by committing genocide in a very efficient manner. In terms of substantive rationality, most of us would call all that fine administration an insane act of barbarism.[4]

The difference between the two types emerges all the time in modern administration. The police who, on a hot summer day in the ghetto, insist on the rigid enforcement of minor laws and thus incite a riot can argue that they are not getting paid to be substantively rational. To take another pathetic example, it was reported that the Illinois Public Aid Department had been sending letters reading, in part, "Beginning Feb. 1, 1976, your medical assistance will be discontinued. . . . It has been reported to our office that you expired on Jan. 1, 1976." If we assume that the officials were not believers in the occult, how do we account for their attempts at communicating with the dead? At a functional level, it makes sense since the agency must communicate with its clients, living or dead. To an outside observer, the exercise must be seen as both tasteless and absurd—in a word, irrational.

We shall see that many of our negative reactions toward bureaucracy result from the pursuit of functional rationality to harmful extremes. At the same time, in a practical sense, substantive is not always preferable to functional rationality. If we were to see our mail carriers sitting on the curb contemplating their role in the cosmic scheme of things, we would probably shout at them to deliver the letter, the sooner the better. It is also doubtful whether any political organization can survive on the basis of substantive rationality. Would the U.S. Corps of Engineers, for example, be so prosperous had it taken the broad view and told members of Congress that the intermittent trickles of water in their home districts were not navigable streams ready for expensive improvements? And how many bureaucratic leaders are there who feel they can afford to turn back unused funds at the end of a fiscal year? Perhaps a major reason for our disillusionment with Washington is that we see that the federal government is a collection of functionally rational bureaucracies, the sum total of which is not the public interest. Why this is so is the subject of later chapters; right now we must place the concept of rationality within the organizational context.

ORGANIZATIONAL RATIONALITY

We are probably lucky that administrators are not philosophers, for they might spend all their time brooding about insoluble metaphysical problems and never get anything accomplished. They know only that they are to get a job done in terms of whatever goals were given to them. The goal, in short, is a statement about how a certain part of the total environment is to be modified, about that part of the entire universe against which rational action is to be applied. But as I said, rationality presupposes the possession of information about the environment. It follows that the environment of any organization must yield a fairly stable, reliable, predictable body of information upon which one can base a rational response.

Only when we can perceive the environment as a stable and predictable thing can we have a rational goal. For example, why has the United States government, until very recently, not included among its many agencies a Bureau of Earthquakes? It is simply because this most devastating of cataclysms was exempt from our way of knowing; earthquakes were an act of God, and it is futile to base an administrative response on the will of the Almighty. Other societies, of course, have not been so inhibited by their knowledge, and they had administrative responses such as sacrificing a virgin or two. Now that our science has accumulated what we feel is reliable information about earthquakes, it is possible to develop an organization to deal with the problem.

Take another example: The person who believes that evil spirits can possess the body has few administrative agencies to turn to. In fact, that person would probably be taken away since the rest of us "know" that the environment does not contain such spirits. But if enough of us become convinced that devils do exist, then we will probably demand the services of some organization to protect us. A Bureau of Exorcism would be created, and a complete procedure for responding to cases of possession would be followed. The example is not that farfetched since this again is an area that other societies, including our ancestors in Salem, have felt obliged to administer.

If everything is known about its share of the environment, the organization can make quite precise calculations. As I said at the outset, such a situation is extremely rare. The environment still keeps some secrets and all manner of unforeseen events occur. But as long as some premises for action are known, the rational organization can function, and it will perform as long as it continues to get reliable information about its environment. Still, in the face of that lurking uncertainty, the intelligent administrators run the risk of nervous breakdowns, particularly when they consider that there is probably an infinite number of things to know about every minor decision.

What do administrators do to preserve some peace of mind? As Herbert Simon put it, each organization creates a limited version of rationality; "Administrative theory is peculiarly the theory of intended and bounded rationality—of the behavior of human beings who *satisfice* because they have not the wits to *maximize*."[5] With his notion of "bounded rationality," Simon is describing a world view which does not include every conceivable variable, but instead provides just enough premises for the organizational member to get by, to "satisfice." It is a most imperfect rationality, but it does prescribe a manageable routine for dealing with the relevant part of the environment so that members can avoid chaos. The organization provides a picture to its members to tell them what is and what is not. It is a formal, precise description in most cases, and although it is not quite the same as "knowing" reality—in fact, it is much closer to "constructing" reality, especially for public organizations which have the power of the state to enforce their pictures—it is usually sufficient to get the job done.

A problem arises when the environment does not coincide with the bounded rationality. Thus we find that organizations have taken a variety of steps to guard against an environment, physical or social, which does not always function according to the established routines.

1 Provide for an "emergency." This is the favorite of the military, with its plans for every possible contingency: e.g., what do we do if Poland invades Bolivia? Unfortunately, so much of this is planning for the unknown in terms of the known. Such planning accounts for the surrealism of civil defense. Most organizations have their plans for what everyone is supposed to do when the H-bomb goes off in the cafeteria. We read them, but we know full well that when the disaster strikes we will all panic.

2 Provide for a new decision about the nature of the world. This is generally difficult since the persons with the authority for changing the bounded rationality tend to be in high and isolated positions, which is understandable because it would not do to have every member capable of redefining what the organization is about. Students who have ever tried to get a waiver of the university's definition of an education so that they can graduate know some of the problems here; there probably has never been a recorded instance of a waiver being granted by the first person contacted.

3 Ignore reality and continue to cram everything into manageable categories, regardless of the environment. Or in the words of the old stationmaster who had only two tariff rates, "Cats is dogs and guineapigs is dogs, but this 'ere tortise is a hinsect." We have all confronted this crabbed picture of reality when we have struggled with filling out forms. It is often hard to distill our existence into the limited number of categories recognized by the organization. For instance, dare José Xavier Francisco O'Hoolihan check the box marked "Spanish Surnamed"?

4 Construct your own reality. This is the most popular administrative solution. Beat down the environment to make sure that it does not provide any surprises. Most of all, if the public is unruly, domesticate them, make them "ruly." The Russians, as the masters of the complete administrative state, have shown us the way. If you do not like Soviet reality, you are obviously sick and must be cured in an institution.[6]

Herbert Simon's speculations about the future of computers in management show how easy it is to think in terms of reality construction. Because of their "flexibility and general purpose applicability," human decision makers are now superior to computers in uncertain situations. One can remove this advantage only if the environment is predictable, so that "environmental control can be a substitute for flexibility"; eliminate the need for people by eliminating the need for flexibility. Already many things formerly done by hand are now processed by machines because we have been taught not to do anything so irrational as fold, bend, spindle, or mutilate our cards. The Internal Revenue Service can handle most tax forms mechanically because we have to confine our discussion of income and expenditures to a very limited number of categories. So Simon concludes, "The stabilization of the environment for productive activity will reduce or eliminate the need for flexible response at many points in the productive process. . . .[7] This is more than homely advice for the good manager, since the environment to be stabilized includes our daily lives.

The bureaucratic construction of reality has happened often enough in history. Karl Wittfogel gives numerous examples in his book on "hydraulic societies." These were the ancient Oriental states in which the only reality was the management of a complex irrigation system. Everything in society, including the people, became part of the administrative machine.[8] Our modern society has not quite reached that stage of development, but there is legitimate cause for concern about the suggestion that Americans adopt the European system of a common identification number for all administrative purposes. That system might tend to shape our self-image as items of administration, as part of a manageable environment.

The impact of the bounded rationality can be crucial for any society, especially if, to use the language of the sociology of knowledge, a single image becomes "reified," in which case the social world "loses its comprehensibility as a human enterprise and becomes fixated as a non-human, non-humanizable, inert facticity."[9] That is, social reality is no longer commonly shared by all, but is rather a form of domination imposed by administrators who have come to view their regulations as immutable absolutes. Conflict is likely when the bounded rationality becomes more and more removed from what common sense tells the rest of us is real. In that case, all the solutions the administrators come up with may be unhealthy and unpleasant.

These solutions are unhealthy because the times do change, and the organization may be too rigid to change accordingly, particularly when the rate and direction of change is controlled by forces outside the society. All of Wittfogel's empires have long since collapsed because they could not respond. Even the Chinese, with their very elegant administrative system, got into trouble because of their oversimplified categories; Westerners were barbarians, but those barbarians had mastered the tools of modern warfare. The phenomenon can explain many military disasters. Take the case of the British General Edward Braddock and his strategy for fighting Indians. In terms of the rationality of his organization, he should have earned high marks for marching his Redcoats through the forest according to all the accepted procedures. The only problem was that the "irrational" Indians did not play by the same rules and wiped out his entire command.

These solutions are unpleasant because then society exists for the convenience of administrators and not the other way around. That is the real political challenge today. Who is actually in charge? When the organizational rationality and the collective rationality of individual citizens do not conform, whose rationality should prevail? We might want to say, the people's, because administration supposedly serves their needs. The job in the following chapters is to suggest that (1) today that is not likely to happen and (2) ways of ensuring that it does happen are not particularly effective.

MANAGEMENT

So far we have dealt with only half the job of administration, i.e., the relationship between the organization and the external environment. There remains the equally difficult problem of making organizational members at least nominal believers in the bounded rationality. The combination of techniques designed to ensure compliance we can identify as "management." It should be noted, however, that the external and internal environments are inextricably united for the administrator. If the organization is blessed with a completely stable environment, there may be no need for anything but the most mechanical response from members. The captains of slave galleys did not face any weighty managerial problems; they could simply tell the crew to row or be thrown overboard, and the whip was usually enough to encourage cooperative human effort. In less secure organizations, one must use more sophisticated methods of obtaining cooperation. Hence we have the need for management, or the rationalization of the internal dynamics of the organization.

In a simplified, two-step organization, we have, first, the administrator—the decision maker, sovereign, boss, honcho, big enchilada—and second, the worker, operative, or delegate. The administrator will know the worker not as an individual but only as a rationally constructed role designed to achieve formal goals. The trouble is that the formal role may not coincide with what the worker wants to do or thinks he or she must do. The worker remains a complex bundle of drives and ideas, quite a few of which may be irrational from the administrator's point of view. How then does the organization control the individual, especially if, as so often happens today, the worker may not care a great deal about the organization or its goals?

Certainly there are a number of formal control techniques, most of them reducible to some form of rewarding workers for good performance and punishing them for poor work. But to regularize these systems, the organization needs precise knowledge about the level of performance and an awareness of how that level relates to the desired modification of the environment. Most organizations have only incomplete information. In many situations, the free contribution of the worker may be the only thing which permits the organization to meet the challenge of the environment. The person on the organization's frontier, on the cutting edge of the organization, must be expected to do more than can be rationally determined beforehand.

Most organizations, therefore, depend upon workers who have the capacity for "self-adjustment."[10] Without that element, the organization is a house built on sand. A few years ago, a survey of Italian government uncovered an obscure bureau whose sole function was to collect and store data on weather conditions in the colonies lost by Italy in World War II. The people were doing no earthly good, but no official had given them the word to knock it off and they did not adjust themselves to changed conditions. A more tragic example occurred in Southern California. A couple went for a Sunday drive and had an apparently minor traffic accident. The husband decided to ride with the ambulance to the hospital just to make sure that there had been no serious injury. The next morning, when he had not returned, the wife called the hospital and was informed rather nonchalantly that her husband had died. When a reporter checked to find why no one had the decency to inform the woman she had become a widow, he was shown chapter and verse of the regulations of all the involved agencies—police, ambulance, hospital, coroner—that at the precise moment of death, the husband was in nobody's jurisdiction and therefore was nobody's responsibility. A rather cold alibi, and surely we would agree that one of the several functionaries could have taken the initiative to do what was humane, even if it was not required by the regs.

In his analysis of life in the bureaucracy, Anthony Downs has described the problem of management: "Every successful organization relies upon the willingness of some of its members to enlarge the scope of their roles voluntarily without being exhorted by their superiors. However, there is a marked variability in such willingness among individual officials."[11] Marked variability! What a foul phrase to throw at an administrator whose whole being craves predictability. No wonder managers wake up in a cold sweat and gnash their teeth at the countless ways in which workers can screw up the most rational plan. But it is easy to see that the net of rationality cannot be knit so tightly as to exclude the need for this variable self-adjustment.

The dread of the unknown can be seen by the tortured language of administration—bureaucratese—a strange form of English much deplored by literate people. But in reality, bureaucrats are generally trying to clarify rather than to obfuscate by their prose. They are striving for complete objectivity and precision, for the unambiguous in a world that is still full of ambiguities. No matter how they try, language remains a gross limitation, since not every contingency can be explained before it happens. Even the ridiculous orders—"Classified material will be considered lost when it cannot be found," or "In case of fire, stand in the hall and shout 'Fire!'"—are open to possible misinterpretation by the workers.[12]

Each misinterpretation demands further clarification, and eventually there are so many directives that there is a need for outright disobedience. Many organizations are so ponderous that they could not move at all if every order were obeyed. We are familiar with the abuse of this technicality by unhappy civil servants who, if they cannot legally strike, can still bring the organization to a standstill by doing what they are supposed to do. In fact, the Germans have become so administratively muscle-bound that one cabinet minister had to warn his subordinates that "strict adherence to the law is a violation of official trust."[13]

Therefore, no organization can depend solely upon the written statements in the job specifications. Not as long as the unexpected might occur, which is why the military, the organization with the most unpredictable environment, has never been an 8-to-5 routine and why generals hand out medals for conduct "above and beyond the call of duty." To lesser degrees, other organizations depend upon behavior above and beyond what is formally required if they are to meet their goals. For the administrator, the frustrating fact is that there is no way to ensure that such behavior will be available when it is needed.

THE DILEMMA OF ADMINISTRATION

If administration is a matter of stabilizing the unstable, rationalizing the irrational, predicting the unpredictable, knowing the unknown, it should be clear that a formally determined bounded rationality, limited in time and space, is not enough. Put another way, the perfect organization would be one in which each member promotes organizational goals without direction from above. But that leads to a contradiction since there would then be total agreement among all members and thus no need for administrators or formal organizations. Human reproduction, to take one notable example, has continued to meet the goal of survival of the species (if not of more limited national goals) without an organizational overhead largely because of the spontaneous desire of participants to cooperate, and it would be superfluous to have a bureau to encourage this activity. The work of most organizations is just not as much fun.

The contention is that the individual remains an individual and the organization remains an organization. Both have their own style of rationality. The point is hardly new since at one time or another all the big names in the study of administration have come across the same problem of meshing individual and organization goals. According to the sociologist Amitai Etzioni, the inevitable result is a persistent "organizational dilemma" consisting of the strains, "which can be reduced but not eliminated," between rationality and nonrationality. That idea is the most concise summary of almost everything written on administration, public or private.[14]

The whole body of administrative theory seems to rest on the organizational dilemma. Take any book on the subject and surely there will be a chapter on the synthesis, the convergence, the integration, or the blending of the extremes of individual and organizational fulfillment. Etzioni is one of the few writers to say quite bluntly that the dilemma cannot be reconciled. The only thing to do is recognize the fact and get on with an approach that balances the two. Anything more profound than that you will not find in this book, since the problem is basically the same one which has perplexed the great social thinkers throughout history: how to be a free individual and a part of the social group. Anton Zijderveld, in his discussion of *homo duplex,* or dual man, quotes Martin Luther: "Each individual human being has on earth two personalities: one for himself, bound to nobody but God alone, but also a worldly personality, through which he is bound to other people."[15] The perpetuation of this uneasy arrangement is the best deal we can ever expect.

THE ADMINISTRATIVE MENTALITY

For many in our society, the call for a truce may seem cowardly and the claim of a hopeless dilemma a sign of defeatism. Western civilization encourages us to see the world through the eyes of the administrator, for whom little is impossible. Max Weber, the great German sociologist, had a wonderful term to describe our progress; he wrote often of "the disenchantment of the world." Our peculiar style of knowing has for centuries been taking affairs out of the hands of gods, witch doctors, experts in evil humors, and even poets. We feel better if things are controlled by learned men and women who supposedly know the facts—the facts derived from a very special mode of perception. We know, or presume to know, how the world works, and we are inspired to do something with this knowledge. We are on the crest of a 500-year wave of rationality.

The relationship to empirical facts is the most striking characteristic of Western thought. Moreover, when we translate these facts into the ultimate abstractions of mathematics, we can replace a lively reality with numbers. Instead of dealing with the world in all its complexity, it is possible for us to manipulate a supposed reality through manageable symbols. To be sure, we are doing what other societies have done; we are providing an order to a disorderly world. People must comprehend their environment and develop ways of coping with it so that they are not completely dependent upon the unknown. Some cultures have relied upon the teachings of custom, others on magic. And we, as Weber put it, depend upon the rational, calculative techniques which have grown out of our belief in an empirically derived understanding of the relationship among things.

There are two particularly significant elements in the administrative mentality. One is the dependence upon a rational science, based upon experimental methods which reject all supernatural or otherworldly explanations; it is a science pursuing an objective causal chain. Theodore Roszak, the chronicler of the counterculture, described this mode of thought as "the myth of objective consciousness" the aim of which is to "cultivate a state of consciousness cleansed of all subjective distortion, all personal involvement."[16] Kenneth Keniston, in his search for the roots of modern alienation, adds further exclusions from reality demanded by the "methaphysic of empiricism": the intangible worlds of poetry, art, feeling, and religion.[17] For administration, such things are important only if they explain what makes the world work.

The second element of the administrative mentality is, in a practical sense, the more important one. It is the feeling that knowledge about the world carries with it an implicit demand for action. If it is technologically feasible to go to the moon, then we must go. If the SST will fly us from New York to London in a few hours, then we must have it, regardless of the damage done to the ecology. Some insist, in fact, that the only real political questions concern when, and not whether, we act on what is known. The pure scientist may show some doubt about what can actually be known, but for the administrator, a vulgar understanding of the scientific enterprise reveals all sorts of possibilities for taming the environment.

There is a body of literature which warns us in the most forceful terms that there is no limit to what is administratable. The French writer Jacques Ellul has been most eloquent in presenting a chilling vision of an autonomous technological impuse which must devour every independent factor in society, up to and including men, women, and children.[18] Roderick Seidenberg, in his *Post-Historic Man,* developed the thesis that "organization demands further organization," and that "perfected organization is conceivable only in terms of universal organization."[19] If we accept the administrative mentality, we can look forward to the perfection of what Lewis Mumford called the "megamachine": the complete system in which there can be no troublesome unknowns.[20]

The administrative mentality is a function of what John Schaar refers to as "the bureaucratic epistemology," in which "the only legitimate instrument of knowledge is objective, technically trained intellect, and the only acceptable mode of discourse is the cognitive mode."[21] Under the influence of this epistemology, all things become possible, and we roll merrily along, figuring that all our problems will yield to some "technological fix." With enough money and talent, we can always build a bigger and better something or other. And superficially, we have succeeded, as our standard of living seems to attest. But now more people are questioning whether all this rationalization process is the sole purpose of human existence. For many, society turns out to be the punch line to a ghastly joke: by behaving very, very rationally, we have created a world which looks like a lunatic's nightmare.

All the old answers seem worthless. We cannot revert to a more tranquil era, nor can we burn it all down by doing the Red Guard number, because we have tasted the good life. As every crisis indicates, the majority of us are not anxious to give up the benefits of technology for the uncertain joys of scrounging for subsistence in a commune. Come what may, our message to our leaders is: "Let the good times roll!" Nor can we trust in God, because somewhere in the process He was defined away or became expendable. Nor can we blame the whole thing on fate, because deep in our hearts we know we are the responsible ones. It would be quite curious if we should destroy ourselves since the problems are very much of our own creation. We thought we knew what we were doing when we did it, and there is nothing to say that our brains and willpower cannot save the day—if we behave in a rational manner.

ADMINISTRATION AND REASON

The study of administration, a relatively new academic discipline, has had as its mission nothing less than the rationalization of this rationalization. It has not been, therefore, a source of consolation for the unhappy or a guide to the perplexed; it has not told us anything about the contradictory elements making up the whole—the *yin* and the *yang* of rationality and irrationality. Administration emphasizes the one side, the side representing order, regularity, predictability, calculability. But what about the antithesis? Students of administration have had little taste for this "something else" because it threatens to negate all their theories. When they try their hand at it, the result is rather awkward—something like inviting the poet Allen Ginsberg to serve on a fifteen-member advisory committee or appointing a vice president in charge of blue-eyed soul.

It comes down to this: Administration is the pursuit of formal goals as required by a limited rationality derived from knowledge about the environment. But what if that knowledge is defective? What if administrators are making rational decisions about a world that does not exist? The inherent weakness of the bureaucratic epistemology can be seen by considering other bases of knowledge which have seldom been incorporated within administrative thought. There is religious knowledge, but no bureaucracy can operate for long from a purely mystical base; one of the constant sources of social conflict has been the bureaucratization of the church and the eruption of resistance caused by a new divinely inspired prophet. There is the truth of art, which is why the artist and the administrator have usually been at odds. And most of all, there is common sense, that great communion with the social world in which we all share, that sense which is, according to Hannah Arendt, "the political sense par excellence."[22] The average person is most likely to be offended by the bureaucratic style when the common sense of things is violated. Not one of these ways of knowing is infallible, and a society based upon a single approach would be as intolerable as one built solely upon scientific rationality. Any social organization which depends upon a single source of knowledge can engage only in functional, and not substantive, rationality.

Joseph Royce, a psychologist, has defined the problem as one of encapsulation. This epistemological disease involves "looking at life partially, but issuing statements concerning the wholeness of living." The term, Royce maintains, "refers to projecting a knowledge of ultimate reality from the perceptual framework of a limited reality image." Because of encapsulation, modern society suffers from an epidemic of the "malady of meaninglessness"; so much of the richness of life has been excised.[23]

The terminally encapsulated individual is perhaps nothing more than tiresome when he is a guy in a bar explaining his view on racial integration or a freak returning from a drug-induced high. Life becomes a little stickier when he is our boss in the organization, able to make decisions about our career goals and beginning to grumble about "wrongthinkers." The problem of encapsulation is most intense when an entire government agency suffers from the malfunction. If we have no means of appeal, the bureaucrat can tell us that black is white and, unless we look forward to a little time in the slammer, we had better respond, "Yes, and ain't it beautiful!"

The obvious prescription here is omniscience. Failing that—as we most certainly will—the next best thing is humility. All people, but most of all those in power, should be reminded of Oliver Cromwell's plea: "I beseech you, in the bowels of Christ, think it possible that you may be mistaken." It would be naïve, however, to believe that exhortation will instill in administrators a feeling of humility. My contention is that a more reliable means must be devised, and as far as the administration of public affairs is concerned, that means should be an operational political overhead.

ON THE NEED FOR LIMITS

There are two things which must be protected from domination by the bureaucratic epistemology and which might be preserved through politics. First, there is the question of "meaning" in life. Management scientists talk much about motivation, but none of them have really come up with a good reason to even begin truckin', let alone for keeping on. If you are only a hunk of "human resources," with a definite market value for the organization, what meaning can life offer? With the nearly complete collapse of the theological assumptions which kept the Protestant Ethic alive, why do we play the game except to accumulate material benefits?

The recent convulsions in postindustrial societies are products of a sense of meaninglessness which cannot be cured by the most soothing techniques of social adjustment. As the wise French humanist Gabriel Marcel wrote of the victims of administration, "this strange reduction of a personality to an official identity must have an inevitable repercussion on the way I am forced to grasp myself."[24] What is that remaining image? It is that of a dehumanized tool. Small wonder then that, in a variety of ways, people are going out of their minds. What solace is there in remaining within a mind that is so deformed by a repressive epistemology?

The social spasm caused by the birth and death of the most recent counterculture will be repeated. In one of the more balanced assessments of the movement, Frank Musgrove argues that the counterculture was a search for ecstasy, "the capacity to stand outside the obvious"; it was an attempt to break out of the "obvious" social reality and to come in contact again with the richness of human life.[25] It seems to have failed, and we are left with little bands of "nay-sayers" who are even more helpless than ever before the process of rationalization. As Jim Hougan describes the sadness of a resistance almost as pointless as the system it rejects:

> Half-baked or boiled Napoleons of one True Faith and another proclaim themselves everywhere—God, Prophet, Healer and General. Never have we had so many, a nation of ultimate solutions. Covens clot in the vicinity of every ersatz insight; movements gather in persecuted queues that go nowhere; salvation boogies behind a thousand psychic corners, illuminated in the flash of specula, bathed in chants and primal screams. Existence becomes increasingly ceremonial, a dance to Reason, part homage, part exorcism.[26]

One hates casting a morbid pall over the discussion, but then what is administration itself if not such a pall? Any study of administration must at least acknowledge the arguments made by such thinkers as Norman O. Brown that work is "effort spent in fighting death" and that our best weapon in this futile effort is the large, impersonal, and presumably immortal organization.[27] Particularly since the publication of Ernest Becker's *The Denial of Death,* administration must be seen as a branch of thanatology. It is today the most powerful "vital lie" we tell ourselves to distract our minds from our horrible fate—we are animals who will die and rot away. Our organizations are gratefully accepted instruments of repression, the value of which "is that is makes it possible to live decisively in an overwhelmingly miraculous and incomprehensible world, a world so full of beauty, majesty, and terror that if animals perceived it all they would be paralyzed to act."[28] Becker is right in maintaining that we cannot achieve a life free of repression since that would expose us to the unspeakable terror of existence. But insofar as administration, as repression, is a form of "normality" based on the "refusal of reality," there is something obscene about the demands which the organization makes of us.

If we must huddle together against the cold of an unfair world, I agree with Miguel de Unamuno that we should not have to put up with a "leader who is not penetrated with the feeling that he who orders a people orders men, men of flesh and bone, men who are born, suffer, and, although they do not wish to die, die."[29] A character in the novel *Bang the Drum Slowly* says, "Everybody knows everybody is dying. That is why people are nice."[30] But that one absolute fact, so awful that it lends dignity to every life and provides us our one common bond, is not so easily acknowledged in an organized world. How empty is Donne's consolation when it is updated to read, "every man is a piece of the machine"; any man's death does not diminish General Widgets or the U.S. Post Office. Just send in a requisition to personnel for another expertly tooled and interchangeable part, and it is business as usual. If our death can never be more than another statistic, why bother?

The second thing to be protected from bureaucratic epistemology is a sense of motion. Administration is necessarily a foe of social movement and strives to create a steady state by the elimination of the tension between what is and what is becoming. Life is a process of becoming and without a recognition of this there is no meaning. Politics represents motion; politics is the sign of a society in flux. To be sure, the practice of politics is frequently in the opposite direction, an instrument of repression. In modern times, in particular, politics is an ally of administration in the work of reproducing the existing reality. Politics, however, should be a means of preserving the life-force of motion, of enabling us to seek meaning and to grow within an expanding universe. Kenneth Dolbeare wrote that the problem of political change is an epistemological one—"A problem of how to think and what to think about."[31] If we are not to be tiny specks caught up on a wheel of fate whose revolutions are measured in eons, politics must show alternatives to the unidimensional path of technological and administrative rationality.

As Herbert Marcuse and others have made clear, our single-minded pursuit of functional rationality has created an irrational society.[32] In the process, we have lost sight of what it is to be human. We have lost our ability to reason, in Alfred North Whitehead's view, the distinctive human trait whose purpose it is to to "promote the art of life." A new set of doctrinaires, their power now immensely greater because they are organized, have stopped our ability to speculate; and, said Whitehead, "to set limits of speculation is treason to the future."[33] The political process is the last best hope for humanity to regain the ability to speculate and to reason.

AN EXAMPLE

After all that profundity, it is now time to return to earth and apply what has been said to a specific example. The Vietnam war, an event which agitated the nation for over a decade, is an excellent case to show the weaknesses of the classic style of administrative rationality. The study of military affairs in general is most instructive for an understanding of people in organizations, because military operations delineate the problematic nature of rational behavior in the face of irrationality. Vietnam gave us a particularly long and painful exposure to the fact that the world is still an intractable thing for the administrator.

Vietnam was a unique event: a bureaucratic war. The most dynamic, the most unpredictable of human activity was being carefully managed by thousands of bureaucrats. In the final analysis, we may be thankful that it was such a disaster. Our efforts may not have broken the will of the Viet Cong, but they did discourage, at least temporarily, an emerging administrative elite. The 1960s, in retrospect, were dangerous years. The "best and the brightest" had convinced the political leadership that they could administer a foreign war while ensuring domestic peace at home. Had they succeeded, there might have been little left to stop them from perfecting a totally administered society. Their most arrogant attempt was in the rationalization of warfare, and the humiliating defeat there has caused a loss of confidence in administration.[34]

This bureaucratic control was a peculiarly civilian addition to the art of war, for stereotypes to the contrary, military professionals are not model bureaucrats. There remains in their thinking a wide streak of mysticism stemming from an appreciation of the unknown factors which can win or lose a battle. The military environment is especially misleading, even beyond the deliberate deceptions of the enemy. By its nature, the business of killing and of getting killed is not a matter of hard and fast rules. Even the diligent work of a host of contracted psychologists has not told officers all the answers about heroism and cowardice in the face of hostile fire.

Thus, throughout history, surprisingly few armies have been completely rational in their orientation. There was one major exception: During much of the eighteenth century, when warfare was the sport of kings, battles were not so much fought as choreographed. These parade-ground machines, however, were effective only when the other side played by the same rules. The Prussian Army, which had been turned into a lifeless marching machine, was torn to pieces when Napoleon unleashed the irrational violence of nationalism. Wild passion and individual enthusiasm found a place in warfare again, but at a loss in administrative elegance. From the Napoleonic Wars until Vietnam, warfare tended to take on the character of an emotional crusade which, once begun, could scarcely be controlled until the bitter end.

In Vietnam, the Pentagon, freshly staffed by a new corps of "take-charge" technocrats, asked whether the bureaucratization of violence was possible. Odd as it seems now, they convinced themselves that the answer was yes. There followed all those strange manifestations of war with bureaucrats in command. There were no front lines and heroic charges. Instead, we had body counts and kill ratios; dispassionate language was used to describe a very passionate situation. No more "we-have-met-the-enemy" rhetoric, but instead press releases telling us, for example, "the number of South Vietnamese living under direct control of the Viet Cong hit the record low of 12.3 percent at the end of 1968, the U.S. Command said Saturday." Now that the figure is 100 percent, we need to reconsider how we were misled.

To see what went wrong, one must go back to the basic premises of foreign policy after Eisenhower. He and his Secretary of State took a frugal approach to national defense by relying on nuclear weapons. Unfortunately, this offered only two choices—World War III or nothing. Policy makers were limited in the sort of responses they could make to foreign events. The theory during the Kennedy-Johnson years was that military power ought to be tailored to respond to a wide range of national security threats. In short, we had the concept of "limited warfare."

Limited warfare is largely a matter of administration. It is governed by the belief that violence can be accurately measured and dispensed without really exciting the domestic political scene. If the Nicaraguans are acting up, send in just enough Marines to bring them back in line. If enough force is applied, the other side will stop doing bad things. From this follows the principle of escalation; if formula X did not bring Hanoi to the conference table, then surely X plus Y will do it. The whole idea sounded so attractive, especially when it was argued that the operations could be carried out without any real political repercussions.

But violence is a volatile commodity, and in Vietnam calculations were made without knowing the effect of a certain level of violence on the enemy, or the enemy's violence on us, or of our own violence on ourselves. The "administration of violence" makes sense when part of an academic theory about international relations. In moments of intense passion, it is not so easy to execute. So while Robert McNamara and his aides were making their elaborate calculations, they oversimplified things by ignoring the crucial factors, the imponderable human elements, which do not fit into a computer program.

As John Sack wrote of the Vietnamese, they were "a wrench in the war machine, the hitch, the fatal insertion of human uncertainty into the System."[35] There is in fact no handy formula to indicate how much punishment a people can take. Some officials were surely deluded in the belief that the placement of a bomb on a target had a direct relation to the will to negotiate. After all, our own history is filled with heroes who did not know that they were beaten. Had George Washington been a systems analyst, he might have concluded that he was finished at Valley Forge. He persevered, and why should it be otherwise with the enemy in Vietnam?

The Vietnamese were a major source of "irrationality." But more importantly, the experts ignored the domestic calculations. They did not foresee the explosive political division between the hawks and doves, with both sides drawing their strength from irrational sources, from morality, from patriotism, from historical myth. The administration of violence was supposed to be just another job. Some people would deliver the mail, some would prepare welfare checks, and some would shoot bullets at those funny little men in the black pajamas. And if, in the course of things, one was shot at, there was still nothing to be alarmed about. Somebody failed to realize the consequences of telling young Americans: "Do be a good bureaucrat and kill this person we have identified as the enemy. Don't hate him, don't feel sorry for him. Just do the job." Muhammad Ali spoke for a generation when he said, "I got no fight with the Cong."

For all the good intentions—and any sane person must admit that limited warfare is preferable to the unlimited version—the country faced a grave political crisis because war cannot be contained within tidy bureaucratic compartments. And so we learned the costs involved when, in the words of one student, "the displacement of political prudence and political process by technical rationality and the processes of the functionary made its farthest advance."[36] The strategists in the Pentagon, State, and Rand did not finish reading their Clausewitz, the German military theorist who was also the greatest administrative thinker of the nineteenth century. They took his dictum that "war is a continuation of political relations by other means" as a justification for limited warfare. Clausewitz went beyond this statement to warn that warfare is conducted in a resistant medium and the element of "friction" is always introduced into grand plans by the individuals who must execute them. If you eliminate that element of irrationality, you also lose the ability to respond. Therefore he cautioned, "Everything is very simple in warfare, but the simplest thing is difficult."[37] That is a point to be remembered by all administrators, civilian or military.

This analysis is not meant to imply that the outcome in Vietnam would have been happier had we engaged in a gung-ho orgy. For present purposes, Vietnam is only a clear example of the weaknesses of a large, complex bureaucracy, grounded in Western technology, when it meets an environment which does not yield reliable information. The military machine was cleverly designed to obtain a large amount of data about the progress of the war, but almost all the indicators were terribly misleading. The bureaucracy on numerous occasions had all the data to indicate that victory had been achieved, and it convinced everyone except the enemy. As we learned in April 1975, this particular piece of bureaucratic reality was the ultimate in functional irrationality.

SO WHAT'S THE POINT?

At this stage in the traditional public administration textbook, the heavy questions will have been touched upon and the reader will be within easy reach of solid answers about the organizational maze—with the prospect that somewhere in the pyramid is a cozy little niche in which one can hide until it is time to collect the pension. How to preserve and defend that cubbyhole is the subject matter of classical public administration. It is the sort of thing that is "useful."

But I have nothing but questions. Just look at that niche one more time. What does it really mean? How will you respond when the Voice asks, "What on earth are you up to?" You can, of course, answer, "Oh, I'm building dams, fighting fires, collecting taxes, inspecting fruit, or stopping crime." That is to say, you are behaving like a good functionally rational bureaucrat, and thus you are probably guilty of a wide variety of crimes of commission and omission. Readers of Franz Kafka's *The Trial* have always wondered why the hero of the novel is taken away by mysterious strangers to be executed; maybe Josef K., just by virtue of being a clerk, was not so innocent.

Consider the pyramid again. Sure you will be rational and efficient and all that. But why? Where does that formal goal you are being rational about actually come from? What relation does it have to your job? Are you committed to it because it is a worthwhile goal or because it is a convenient excuse to justify your workload? And how much of that goal is a product of your own imagination? Is it not possible that you have convinced yourself that your work is important simply because it is being done?

There are plenty of excuses. You can claim to be carrying out "the will of the people." But who are these people? Your neighbors in Twin Oaks Estates? The boys at the Elks Club? The agent of a friendly interest group? Other bureaucrats? After all, nothing will ever come up to you and whisper, "I am the will of the people."

You can say that you are a public servant (a noble but meaningless title) and that you are necessarily committed to the Public Interest. And what does that mean? Not much, when you consider the crimes that are committed daily in the name of the public interest. The Watergate gang was only the latest in a long line to give hanky-panky in the public interest a bad name. Besides, hidden away in your air-conditioned office on the twenty-fifth floor, you will know of the public only by hearsay.

In short, how does society control you and your vision of reality? How do we poor citizens who are hardly rational by your standards live with all that awesome rationality you represent? How are you made responsible?

There are no easy routes to bureaucratic responsibility. Some procedural devices may be useful, but procedures are always capable of being incorporated within the bureaucracy itself, of becoming part of the system. The only sure way to administrative responsibility is through the conscience of the bureaucrat. And that is not much, since the perfect bureaucrat does not have anything so insubstantial and unreliable as a conscience. The only suggestion is that the best way to stimulate the rebirth of the conscience of the bureaucrat (and we are all bureaucrats today) is through politics.

REFERENCES

1 A. Dunsire, *Administration: The Word and the Science* (London: Martin Robertson, 1973), pp. 228–229.

2 Carl Becker, *Progress and Power* (Stanford, Calif.: Stanford University Press, 1936), p. 37.

3 Edward Friedland, "Introduction to the Concept of Rationality in Political Science," *University Programs Modular Studies* (Morristown, N.J.: General Learning Press, 1974), pp. 22–24.

4 Karl Mannheim, *Man and Society in an Age of Reconstruction* (New York: Harcourt, Brace, 1941), pp. 39–75.

5 Herbert Simon, *Administrative Behavior* (New York: Macmillan, 1960), p. xxiv.
6 For one man's ordeal, see Zhores and Roy Medvedev, *A Question of Madness* (New York: Knopf, 1971).
7 Herbert Simon, *The Shape of Automation for Men and Management* (New York: Harper & Row, 1965), pp. 40–42.
8 Karl Wittfogel, *Oriental Despotism* (New Haven, Conn.: Yale University Press, 1957).
9 Peter Berger and Thomas Luckmann, *The Social Construction of Reality* (Garden City, N.Y.: Doubleday, 1967), p. 83.
10 This term is taken from Peter Blau, *Bureaucracy in Modern Society* (New York: Random House, 1956), p. 61.
11 Anthony Downs, *Inside Bureaucracy* (Boston: Little, Brown, 1967), p. 78.
12 These and similar bits of bureaucratic idiocy are found in John Kidner, *The Kidner Report* (Washington: Acropolis, 1972).
13 Frieder Lauxmann, *Die kranke Hierarchie* (Stuttgart: Deutsche Verlags-Anstalt, 1971), p. 128.
14 Amitai Etzioni, *Modern Organizations* (Englewood Cliffs, N.J.: Prentice-Hall, 1964), pp. 1–4.
15 Anton Zijderveld, *The Abstract Society* (Garden City, N.Y.: Doubleday, 1970), p. 16.
16 Theodore Roszak, *The Making of a Counter Culture* (Garden City, N.Y.: Anchor Books, 1969), p. 208.
17 Kenneth Keniston, *The Uncommitted* (New York: Harcourt, Brace, 1965), pp. 253–254.
18 Jacques Ellul, *The Technological Society* (New York: Knopf, 1964).
19 Roderick Seidenberg, *Post-Historic Man* (Boston: Beacon Press, 1957).
20 Lewis Mumford, *The Pentagon of Power* (New York: Harcourt, Brace, 1970).
21 John Schaar, "Reflections on Authority," *New American Review* (New York: Signet Books, 1970), p. 70.
22 Hannah Arendt, "Understanding and Politics," *Partisan Review,* 20 (1953), p. 387.
23 Joseph Royce, *The Encapsulated Man* (Princeton, N.J.: Van Nostrand, 1964), p. 2.
24 Gabriel Marcel, *The Mystery of Being* (Chicago: Regnery, 1951), p. 29.
25 Frank Musgrove, *Ecstasy and Holiness* (Bloomington: Indiana University Press, 1974), p. 148.
26 Jim Hougan, *Decadence* (New York: Morrow, 1975), pp. 123–124.
27 Norman Brown, *Life Against Death* (New York: Vintage Books, 1959), p. 285.
28 Ernest Becker, *The Denial of Death* (New York: Free Press, 1973), p. 50.
29 Miguel de Unamuno, *Tragic Sense of Life* (New York: Dover, 1954), p. 16.
30 Mark Harris, *Bang the Drum Slowly* (New York: Anchor Books, 1962), p. 129.
31 Kenneth Dolbeare, *Political Change in the United States* (New York: McGraw-Hill, 1974), p. 209.
32 Herbert Marcuse, *One-Dimensional Man* (Boston: Beacon Press, 1964), and *Negations* (Boston: Beacon Press, 1968).
33 A. N. Whitehead, *The Function of Reason* (Princeton, N.J.: Princeton University Press, 1929), p. 60.

34 Required reading here is David Halberstam, *The Best and the Brightest* (New York: Random House, 1972).

35 John Sack, *The Man-eating Machine* (New York: Farrar, Straus & Giroux, 1973), p. 13.

36 James Roherty, *Decisions of Robert S. McNamara* (Coral Gables, Fla.: University of Miami Press, 1970), p. 19.

37 Karl von Clausewitz, *On War* (Washington: Combat, 1953), pp. 53–55.

Chapter 2

Politics and Administration

The thing that is most fatal to the political process is conclusions; when once the train of thought has reached a terminus, everybody might just as well get off it.

Kenneth Boulding
The Organizational Revolution

It may seem painfully repetitive, but this chapter will continue to stress the dichotomy of the rational and irrational. Until that division is firmly fixed in the mind, both in a conceptual and a pragmatic sense, it is difficult, perhaps impossible, to defend anything really worthwhile against the drive toward administration. If everything is potentially a matter of administration, what then is human existence except a calculable factor in a smoothly functioning, fictionless machine? How can one find meaning in a thoroughly "disenchanted" world?

Let me recapitulate the argument of Chapter 1. Human behavior is rational, but the body of knowledge from which rational premises are derived is necessarily limited; the human mind is too puny a vessel for complete rationality. The same is true of organizations. Through a basically arbitrary process, some organizationally sanctioned patterns of behavior are deemed rational. All else is considered "irrational" (or "nonrational," but I am not convinced that, outside of hairsplitting debates among philosophers, there is much difference between the two words).

In the modern world, the foundation of rationality is in the objective consciousness which rejects anything not verifiable by scientific methods. It is a rationality dedicated to the domination of the physical and social universe. Because it has shown its utility in the manipulation of tangible things for productive purposes, this rationality has driven from our consciousness other ways of viewing the world.[1] When a number of individuals indoctrinated with such an expansionist epistemology are united in an organization, a unilinear development of society accelerates. As sociologists describe the "imperialistic mode" of bureaucracy: "There is a bureaucratic demiurge who views the universe as dumb chaos waiting to be brought into the redeeming order of bureaucratic administration."[2] The purpose of this chapter is to look at politics as a way of slowing the seemingly inexorable march of this sort of rationalization and to see if we can ever hope to expand the content of rationality.

Some may feel this is fearmongering. That might be so if so many good minds had not already urged the perfection of the megamachine. And in times of stress, when nothing seems to go right and things are helplessly out of joint, the message of administration is so soothing, so confident, so promising. Thomas Huxley, the nineteenth-century biologist, made the most unabashed statement of the administrative creed:

> I protest that if some great Power would agree to make me always think what is true and do what is right, on condition of being turned into a sort of clock and wound up every morning before I got out of bed, I should instantly close with the offer. The only freedom I care about is the freedom to do right; the freedom to do wrong I am ready to part with on the cheapest terms to any one who will take it of me.[3]

The freedom to do right! How can one beat a deal like that? Do we not yearn for that? Is that not what we expect from administration? How nice to have the great Power lay the word on us so that we could always do the one best thing. Surely this is the lure of a B. F. Skinner. Give up all this nonsense about freedom and dignity. We have never enjoyed those two nebulous items anyway; and even if we did have them, we would be horrified.[4] It is much more practical to hire experts who can make us fat and happy. Allow the administrators to perfect the completely predictable society in which we all receive our minimum daily requirement of contentedness. A bovine existence, no doubt, but at least we will not suffer from that gnawing anxiety caused by individual responsibility.

Getting several million people into line, of course, requires at least a little coercion, and the more nervous observers paint an ugly picture of the techniques for ensuring control. There are already available a number of science-fiction inventions which could be used to pacify the public, such as frontal lobotomies, behavior modification through drugs or conditioning, and machines for changing brain waves. But these are only superficial signs of administrative domination. The basic tool is still in the realm of ideas, in our failure to see what choices are available to us. Two hundred years ago, William Pitt warned, "Necessity is the argument of tyrants; it is the creed of slaves." Today, most of us willingly accept the tyranny of a functionally rational necessity.

But maybe it is not too late. Maybe enough of us are questioning the wisdom of pursuing the line of administrative feasibility. The turmoil of the past decade can be taken as a hopeful sign that we have not been entirely remade as items of administration, but politically it is quite depressing. The militant leaders of the counterculture are nothing more than a modern version of the Luddites, those English workers who tried to stop the industrial revolution by smashing the machines. To say that the Weathermen or the Symbionese Liberation Army are solutions is like saying that acne is a solution for eating candy. They are symptoms and not cures.

What, then, is a workable political solution to the problem? Or more precisely, what is a political theory for an age of administration? Other than occasionally lynching the administrators—and becoming the new bureaucratic elite ourselves? When we think of tyranny, we think of individuals such as George III or Joseph Stalin, and our political institutions are designed to control specific individuals. But the monstrous despot is obsolete (except for an Amin of Uganda who is so uncool that he shocks even his fellow dictators). Tyranny today is largely software. It is the "necessity" which guides our everyday action. There is no sense in denouncing the power elite, establishment, or similar coterie of evil schemers. Nuts who wanted to destroy the system could exhaust themselves by blowing up any 1,000 or 100,000 or 1,000,000 clerks and still not make a dent. Personnel offices across the land would work overtime and next morning the survivors would take one step forward to keep operations going.

We cannot resist administration if we do not know what nonadministration looks like. If you view the existing reality only from within, you will see only the acceptable solutions, which are not real alternatives but a paraphrase of what is bugging you in the first place. We need other ways of knowing and, more, ways of ensuring that those who hear the different drummer are legitimate political actors and not candidates for therapy at some public institution. We need, that is, a truly effective political system.

THE ROOTS OF PUBLIC ADMINISTRATION

The job of illuminating the nature of politics would be much easier if we could just dip into the literature of public administration to pick out the proper conceptual model. That we cannot turn to any public administration textbook and find an entry in the index on "Politics: how to integrate with administration" is indicative of some severe problems in the discipline. It may be instructive, therefore, to begin a discussion of politics through a review of the study of public administration and the way in which, for many years, the issue was avoided. In that way, we can better appreciate the difficulty of uniting administration with politics—whatever it is.

In his classic "study of the political theory of American public administration," published in 1948, Dwight Waldo's judgment was that students of administration "have simply been willing to accept the verdict of science—or more accurately, popular conceptions of the verdict of science—as to the nature of reality."[5] This view of reality was mixed with the political biases of the early writers at the time when people were becoming aware that there was such a thing as administration and that it was worthy of serious study. A brief survey of these biases might provide us with some insights into why the values of public administration have usually been most appropriate for a rather sterilized form of politics.

Return with us then to those days of yesteryear, say, to about 1890. Not that there was no administration before then, but it was around that time that a number of ideas began to coalesce. Why? The year will sound familiar to veterans of introductory classes in American history; it was the year, according to the famous thesis of Frederick Turner, that the frontiers closed for Americans. The pioneers in public administration were concerned with the waste and inefficiency which had characterized the march across the continent of the "people of plenty." To some, they were noble conservationists; to others, they were a bunch of fussy spoilsports. But they were among the first to realize that the good old days were gone forever and so they brought us the saddest message about the loss of innocence: "We've got to get organized!"

We had to get organized, to stop fooling around, to get the whole country rationalized. Around 1890, a number of movements sprang up, all having as their goal the introduction of more efficiency into the management of public and private organizations which, during the Gilded Age, had experimented with about every conceivable form of graft, corruption, and prodigality. Among these movements were the following.

The Civil Service Movement Beginning as a reaction to the gross corruption of the spoils system, the movement attacked the bosses with an evangelical zeal. Eventually the emphasis changed, and a professional civil service was sold as a means of achieving neutral competence in government. This was the consummation of our love affair with the experts, a blind affair which has seldom let us recognize that expertise carries its own political premises.

The Progressives This movement was for the middle-class reformers with a desire for organizational tidiness. The structure of American government was a mess, and so research bureaus, voters' leagues, and other good-government groups stressed the need for reorganization to elimate all those rules of the game which had encouraged the political machines. Typically, reform was not advocated on the basis of "our policies versus yours." Instead it was a purely technical matter of instituting rational proposals which any reasonable citizen could endorse. Only the stubborn and selfish could resist the light of reason.

Scientific Management Originally an invention of business administration, it became a coherent managerial ideology with considerable spill-over into the public sphere. The early effort was directed at identifying work patterns which would make cooperative human effort more efficient. Both managers and workers were ignorant and shortsighted. There was, after all, only one best way to tote a barge or lift a bale, and through scientific investigation one could find that way. Experts should discover the fundamental requirements of any job so that the worker could be placed in an exactly defined role. To an extent, the basic proposition of scientific management is acceptable. There probably is one best way to hoist a 50-pound garbage can, assuming the workers are not after hernias. But does a whole social theory follow from that simple notion? Some people have felt so, as they identified "laws" in situations where it might be argued there is still room for personal choice. But personal choice was seen as irrelevant when efficiency became the highest good, and efficiency was the province of the expert.

Scientific management as political ideology, as a statement about how the whole world should be run, deteriorated rather quickly and was unimportant in American politics (but not in the Soviet Union as Lenin was an admirer of the method.)[6] However, it is possible to trace where too much faith in the ability of the trained manager can lead. A case in point is Thorstein Veblen, the economist, who urged that a new class, the "Soviet of technicians," should be permitted to take over the operation of society. They had studied the situation; they knew what was best. Because of their training, they had the qualifications to lead the rest of us down the road of necessity.[7] Veblen did not persuade many; but during the economic dislocations of the 1930s, a minor ripple was caused by the Technocracy party, whose platform was to turn everything over to the engineers or "technocrats" and to eliminate our reliance on politicians.

The Study of Public Administration Public administration began to emerge as a distinct branch of political science. Woodrow Wilson and Frank Goodnow are usually charged with the paternity of the new discipline. In particular, to them is attributed the basic theoretical premise; namely, politics and administration are two separable elements of the governmental whole. Wilson's essay on "The Study of Administration" can be easily read as the source of the idea that "administration lies outside the proper sphere of politics."[8] Politics decides and administration carries out the decision. However, a careful reading of the complete works of both scholars shows that they were not all that naïve and that they appreciated the political role of the administrator. The fact that even today authors must continue to beat down the idea indicates its powerful attraction. Life would be so simple and a science of administration attainable if only the division could be made. Moreover, the notion took concrete shape in a number of important institutions, such as the council-manager form of municipal government and the structure of the public schools.

In light of this intellectual heritage, it is not odd that the mainstream of public administration thought has contributed little to the development of an effective political theory. The advocates of the old methods have been replaced by new waves of zealots, such as those who claim to have found the path to efficiency in systems analysis or budgetary reform. Their claims boil down to a matter of solving our programmatic problems without political confusion. Hard-core public administration, as preparation for a vocation, does not promote politics, for to open the door to politics threatens the return of the irrational it has tried so hard to eliminate. Much of public administration remains the science of "necessity."

Even though many leaders in the field call for the total divorce of public administration from political science, a number of scholars still try to bridge the two. They have produced many works detailing the role of administration in shaping public policy. Much of this, however, remains within the confines of the traditional paradigm and thus is incapable of provoking a truly critical consideration of the problem. As two foreign observers noted about American social science, while the dissidents challenge the very foundations of the "system," the scholars continue "unperturbedly to spin their theories within the parameters of the status quo, apparently accepting these as the only frame of reference for their scientific discourse."[9] In an attempt to break out of a barren intellectual legacy, the advocates of a "New Public Administration" take the most drastic way to resolve the politics-administration problem: forget about the niceties of theory, which can only induce a debilitating sense of vertigo, and advise administrators to do whatever they feel is best—so long as it is "right." It is an impossibly dangerous approach, but one which indicates the frustration felt by younger scholars who cannot bear to be part of a perpetuation of an irrational rationality.[10]

IN PRAISE OF POLITICS

We shall eventually get to the operational definition of politics, but first politics must be praised so that the reader can understand why some are concerned about its demise. Throughout history, the enemies of politics have always outnumbered its friends, and so one is obligated to put forward convincing reasons for liking politics. Of course, the simple reason for praising politics is that it offers to individuals a way of opposing organized dogma, including that of administrators. But since the administrative mentality is so widespread—and one takes classes in public administration to sharpen rather than dull it—a philosophical justification for politics should be provided.

Human Dignity Is All The individual must be the absolute ingredient of any social philosophy. According to Henry Kariel, the human is the "irreducible phenomenon" whose "conduct is ineradicably colored by freedom."[11] One must reject as an affront to human dignity the idea that people are mere objects. This is an existentialist view, the intellectual "resistance movement" in an age of organization.[12] Of course, if taken too far, it is a purely negative philosophy in which the world is living with the individual, rather than the other way around. It becomes an excuse for selfishness and the rejection of all authority. But the political actor can be an individual only while understanding that "we are all in this together." The futility of an atomistic individualism is one more cost of the organization. Like it or not, there is a bond among all members of the polity, and that bond must prove a boundary to individual rationality. The political hero is faced with all sorts of hard, if not impossible, choices, and being true to oneself is always an expensive proposition.

An Infinity of Values Because all values are equally unprovable, the individual is free to choose his or her own and to defend them against all challengers. Our values are moral absolutes only for ourselves. They are not universal truths; but still no scientist, no pedant, no bureaucrat can deprive us of them. It is up to each of us to decide what is good and true. Or in the words of Davy Crockett, "Be sure you're right, and then go ahead." Ahead to where? That brings up a host of unanswerable questions. For example, can I destroy a political system that threatens my cherished values? If yes, am I not then denying to others what I demand for myself? There are no book solutions to such questions.

One must, it appears, compromise to live, and we need a political system which can accommodate compromise. For some, compromise implies the acceptance of a wishy-washy relativism. True, there are some sticky problems involved in arguing the relativity of values; I would not myself assure a Heinrich Himmler, "Whatever gets you through the night, baby." I am only suggesting that it is still up to us as individuals to validate our sense of what is right or wrong. We have the right to listen to all the arguments of others, but we are still responsible for the set of values which will guide our behavior. We hold our truths, but with a hand palsied by uncertainty. And so I agree with Robert Pirsig that, whether repairing Harleys or coping with life, the great threat is "an inability to revalue what one sees because of commitment to previous values."[13]

Academic arguments about whether there are moral absolutes and about what they tell us do not face the central reality of what someone called "our worst century so far." As Charles Reich wrote, the danger is:

> . . . that evil today is the product of our system of organization and our technology, and that it occurs because personal responsibility and personal awareness have been obliterated by a system deliberately designed to do just that—eliminate or minimize the human element and insure the supremacy of the system.[14]

The possibility for evil is greatly increased when officials are either fanatic adherents of a single value or, at the other extreme, moral neuters who see themselves as the agents of another's truth. Bureaucracy is wonderfully constructed to obscure the fact that individuals are responsible for their acts; it encourages members to suspend their capacity for an independent moral judgment. Our survival may depend upon a reawakening of the idea that each individual is ultimately responsible for the morality of her or his acts.

Uncertainty I take it as given that we cannot know all, simply because there is no way in which all modes of perception can be consolidated. The best we can say is that, at this particular time, we will act as if certain things are true, even though our knowledge is incomplete. We will, however, change our minds when further evidence, of whatever nature, is contributed. If, as I am certain, it is a world of uncertainty, we must agree with Ralf Dahrendorf that "the supreme moral consequence of our assumption of the principle of uncertainty is the necessity of maintaining a plurality of decision patterns and an opportunity for them to interact and compete. . . . "[15] That means there must be room for politics.

WHAT IS POLITICS?

I have intimated all along that politics has something to do with the sort of speculation which is the highest function of human reason. Politics is collective choice, and a free politics is not bounded by any predetermined concept of rationality. We are still, however, a far step from a formal definition of the word and an understanding of how one "does" politics. There also remains the critical question of what forms or institutions best serve the political process.

Politics concerns the attempt for social order in the absence of certitude about the nature of that order. When a people engage in politics, whether joyfully or reluctantly, they have to some extent conceded the absence of absolute truth. In politics, we are like trapeze artists working without a net. It is not surprising, therefore, that politics is a very disturbing phenomenon for many people. The void threatens to overwhelm us with an infinity of choices; if a person does not wish to view this situation as an opportunity for the cultivation of the self, then administration, built on the bedrock of certitude, "will be only too ready to come to his aid by limiting his options."[16] Perhaps we scared sojourners in a pitiless cosmos should be proud of the limited amount of politics we have dared to tolerate.

Since it does involve choice, politics is inextricably bound up with values. Values are subjective estimates of worth; they pertain not only to the ends of government (or in less abstract terms, to the policies and programs), but also the means to achieve the ends. One definition that integrates values in the political process is posed by David Easton. He maintains that "in all societies, one fact dominates political life; scarcity prevails with regard to most valued things." That is, there is never enough to go around. Valued things can be either tangible or intangible. Whatever the case, there must be a process of getting and giving in any society; so Easton states, "the study of politics is concerned with understanding how authoritative decisions concerning the allocation of values are made and executed for a society."[17]

This skeletal definition of politics could apply to a number of social institutions, and it is not too far in the past that most people attained their values through nonpublic means. They disposed of their own garbage, took care of their own sanitation problems, protected their own property, and educated their own children. Private organizations such as the church provided other services. Today, these and innumerable other functions requiring the distribution of scarce resources are performed by government because government is perceived by most people as the proper arena in which to strive for the maximization of their values.

Citizens therefore make demands on the political system for a preferred outcome. Since people are unique, there may theoretically be as many demands as there are individuals. Most of us, of course, learn what to demand from the system so that there is regularity in expressed desires; Americans, for example, have been taught that only someone of the Bolshevik persuasion could believe that government should provide medical services. In addition, not everyone has equal amounts of power to back up demands or equal access to the system. The actual distribution of valued things will depend upon the relative power, however defined by a society, of the makers of demands. The important point is that the outcome of the political struggle is accepted by winners and losers as "authoritative." An authoritative decision is one which it is felt must be obeyed because of the rightness of the means or ends or both. We obey because the decision fits into our sense of social reality.

In this sketch, the "politician" will be regarded as an individual within government who, wholly or in part, influences the making of a new allocative decision. In most complex systems, there is a differentiation of roles to the extent that there is some justification for our lingering belief in the politics-administration dichotomy; the politicians bear the primary responsibility for balancing the demands and power inputs, thus keeping the system in a state of equilibrium. Administration is the instrument which modifies the environment in accordance with the values of the dominant political forces in the society. Ideally, bureaucrats should be able to change their vision of the environment in response to the politician's assessment of a fluid situation. This presupposes much dexterity on the part of bureaucrats, and it is often more convenient for them to shape rather than reflect reality.

Public administration is a function of that concrete institution known as "the state." The state has several attributes, the most important being, in Weber's terms, its successful claim to a monopoly of the legitimate use of force. In other words, the state has the right to apply pain to your body, which tends to be the ultimate clincher in any argument. This power, particularly in a sophisticated political system, may be seldom used. However, the association of even the most mundane activities of government with the awesome power of the state supports the claim that "the distinctive characteristic of activities in the public sector lie in their relation to state action."[18]

In terms of the present analysis, that means that when a citizen engages a bureaucrat in a discussion of reality, it is not always on an equal footing. You and the narcotic agent may disagree about the medicinal benefits of *cannabis sativa,* but unless you are eager to serve time, you will probably be persuaded to the agent's point of view. Conversely, a lone revenuer stupid enough to pull a bust in a convention of armed moonshiners may find his claim to the legitimate use of force is overlooked.

Politics, then, is the striving by groups and individuals for control of the legitimate power of the state so that favorable allocative decisions can be made. The political struggle has been regularized in order to avoid "the war of all against all." Citizens have surrendered their claims to the final persuader in changing the behavior of others and accept the state agents as the ones who can apply the extreme sanction of physical force. Although the state has great power, it could not exist if all its energies were channeled into maintaining order by coercion. The frustration of the police in enforcing the reduced speed limits is one illustration of the dependency of administrators on the citizens' willing acceptance of authority.

What are the actual missions of public administration? John Dewey, in his *The Public and Its Problems,* offered a flexible concept of matters public. He argued that a public is based upon the perceived consequences of an act. When the consequences are confined to the immediate participants, it is a private act and is subject to the rules governing private conduct. When others than the direct participants feel some impact, we have the beginnings of a public. Dewey's thesis was that the public becomes concrete when specific agencies are set up to regulate the consequences. The bureaucracy is the major instrument for controlling the perceived consequences through, if need be, the application of force.

But note that we are talking about the perceptions of the dominant political force in the society. It is not a matter of right or wrong, or of consenting adults. If Mr. Big in a community is upset by the thought of unmarried couples living together, then steps will be taken, even though the other citizens may not find the act offensive. Depending upon the distribution of political power, there can be bigger or smaller publics, each of which, "being unable to forecast and estimate all consequences, establishes certain dikes and channels so that actions are confined within prescribed limits and, insofar have moderately predictable consequences."[19] If the administrator always remained a humble ditchwalker for society, keeping the channels in repair and changing them when desired, the problem of politics and administration would not be so complex.

In an open society, where citizens are trying to expand the perceptions of their fellows, bureaucracy should reject any idea of permanency. But bureaucrats have a hard time in assuming the role of a societal scoreboard, reflecting the latest political settlement. Part of the problem today is that politicians have more trouble in providing the proper cues to administrators about what is desired. More important, bureaucrats perceive consequences; in fact, they probably do so more quickly than the rest of us because their bounded rationality provides all sorts of guidelines about needed extensions of control. When the bureaucracy settles on a limited perception, compatible with its view of the world, the result is rigidity rather than openness. The single-minded pursuit of a limited perception inhibits the emergence of new publics.

THE END OF POLITICS

Politics is a strenuous, confusing business. Just because of that it deserves praise. In the words of one of its more eloquent defenders, "to renounce or destroy politics is to destroy the very thing which gives order to the pluralism and variety of civilized society, the thing which enables us to enjoy variety without suffering either anarchy or the tyranny of single truths."[20] Politics extends an umbrella of civility over a people so that as many perceptions of reality as possible can be accommodated. Despite these merits, is it possible to eliminate politics, to replace it with the routines of administration? Certainly it is possible to try; the paradoxical tragedy of politics is that almost every politician would like to be the last one. Unfortunately, the hardest thing for a friend of politics is the caliber of people who go into that line of work. Beyond these human frailities, however, there is the larger danger to politics posed by the drive toward administration. The urge for greater rationality is denying opportunities for other ways of perceiving the world.

There is something that does not like politics, that does not want the individual to exercise too many options, that does not appreciate the disorderly, raucous life of conflicting values. Karl Popper put it nicely when he said that the "open society" has always had its enemies, the first of whom was Plato. Plato, the eminence who still colors our political thought—the first philosopher and maybe the last, with his seductive insinuations about ultimate truth.[21] His "philosopher kings" offer a safe haven for us in our escape from freedom. After all, freedom does require us to depend upon our own critical abilities and permits us to make mistakes in pursuit of our various goals; it does involve the "freedom to do wrong." The possibility of error has always been disliked, especially by those who are certain they have discovered the demands of necessity.

Most Americans, secure in a faith produced by 200 years of hard practice that they are artful politicians, might assume that the major antipolitical threats come from alien ideological forms of totalitarianism. In the totalitarian ideal, there is no room for politics because the one true way has been discovered. Just refer to the works of the Master, of Marx or the Führer or Chairman Mao. There is no part of human life that need be opened to honest debate. All policy has been determined by whoever stumbled across the truth, and governmental activity is mere administration. The result is an administered society, "defined as one in which an entrenched and extraordinarily powerful ruling group lays claim to ultimate and exclusive scientific knowledge of social and historical laws. . . ."[22]

An intermediate type of apolitical society is represented by those Western European countries which have opted for all the bourgeois comforts through a managed economy and welfare government. Consequently, "political government is becoming greatly restricted in view of the requirements of an agreed economic system";[23] allocative decisions must be made according to the trained judgment of a new breed of technicians. This type of society has an appeal, and one American visitor to Sweden was enthusiastic about the "organized humanitarianism" of that country where political debate has been turned into "seminars on economics, political science and sociology" after the retreat of "the rabble-rousing, folksy, electioneering politicians."[24]

At least one recent President—the only one, in fact, to be called "charismatic"—endorsed the technocratic creed as the most reasonable alternative to an outmoded partisanship:

> The fact of the matter is that most of the problems, or at least many of them, that we now face are technical problems, are administrative problems. They are very sophisticated judgments which do not lend themselves to the great sort of "passionate movements" which have stirred this country so often in the past.[25]

So while Americans still seem to cherish the notion of politics and would refuse to endorse any ideology, we have been lured into placing our trust in the scientist, the expert, the administrator.

Modern life is so full of examples of the narrowing of politics by the expert that one hardly knows where to begin an account. The bumbling but lovable amateur is on the defensive everywhere as we abdicate our responsibility to the experts, and the politicians have done little to protect us. In fact, some political campaigns have turned into contests to see who can nominate the most prestigious scientists to this or that "blue ribbon commission" which will come up with all the answers.

We are smothered in expertise and are controlled by people who pride themselves on not being politicians. Their battle cry, which has shaped the structure of American government, is: "Get——out of politics!" Get education, get the military, get the police, get sanitation out of politics! Put them all together and you get the message: Get government out of politics!

Is there much difference then between, on the one hand, a marxist or welfare economist and, on the other hand, a city planner, a fire fighter, or a high school teacher? All seem convinced about what has to be done and are confident about the righteousness of their work. The major difference is that the "isms" and the doctrines of the welfare state are wholes. Technical expertise, by its very nature, is fragmented, although the idea of putting all the experts together is often attractive.[26] Some say that the consolidation has already happened without our really noticing it. In 1941, James Burnham described a quiet revolution which had brought to power a managerial elite.[27] More recently, John Kenneth Galbraith described the managers of the technostructure as the ruling class of the New Industrial State.[28]

All of which leads to a natural question: Are the American and Russian bureaucrats any different? In view of the famous wheat deals, many might respond, "No, except theirs are smarter." But before we endorse the so-called convergence theory, which holds that both capitalist and communist systems must follow the same technological dynamics to a common conclusion, reconsider that there is at least one major difference in the American system which holds some promise for the perpetuation of a workable political system. Democracy is still a legitimate political concept in the United States.

DEMOCRACY

I have painted a drab picture of a nonpolitical world in which all values have been established and there is nothing left but their administration in the most rational manner. Is it such an impossibility? The same situation is precisely what makes college student government so contemptible. Everything has been decided by the administration, and it does not appreciate too many comments from the bottom. Student politicos get together to decide the homecoming theme, while the experts decide admission policy, tuition, curriculum, and all the other important issues. Perhaps being student body president is excellent preparation for the work of real politics.

I have also suggested that American public administration has seldom shown a great deal of sympathy for politics, which is a pity because you cannot have democracy without a lively politics. Democracy is a process of constructing a temporary alliance of supporters around a very transitory idea. It is a matter of constant brawling about the truth but never of establishing it once and for all. Rationality in a democracy is a fleeting thing, for democracy is a nearly value-free system with only one inviolable rule: Preserve the system. All else is open to serious debate.

Our problem is how to harness bureaucracy to democracy, how to have rationality and irrationality at the same time. Perhaps it is impossible, but when we get to the traditional subject matter of public administration, our main concern will be how to facilitate that combination.

Democracy is endorsed for quite practical reasons. It is more likely, in the long run, to guarantee better administration. As Herman van Gunsteren has shown, a centralized, hierarchical system of administration is inferior to one based in politics because "the rationality of politics, of living together, is a historically situated rationality that is continually in the making, that is kept alive by discourse and interaction between a plurality of citizens."[29] Democracy will bring us closer to true rationality than will the dogma of bureaucracy; it is the most constructive way for a people to cooperate in the modification of their environment. Democracy does have its defects, but it may be proper to update Fisher Ames to the effect that "Bureaucracy is a great ship which sails smoothly until it hits a rock, and then it sinks out of sight. Democracy is a raft: it will not sink but damn it sir, your feet are always wet." Wet feet is not an unreasonable condition for the survival of society.

This is not the place for an involved discussion of the determinants of democratic government such as economic and social factors. Here we need only a sketch of democracy as a political decision-making process where normal people can participate in government on a regular basis. Democracy is not self-government. It is a system in which decision makers—those who determine the distribution of valued things—are responsible to the citizens. Political decisions must eventually be judged by the people.

It will be helpful if we can keep in mind an objective standard of democracy so that we can evaluate politics in the United States. For this purpose, we can do no better than borrow Henry Mayo's four components of democratic government. These include:[30]

1 *Popular control of decision makers.* The citizens enter the process primarily in the selection of those who will be entrusted with the making of decisions over a certain period of time.

2 *Political equality.* In terms of the most abstract form of political power—the vote in the selection of decision makers—all citizens are equal. This does not overlook the fact that the rich and influential are probably "more equal" than others. The formal power, however, remains through the ballot.

3 *Effective instruments of popular control.* There must be alternatives presented and procedures guaranteed so that an effective judgment can be made. This includes the protection of the political liberties necessary for a free and open discussion of governmental decisions.

4 *Majority rule.* We accept majority rule simply because there is no alternative. Unanimity is unattainable, and no minority can justify the exclusion of other participants. Majority rule, of course, presupposes the protection of minorities, and a majority's power does not entitle it to destroy the losers of the last election.

Democratic politics demands that political decisions reflect the values of a majority of voters, acting in free elections. The governors will be given time to do their work; and, at the next election, if the majority is displeased with the decisions they have made, new officials can be brought into government.

I assume a radically democratic stance. For the sake of future argument, I shall be concerned with the preservation of only one value—the continued operation of the democratic system. Once that is assured, I must go along with the majority decision. Anyone wishing to challenge that stance would seem to face an impossible chore. It must be proved that there are some decisions which the majority is incompetent to make. That is, some values must be declared off limits, and it is only the sin of haughtiness, not infallibility, that would enable anyone to make such a claim. Of course, you are free to be an elitist of whatever stripe, but the rest of us should be able to demand that you explain how it is that you happen to be tuned into the truth.

Many of us are probably uneasy with the idea of democracy. In America we are a bit Whiggish, and lurking in our minds is the idea that democracy is akin to mobocracy. The mass, many fear, is full of all sorts of destructive urges, and it will inevitably destroy minorities in its uncontrollable lust for power. We have failed to appreciate which is the lesser of political evils. We can ignore the validity of the conservative criticisms of democracy and ask instead what does pose the greatest danger to minorities. If the system is democratic, I believe that the minority will at least have a fighting chance. If nothing else, one can be consoled with the belief that a crazed mob will eventually exhaust itself.

The alternative—bureaucracy—is inexorable, relentless, inflexible. Bureaucracy never forgets, never gets distracted; it always gets whomever it's after. The technological state has to eliminate all minorities in order to homogenize its environment and its inner workings. Anything autonomous is a potential threat to its control and must be encompassed by the system. Take a hard look at the sources of "minorityness" and see if bureaucracy is not the greater hazard.

1 *Politics.* This follows from other sources, but we have become aware that there are fewer differences within and among nations. Politics is now a matter of picking an attractive figurehead who needs only an ability to kiss babies, open supermarkets, and ratify decisions made by the bureaucracy. A more primitive politician such as George Wallace can attract support by his vows to throw the bureaucrats with their briefcases full of guidelines into the Potomac, but we know in our heart of hearts that things would not change if he were elected. Moreover, if a political minority is too obstreperous, too "radical," it becomes a problem for the bureaucracy to administer through surveillance and harassment.

2 *Race.* To the extent that race is not made an important variable within the bounded rationality, bureaucracy is probably color-blind; ordinarily, achieved factors are more important than ascribed. If race is important, God help the minority. All technocrats must be asked to brood about one dreadful fact: the worst racial crimes—the worst crimes, period—were possible only because of the existence of a thoroughly rational administrative machine. Adolf Eichmann, hanged for his mass murders, was not a sadistic monster; he was a company man who, in contemporary America, would probably be the manager of a department store. Without rage or passion, he managed the extermination of millions of people. He was, Hannah Arendt wrote, "terribly and terrifyingly normal."[31]

3 *Religion.* Technology, the antithesis of religious faith, has squeezed religion out of our daily lives. The ecumenical spirit seems related to the spread of technology; eventually, we will be left with a bloodless religion as in the military, where it is utilitarian "character guidance" and not a source of inner direction. As we saw in the campaign of 1976, many Americans are uneasy when it appears that a President might make decisions based upon deeply held religious convictions.

4 *Culture.* The history of the past 500 years is largely a story of the futile resistance of nontechnological cultures to Western civilization. All peoples must conform to the demands of the machine. If anything remains of a culture, it is in ornamental form, as in Southern California where the Mexican heritage has been reduced to the ubiquitous Taco Bell—safe, bland, and consumable by millions. There has been a resurgence of ethnic pride in the past few years, but one must wonder whether there is enough vitality in these subcultures to ensure their survival once its members have really made it in the dominant culture. There is no black, Chicano, or Polish way to operate a computer or do accounting.

5 *Sex.* Perhaps males, as a minority, will eventually need their own liberation movement since they are not all that indispensable in the biology of reproduction. One can think of a number of efficiencies to be achieved in a unisex society.

6 *The individual.* And what about the most important minority, the minority of one? It is unnecessary to spend time reviewing the reality of conformity. People have always yielded to the group, but today it is not simply a matter of cowardice. Nonconformity is administratively dysfunctional. It is a sign that individuals might start thinking for themselves.

There are those who despise individuals because of the mistakes they can make, the waves they can create. A philosopher said, "The rationalism born of technological pride hates human liberty both on account of its excellence and on account of its wretchedness."[32] By our attempt to cure people of their wretchedness, we have created a far greater danger. In his comparison of personal crimes and those conducted in the name of this or that glorious ideal, Arthur Koestler concluded that "the tragedy of man is not his truculence, but his proneness to delusions."[33] The most widespread delusion today is the one encouraged by scientific arrogance and administrative naïveté. To stop the relatively harmless meanness of people we would allow ourselves to be blinded by a most monstrous delusion.

All minorities will be better protected by democracy. Of course there will be threats; but I do not understand that the purpose of democracy is the creation of a no-sweat, Endless Summer utopia, just as I do not understand that the business of living is simply a matter of happiness. As we said, there is already a technology of happiness available; give us this day our daily Soma. Life is not an easy proposition, and we must be content to coexist in a world where people do silly things, even make monumental mistakes. In all good conscience, I do not know how to prevent others from making these mistakes, and I hope others are not busily engaged in keeping me from my errors. Insofar as those others are bureaucrats, they are probably up to just that, and so we must look more closely at that alternative.

BUREAUCRACY

We have used the word "bureaucracy" and its derivatives widely so far without benefit of an extended definition. Because I feel that the commonsense understanding is as reliable a guide as much of the literature on the subject, I do not think there has been much chance for confusion. Few will have mistaken its meaning, and, in fact, to bring in much of the modern scholarship on bureaucracy may be less than helpful because, as C. Wright Mills noted, social science today is firmly embedded in the same intellectual matrix as the forces which encourage bureaucratization.[34] However, no discussion of the concept is complete without mentioning the contribution of Max Weber.

Weber was the first, and so far the most successful, in placing bureaucracy within a world historical context. There has been much carping about the Weberian definition, just as there is about any great intellectual monument, but no one has come close to repealing it. Much of the confusion results from a failure to grasp what he was trying to do, namely, to find out why Western civilization is moving in its particular direction. His bureaucracy is not descriptive. No such institution as he describes has ever existed. Bureaucracy was for him an analytical category for studying the real world and not reality itself. The abstraction which he called bureaucracy was based on the first premise of modern organizational behavior: What is the most rational method of conducting large-scale, complex administration? He was trying to identify the material of that so very tangible "iron cage" which, "as soon as it segregates itself from non-reason," must push "nonrational values and behaviour into the ghettoes of madness, crime, and disease."[35]

Weber simply asked, in an ideal world of complete rationality as we in the West understand the term, what things are necessary for the most rational achievement of collective goals? He certainly did not overlook, as some assume, that the world is not ideal and that people and groups are dubious instruments for the manifestation of rationality. The complete abstraction of rational behavior—the "ideal type" of bureaucracy—was made up of several characteristics:

1 Each member has a defined jurisdiction. Subordinates are not expected to be concerned with the total work of the bureaucracy.
2 Authority is defined according to very precise rules. Each member has power only over those aspects pertinent to his or her jurisdiction.
3 Hierarchy—a system of graded authority—is necessary to bring the separate jurisdictions back together again.
4 Administration is based on written documents. Decisions are based on objective information which, in the files as the organizational memory, makes the organization immortal, i.e., independent of the life of any individual.
5 Members conduct their duties with a sense of personal detachment. Bureaucrats do not get personally involved with other people while on the job.
6 Members are trained for their specific role. Employees become interchangeable units depending upon their acquired knowledge.
7 Members are professionals, i.e., not amateurs or dilettantes. They spend their lives in the organization, and their career is determined by rational personnel practices.
8 Members are detached from ownership of the organization. They cannot pick up their tools and go home, for all means of production are controlled by the organization.

As Weber described the results of such an organization:

> Precision, speed, unambiguity, knowledge of the files, continuity, discretion, unity, strict subordination, reduction of friction and of material and personal costs—these are raised to the optimum point in the strictly bureaucratic administration, and especially in the monocratic form.

In a demystified world, the fully formed bureaucracy "compares with other organizations exactly as does the machine with the non-mechanical modes of production."[36]

Simply because it is such a marvelously efficient social invention, bureaucracy has driven out other forms of organization. The real causes of bureaucracy, therefore, are quite evident. As we saw from Dewey, the public and its administration are matters of perceived consequences. Today there is just so much more to be perceived, and these perceptions inform us that action to control the consequences are practicable. For example, there was no sense in having a massive welfare bureaucracy when people believed that the poor were suffering from a lack of divine grace. Only when poverty is seen as the consequences of certain ameliorable social conditions is a bureaucracy able to function.

We will live in an age of bureaucratization as long as the dominant scientific mentality rips apart the mysteries of life and turns them into objects of administration. Thus, to dismantle bureaucracy, we would have to develop an entirely new way of knowing things—and in the process lose all the material benefits produced by bureaucracy. Faceless clerks do keep the world humming for us. There could have been no better argument for bureaucracy than the Big Blackout on the East coast in 1965. Even fanatic libertarians who were trapped in the elevator on the fiftieth floor must have been praying that some bureaucrat would finally push the right buttons to get things moving again. Simply—and sadly perhaps—if you want seventeeth-century government, you should be prepared to accept seventeenth-century living conditions.

POLITICS AND RATIONALITY

Albert Camus has one of his bureaucrats tell the citizens, "Good governments are governments under which nothing happens."[37] Things will necessarily happen, to the despair of the bureaucrats, when people speculate about all the possibilities they could pursue, and so bureaucracy has its chilling effect on changes in perception. Preaching revolution is no cure for bureaucracy, even if a revolution against a technically proficient state had any chance of success. Lenin, the most effective of modern revolutionaries, warned that "all revolutions which have taken place up to the present have helped to perfect the state machinery, whereas it must be shattered, broken to pieces."[38] He found that easier to say than to do, and the Soviet bureaucracy has surpassed that of the czars in the totality of its control. As a marxist philosopher recently put it, even marxists assume that, after the revolution, social thought must "concentrate upon the study and evaluation of the stability, organization and functioning of the new system."[39] Come the revolution, of whatever nature, and somebody is sure to blow it by saying, "We've got to get organized!"

And as we get organized, the new idea is embodied in a bureaucracy which proceeds to rationalize the social world, intruding into, and subjugating, what is now officially defined as "irrational." When the rationalization process is not successful, which seems likely since the bounded rationality becomes more unrealistic as it is used and codified, pressures for the next revolution will mount. The circle is completed as again the streets are full of howling citizens demanding that the last police officer be hanged with the entrails of the last bureaucrat. What we need obviously is a surrogate for revolution, a method of change which does not lose itself in mere change of form, but rather one which opens up new vistas on what is becoming.

Therefore, I recommend that anyone seeking a placid occupation go into TV repairs or motel management. The civil servant plays the pivotal role in most social processes, which, Karl Mannheim rightly understood, are divided "into a rationalized sphere consisting of settled and routinized procedures in dealing with situations that recur in an orderly fashion, and the 'irrational' by which it is surrounded."[40] We are in trouble if our administrators believe that by virtue of their title they are responsible only for the "administrative situation" through stable and programmed patterns of performanced based on the presumption that "a working consensus exists among participants over the important value premises of action."[41]

That administrators can delude themselves accounts for Brian Chapman's conclusion about a remarkable feature of European bureaucrats: "their wish to use the term administration for the respectable part of government business, and politics for the less respectable part."[42] People who are nice and think pure thoughts—who are rational—do not get involved in politics. But there can be no question that bureaucrats are politicians and will remain so until there is no disagreement about values. We must urge them to be conscious politicians and, most of all, democratic politicians.

It is not very important to conclude a chapter on politics and administration with bold words about how we shall control this thing called bureaucracy. We are all implicated in the situation. The only real hope is that we, either as administrators or administratees, will appreciate that a democratic system is the best suggestion for societal cooperation in view of the transitory nature of our joint venture in existence. Control of bureaucracy is, in the end, self-control, induced by a sense that others, through their politicians, might have something to say about what is rational.

REFERENCES

1 See Jürgen Habermas, *Toward a Rational Society* (Boston: Beacon Press, 1970).

2 Peter Berger, Brigitte Berger, and Hansfried Kellner, *The Homeless Mind* (New York: Vintage Books, 1973), p. 49.

3 Thomas Huxley, *Methods and Results* (New York: Appleton, 1893), p. 192.

4 B. F. Skinner, *Beyond Freedom and Dignity* (New York: Knopf, 1971).

5 Dwight Waldo, *The Administrative State* (New York: Ronald, 1948), p. 21.

6 V. I. Lenin, *Collected Works*, vol. 42 (London: Lawrence and Wishart, 1969), pp. 68–84.

7 Thorstein Veblen, *The Engineers and the Price System* (New York: B. W. Huebsch, 1921).

8 Woodrow Wilson, "The Study of Administration," *Political Science Quarterly*, 56 (1941), pp. 481–506. But see his "Lectures on Administration," in *The Papers*

of Woodrow Wilson, vol. 7 (Princeton, N.J.: Princeton University Press, 1969), pp. 112–158.

9 Marlis Krueger and Frieda Silvert, *Dissent Denied* (New York: Elsevier, 1975), p. 100.

10 Frank Marini (ed.), *Toward a New Public Administration* (Scranton, Pa.: Chandler, 1971).

11 Henry Kariel, "The Political Relevance of Behavioral and Existential Psychology," *American Political Science Review,* 61 (1967), p. 338.

12 James Davis, "Existentialism: A Reaction to the Age of Organization," *Western Political Quarterly,* 16 (1963), pp. 541–547.

13 Robert Pirsig, *Zen and the Art of Motorcycle Maintenance* (New York: Morrow, 1974), p. 304.

14 Charles Reich, "The Limits of Duty," *New Yorker,* 47 (June 19, 1971), p. 52.

15 Ralf Dahrendorf, "Uncertainty, Science, and Democracy," in *Essays in the Theory of Society* (Stanford, Calif.: Stanford University Press, 1968), p. 240.

16 Henry Kariel, *The Promise of Politics* (Englewood Cliffs, N.J.: Prentice-Hall, 1966), p. 50.

17 David Easton, "An Approach to the Analysis of Political Systems," *World Politics,* 9 (1957), pp. 383–400.

18 Gary Wamsley and Mayer Zald, *The Political Economy of Public Organizations* (Lexington, Mass.: Lexington Books, 1973), p. 12.

19 John Dewey, *The Public and Its Problems* (New York: Henry Holt, 1927), p. 53.

20 Bernard Crick, *In Defense of Politics* (Baltimore: Penguin, 1964), p. 26.

21 Karl Popper, *The Open Society and Its Enemies* (London: George Routledge & Sons, 1947).

22 Allen Kassof, "The Administered Society: Totalitarianism without Terror," *World Politics,* 16 (1964), p. 558.

23 Piet Thoenes, *The Elite in the Welfare State* (New York: Free Press, 1966), p. 146.

24 Hans Zetterberg, "Sweden—A Land of Tomorrow?" in Ingemar Wizelius (ed.), *Sweden in the Sixties* (Stockholm; Almqvist and Wiksell, 1967), p. 15.

25 John F. Kennedy, *Public Papers* (Washington: GPO, 1963), p. 422.

26 See Guy Benveniste, *The Politics of Expertise* (Berkeley, Calif.: Glendessary, 1972).

27 James Burnham, *The Managerial Revolution* (New York: John Day, 1941).

28 John Kenneth Galbraith, *The New Industrial State* (Boston: Houghton Mifflin, 1967).

29 Herman van Gunsteren, *The Quest for Control* (New York: Wiley, 1976), p. 151.

30 Henry Mayo, *An Introduction to Democratic Theory* (New York: Oxford University Press, 1960), pp. 58–71.

31 Hannah Arendt, *Eichmann in Jerusalem* (New York: Viking, 1964), p. 276.

32 Yves Simon, *Philosophy of Democratic Government* (Chicago: University of Chicago Press, 1951), p. 278.

33 Arthur Koestler, *The Ghost in the Machine* (New York: Macmillan, 1967), p. 214.

34 C. Wright Mills, *The Sociological Imagination* (New York: Oxford University Press, 1959), chap. 5.

35 John O'Neill, *Sociology as a Skin Trade* (New York: Harper & Row, 1972), p. 14.

36 This synopsis is drawn from H. Gerth and C. Wright Mills (eds.), *From Max Weber* (New York: Oxford University Press, 1946), pp. 196–244.

37 Albert Camus, "State of Siege," in *Caligula and Three Other Plays* (New York: Vintage Books, 1958), p. 141.

38 V. I. Lenin, *The State and Revolution* (New York: International Publishers, 1932), p. 25.

39 Svetozar Stojanovic, *Between Ideals and Reality* (New York: Oxford University Press, 1973), p. 14.

40 Karl Mannheim, *Ideology and Utopia* (New York: Harcourt, Brace, 1936), p. 101.

41 Philip Kronenberg, "The Scientific and Moral Authority of Empirical Theory of Public Administration," in Marini, op. cit., pp. 221–222.

42 Brian Chapman, *The Profession of Government* (London: Allen, 1959), p. 274.

Chapter 3

Bureaucratic Politics in American Government

"The idea of pressures—order establishing itself that way—as if society were a pond in a field, where natural balance comes about by itself—so many tadpoles, so many water bugs, so many thises, so many thats—that is to say . . ." He paused, searching. "Things kill each other," he said at last. "You look at a pond and you think, 'How calm,' but things are eating things all the time."

John Gardner
The Sunlight Dialogues

Enough of airy concepts. It is time now to descend into the bowels of American government in order to see the ongoing struggle between bureaucracy and democracy. To give these generalizations more human form, let us look at the two main antagonists.

The hero is the politician, the person to whom we should return American government, the person who can somehow reflect the public's notion of what is real and who must suffer the consequences if that reflection is incorrect. Of course, now is an inauspicious time to make the argument since politicians, as an occupational group, are in even lower repute than is usual. But perhaps some of the excesses which have led to a revulsion against politicians can be charged to the antics of nonpoliticians. One is reminded of Sam Rayburn's assessment of those wonderful folks who brought us Vietnam: "I'd feel better if at least one of them had ever been elected sheriff." In the past decade, our political leadership has been supplied by technocrats who ignored the public or amoral crooks whose interest in the bureaucracy was expressed in terms of the desire, in their elegant prose, "to use the available federal machinery to screw our political enemies." Neither type did much to promote domestic tranquility.

Politicians should know only one truth: Preserve a system open to all aspirants to the truth. Abraham Lincoln was a classic example. Beleaguered by encapsulated zealots of every stripe—party hacks, abolitionists, military experts—he kept his eye on the main job and was able to preserve the basic form of government. A Lincoln does not emerge in every generation, and so I am not confident that the odds are favorable even under the best of circumstances. And one must wonder whether Lincoln would have had the patience to contend with the major opponent of the modern politician.

The bureaucrat will be the heavy in this sketch of American government. Or better, we should begin to refer to the bureaucrat as the "professional." I have argued that bureaucrats have a special relationship to knowledge; in the bureaucracy, knowledge is power. That assertion, however, may give the impression that our several million bureaucrats are all imbued with a common body of knowledge. The most salient characteristic of modern administrators is their relationship to a limited body of knowledge, to knowledge not readily accessible to others, including bureaucrats from other departments. It is necessary to comprehend the elements of professionalism since it is the thing which makes a mockery of our political forms.

PROFESSIONALISM

Alfred North Whitehead characterized professionalism as thinking in a groove—which, I hasten to add, is not the same as groovy thinking. The sociology of professions is a bit more analytical; there seems to be general agreement that the basic components of professionalism include the following:[1]

1 *A high degree of generalized and systematic knowledge.* We refer to the more established groups as the "learned professions." One becomes a professional only after a long training period. Because they have not been exposed to that training, laypersons cannot really argue with the professional about matters of professional concern. I imagine that just about everyone has, at one time or another, been intimidated into silence by the professional behind the desk, flanked by row upon row of diplomas, certificates, licenses, and honors; who would dare question the wisdom of a person who can paper the walls with all the right symbols?

2 *Stress on community interest.* The cynic who has recently paid a dentist bill will respond that dentists surely have not taken any vows of poverty. However, I must concede that professionals are sincere in the belief that professionalism is for the good of the public. The argument that an occupational group must become better organized is usually prefaced by remarks about "upgrading the profession" in order to provide improved services. And one upgrades a profession by keeping out those who do not have the systematic knowledge—the quacks.

3 *A high degree of internal control.* Professional groups strive to become self-governing, a natural urge since the members are the only ones with the ability to judge professional work. There must be methods to encourage good performance and, if necessary, keep the bad professional from practicing. Ideally, the control is provided by the internalization of professional values; part of the systematic knowledge imparted in the training period is a sense of professional norms. A sure sign that a new profession is being born is the promulgation of a "code of ethics." But these intangible forces are seldom sufficient and therefore the professional organization assumes the job of policing its membership.

4 *Rewards not based on individual self-interest.* Again, it may be true that there are few poor heart surgeons, but consider how much they could extort if their services went only to the highest bidder. The professionals do not believe that they are vulgar moneygrubbers. The most important reward is the approbation of one's colleagues.

Not exactly revealed in the above model is one factor of professionalism which poses special problems for an outsider trying to control an agency staffed by professionals. The professional mystique is not reducible to a pure science and "successful practice depends as much on intuition as on recall."[2] One can read every medical book and still not have that certain something which distinguishes the true physician. "Professional judgment" is a wild card to be played any time the outsiders get too close.

The pattern of professionalization is by now quite clear and, although the process is incomplete in many areas, we may expect more groups to follow the path beaten down by such powerful pioneers as doctors, lawyers, and educators. As unskilled labor vanishes, it may be realistic to expect the eventual professionalization of everyone. To summarize the work of Corinne Gilb, there are a number of discernible steps on the way to becoming a profession.[3]

1 *Formation of the formal association.* Through this instrument of control, the image of "us" versus "them" can be enforced.

2 *Infiltration of the educational system.* This step is essential if the truth is to be formalized. Through curricular control by accreditation, it can be ensured that only approved professional knowledge is passed on to novices. The incredible increase in college programs of criminology or police science is one of the more recent developments in this area.

3 *Association with government.* In the United States, this generally takes the form of a licensing board. Government now puts its power behind a formal rite of passage. The licensed practitioner is anointed as a Knower of Truth. The purity of that truth will be assured because the board will be dominated by members of the profession.

4 *Creation of a government agency to regulate the work conditions and to protect the boundaries against other professions.* In this ultimate stage, the profession is government and government is the profession. For example, the educational profession is the public school system and vice versa; a "nonprofessional" teacher will never get a job in the public schools.

Through this basic process, some professions have already made their domain off limits to the politician. Almost every other conceivable group is moving in the same direction. A few years ago, it was proposed that the state of California create a board to license astrologers. This was needed, so the usual argument went, to protect the public from nuts, frauds, and weirdoes. The image of a board dressed up in wizard hats testing the applicants on their knowledge of incantations was apparently too much for the legislature, but the case does illustrate the lure of professional status.

THE POLITICS OF PROFESSIONALISM

The professionals, so empowered, are diametrically opposed to the open political process, to any process in which the public can participate on equal terms. Being professionals (see that license?), they need not engage in a dialogue with anyone, and least of all with misguided politicians. "Politics," wrote Frederick Mosher, "is seen as constituting negotiation, elections, votes, compromises—all carried on by subject-matter amateurs. Politics is to the profession as ambiguity to truth, expediency to rightness, heresy to true belief."[4] There is no need for the hassle of politics which can only obscure the general interest. After all, if the professionals did not know what the general interest looked like, they would not be professionals. The logic is unbeatable, and insofar as government is a collection of professions, there is no room for political debate.

Government will ultimately become a self-perpetuating machine, dominated by sets of functional rationality. A dependence on functional rationality is the nub of the matter. When the announcer says—"Kowalski is playing a great game despite a separated shoulder and a deviated septum. *He's a real pro*!"—we have a succinct portrait of some kind of nut or, in more pedantic terms, a person suffering from "professional deformity." The "real pro" is something less than a normal human being who can appreciate life in all its rich detail. But if one is convinced that his or her particular technique holds the key to the universe, why look for guidance from a bunch of ignorent laypersons? In view of that attitude, how can one talk about popular control of government?

An illustration is provided by the "Astin Case." Dr. Astin was the "temporary" director of the U.S. Bureau of Standards when the Eisenhower administration took office in 1953. After twenty years in the wilderness, the

Republicans finally had a mandate to determine public policy. One of their party goals was aid to the small businessperson and one such entrepreneur had developed a battery additive which was sent to the Bureau for analysis. Bureau scientists ruled that the additive, although not harmful, did not add to motor performance. Eisenhower, his Secretary of Commerce, and the political leaders of the Bureau pressured for a favorable ruling. Astin stood by his scientific grounds and was backed by several hundred scientists who threatened to resign if he were replaced. The decision stood, Ike and his Secretary passed from the scene, and Astin remained in charge of the Bureau for many more years.[5]

Now, if you will recall, the subject was democracy, a political decision-making system in which officials are responsible to a majority of the public. In other words, the majority, whether for rational or irrational, professional or unprofessional reasons, has the power to construct reality. Is the situation as bleak as the Astin case indicates? No. It is bleaker, for the case represents only the veto power of professional groups. The professions have become more aggressive and are now on the offensive against the rest of society. It is not enough for the profession to resist ignorant assaults on what is good and true. As Robert Lane predicted about the "Knowledgeable Society," the professions have a vision of what should be and "the gap between the actual and the ideal creates within the profession a kind of strain towards remedial action."[6] The world is not good enough and light must be brought to the benighted. If the public or its representatives do not want to listen to reason, the profession can say, "We have ways. . . ."

The tension between the professions and democracy was revealed by a school election in Lawndale, California. Twice the voters of Lawndale went to the polls and rejected a bond issue for the improvement of the schools. The voters said, in effect, "OK, we do not want to pay for good schools so we'll make do with what we've got." A regrettable decision, we might agree, but one with impeccable democratic credentials. Professional teachers did not accept the decision and the California Teacher's Association blacklisted the school district because it "did not offer an acceptable level for professional service." The errors of democracy would have to be rectified by those who knew better. But how else should teachers respond when they are taught, in the words of a professor of secondary education, that:

> Teachers yield to no group in their concern for the welfare of students, since their lives are spent in schools, and it is this professional concern which imposes an obligation to resist rather than follow the spokesmen of actual or imaginary ethics or "public opinion" should this counsel be contrary to the success of the profession, its members, or their charges.[7]

Of course, this attitude is not the end of politics. Rather, as Lane rightly put it, it is more a change of venue. Somewhere in the shuffle, the public, with all its "actual or imaginary" opinions, is left out. It may be old-fashioned to argue so, but I still hope it is possible for a political community to enable all people to seek a good life together. Such unity can be achieved only if the impact of a fragmenting professionalism is curbed.

AMERICAN BUREAUCRACY

So far, I have said little about the exact relationship between democracy and bureaucracy in the American context. But then such silence is the American way since neither our political theory nor our Constitution tell us much. What passes for American political theory conveniently ignores administrative matters. In the fount of American political forms—the Constitution—administration is not really considered. The authors of the *Federalist Papers*, in their enduring defense of the document, envisioned a President in charge of something innocently called "execution." The decision to be executed was the result of a nicely balanced mechanism built into the Constitution. The three coequal branches act and interact to keep the whole system in equilibrium. Even if that traditional view were ever realistic, it is sadly out of whack today. The tripartite division of powers has not taken into account the growth of a fourth branch—a "headless fourth branch," as journalists like to exclaim—the bureaucracy. The other three branches have responded ineffectively to this intruder.

Some claim the judiciary has worked well in controlling the bureaucracy. At least it has held the line in some areas, and administrators can scarcely ignore the courts. However, the long view shows that courts have never really understood the nature of administration. After a long period of saying no, in the present era of what Nathan Glazer calls the "imperial judiciary" the courts are asking (or telling) administrators to do too much.[8] But these are the concerns of administrative law, a topic to be taken up in Chapter 11.

Congress was to be the branch which formally determined the policy to be executed by administration. Even if we accept the fiction that there is no delegation of legislative authority and that all law is an act of Congress, there are still some serious defects in the theory. First, the subject matter before Congress is so complex that even a general formulation of policy is beyond the capacity of the legislators. When reminded of their intellectual deficiencies by the professionals, legislators are generally willing to be guided by the expert advice of administrators. Second, Congress is not a monolithic unit of decision making in which 435 representatives and 100 senators pool their collective wisdom for the benefit of all the people. Congress is a loose coalition of feudal domains. Real decision making takes place within the specialized committees and subcommittees.

The executive branch is far more than a dignified chief of state and a handful of clerks. Today it is grossly inaccurate to think of the President as a monocratic ruler at the pinnacle of a coherent administrative hierarchy.

What we call the executive branch is better represented as a series of concentric circles, with presidential authority radiating out from the center, through the closest advisers, through the Executive Office of the President to, at best, the department heads. That model would include most of the people likely to respond immediately to the will of the Chief Executive.

Where, then, are the bureaucrats? In a very general sense, they are members of the units which make up the departmental holding companies. But this generalization is awfully misleading because of the bewildering variety of institutional forms in the federal government. Harold Seidman identifies at least fifteen major forms of organizational structure, including one he calls the "twilight zone."[9] In this jungle, the individual bureaus emerge as the real centers of power. The bureaus are the functional areas dominated by specific professions. They come in all flavors: Bureau of Mines, National Guard Bureau, Bureau of Prisons, Bureau of Labor Statistics, Foreign Service, Forest Service, Bureau of Post Office Facilities, Office of Education, Federal Housing Administration, National Science Foundation, National Cancer Institute, Federal Trade Commission, St. Lawrence Seaway Development Corporation, Federal Records Council, Flood Insurance Advisory Committee, Corporation for Public Broadcasting, the Migratory Bird Conservation Commission, and so on.

Does the President have any or all of these under firm control? Not very likely, I should think. In reality, we must cut the executive branch into two parts. One part is the President, who serves as a spokesperson for a national constituency—speaks, but not necessarily acts. The rest is the bureaucracy, the administrative branch, and whatever control exists comes from a variety of sources. The main point is that the bureaucracy remains outside the Constitution and outside its democratic requirements.

To those who would wail, "Oh lordie, the Constitution doesn't work anymore and we'll all be killed!" the students of American government have a reassuring answer. Social scientists have investigated the problem to find out how things do work and, in finding out, are obliged to confess that it is exactly the way it should be. We ought not hope for something better because realistically we have the best possible system. The sober students of the administrative process have weighed the bureaucracy and found it to be just a little bit of all right. The bureaucracy is a vital part of the dominant theory of American democracy—the pluralist approach.

PLURALISM AND ITS PROBLEMS

Pluralist theory sees the polity as composed of a number of conflicting groups. As groups pursue their special interests, they collide with one another in a political arena designed to provide access to the relevant government agencies. In this view, there is no "public" but instead an infinite number of publics, each one concerned with a narrow range of interests. A variety of factors—overlapping memberships, an appreciation of the rules of the game, a fear of the threat posed by yet unorganized groups—ameliorates the intensity of the struggle and, as a result, we have a political system which almost automatically satisfies the most urgent demands of important citizens. That is, the right people get their payoffs on a regular basis.

I can accept this theory as descriptive. It is all too obvious that American public policy is the product of the machinations of special interests. But I join with an increasing number of social scientists who question whether the "is" can be translated into an "ought." Specifically, does pluralism as an ideology fit into our concept of democracy? The defenders of pluralism argue that it is democratic, or at least as democratic as any system in a world dominated by powerful administrative institutions. It is in fact the only form of democracy which can survive in the face of modern complexity.

Peter Woll has been a persuasive advocate of the theory that the American political system blundered into the best possible arrangement for the control of bureaucracy. After proving that the bureaucracy is indeed an independent branch of government, he argues that it is quite responsive to public demands and is compatible with the Constitution. In his view, "the bureaucracy, which is actually a more representative body than Congress, combines essential democratic ingredients at the same time that it formulates important policy."[10] Moreover, precisely because bureaucracy is free of the electoral process, it is often as responsive as the politicians to public demands and needs.

True, interests do find representation in the bureaus, but is that all we expect from democratic government? Is the bureau representative of the public interest or of a special interest? Obviously, it is the latter. Woll and the other pluralists are able to make their arguments because they have written out of the political equation the "irrational citizen." By irrational, I mean someone who does not accept the bounded rationality of the bureau, someone who has a different concept of what government should do. By citizen, I mean a person whose only qualification for contacting government is membership in the polity. When the Nader study group began its investigation of the Interstate Commerce Commission, they were regarded by the bureaucrats as the first citizens ever to enter there; here were people with no direct business with the ICC wanting to know what is going on, and it upset the staff.[11] That seems a remarkable situation in a democracy.

We need a political system in which irrational citizens can approach government at their pleasure, even though their strolling in through the door may cause cardiac arrest among the clerks. Bull Connor of Birmingham coined the phrase to describe the irrational citizens: These are the no-count, outside agitators. The administrators, after all, are so full of sweetness and light that only the maladjusted would want to stir up trouble. But government is not meant to be a closed system in which only "nice" people are entitled to participate. Nor should the American political system be a modern version of the medieval guild system, in which each little group claims its piece of sovereignty.

One cannot really condemn the interest groups for their actions in this matter. The promotion of special interests is their sole reason for existence. What we can question is the wisdom of those social scientists, and particularly students of administration, who insist that this is a healthy situation and that indeed the business of public administration is to ensure that the pressure groups have access to the policy machinery.

Theodore Lowi's well-known critique of the pluralist ideology summarizes the defects of such a system in operation:

1 It leads to the atrophy of institutions of public control. Both the public and its politicians become less concerned with the maintenance of more open methods of articulating larger interests. The reform of the legislature and executive is not seen as urgent since supposedly alternatives exist.

2 It creates rigid structures of privilege. Those who have, keep; and they resist the entrance of new participants with whom they might have to share. New players have to make very strenuous efforts if they are to receive a piece of the action.

3 It promotes conservatism in the deepest sense, in the sense of inertia.[12]

As Henry Kariel put it, public policies are determined by standards which are "professional ones professionally arrived at; they are organizational imperatives interpreted by officials whose interest lies in the exclusion of competing interests."[13]

Robert Paul Wolff calls pluralism "a philosophy of equality and justice whose *concrete application* supports inequality by ignoring the existence of certain legitimate social groups."[14] The problem in application is, as we shall see, the bureaucracy itself. Because of pluralism's epistemology, some groups will be seen as irrational. Paul Goodman was correct in noting "the metaphysical defect in our pluralism."[15] It provides all sorts of choice as long as everyone wants more or less the same thing. The freedom of pluralism is much like that freedom of choice hailed by friends of technology such as Alvin Toffler. We can choose among 156 different brands of cereal; the only difference, however, is the amount of Red Dye No. 2 each contains. And so in government, pluralism provides all sorts of choice as long as nothing changes.

AMERICAN GOVERNMENT IN ACTION

We are somewhat closer now to an understanding of how American government acts or, more commonly, does not act. The real engine is the so-called governmental subsystem.[16] Called "the triple alliance," "the cozy triangle," or "the unholy trinity," it is composed of "the expert, the interested, and the engaged" in the bureaus, interest groups, and congressional committees concerned with a specific policy.[17] The subsystems are more important in the day-to-day operations of government than the more visible actors such as the President and congressional leaders. The President and Congress may clash dramatically on major issues, but the great bulk of decisions is made by the less publicized participants. The policies that affect our lives tend to be the product of people who, regardless of their place within the constitutional division of powers, form a community of interest along functional lines.

The public roads subsystem is one example among many. It is dominated by a number of people from various backgrounds, all of whom see a great deal of merit in the completion of the interstate highway system. The professional engineers at the federal and state level are interested in pouring eight lanes of blacktop between any two given points. Labor unions and construction firms, together with a number of subsidiary economic interests, are concerned with keeping the billions of dollars flowing. The trucking industry is delighted with the subsidy. Automobile associations support the project. And as a widely dispersed public works project—an ideal pork-barrel operation—almost all member of Congress have been happy with the tangible payoffs in their home districts. When these people get together to discuss the future of the program, the question of whether it should be done at all seldom arises; and it is not odd that they should agree among themselves that all is in order. Dissenters who would, for example, argue in favor of mass transit have had a hard time making themselves heard. There have recently been some significant inroads made into this subsystem through an assault on the big honey pot holding it all together—the Highway Trust Fund. But changes have come about only after it is no longer possible to deny that the private automobile is ruining our health, our environment, and our economy. To argue, as some pluralists undoubtedly would, that the subsystem did after all respond to the possibility of the end of the world as we know it is not particularly encouraging.

A more notorious subsystem is the "military-industrial complex." It is quite unfair to picture the members of the complex as bloodthirsty merchants of death. Instead, they are influential people with a fairly uniform vision of the reality of national defense. Defense contractors, after all, are interested in bigger and better defense systems. We would hope that the military professionals are equally concerned with the procurement of the latest tools of their trade. Finally, members of Congress, and especially those in defense-related committees, tend to be sympathetic to the needs of an adequate national defense. All these people are, we must assume, basically decent individuals; their only weakness is a collective one—taken as a whole, there is little room for a radically different approach. They are a closed group who have been telling each other essentially the same thing for the past thirty years. Senator Eugene McCarthy was not entirely facetious when he responded to a question about the first thing he would do if elected President. He answered that he would try to establish diplomatic relations with the Pentagon.

This leads to the natural question of where the Chief Executive fits into all of this. According to Senator Barry Goldwater, the President does not fit in; "It would be downright laughable," he said, "if it were not so serious to consider how many of our people actually believe that a national administration firmly controls the Federal Government."[18] Conservative hyperbole aside, the President is far from powerless and if it comes down to a one-on-one contest between the President of the United States of America and the letter carrier on your block, the smart money would be on the White House. But a President has only so much time and energy and cannot ride constant herd on the millions of federal employees and their diverse activities. The report of criminal acts by the CIA cannot be overlooked, and some time will have to be spent on bringing them back under control. While that sticky problem is being dealt with, what will the Bureau of Indian Affairs be up to? If militants take over another reservation, the President's attention will be diverted in that direction.

It is not, in other words, a matter of the President's issuing a coherent set of orders. The best summary of the futility of that approach came from a man who ought to know, Harry Truman. Sitting in the Oval Office just before the inauguration of Eisenhower, he said, "He'll sit here and he'll say 'Do this! Do that!' And nothing will happen. Poor Ike—it won't be a bit like the Army. He'll find it very frustrating."[19] Truman could vouch for that from his own experiences, such as the dismissal of his supposed subordinate, General MacArthur. Formal orders can be thwarted by something so simple as the "rule of three." According to veteran bureaucrats, the first time an executive asks for something, just ignore it; the second time, say you are working on it. A third request means the matter is probably serious, and so some action had better be taken. But few have the perseverance to follow it through that far. Some bureau chiefs, of course, are so powerful that they do not need to bother with such ploys. They simply tell the President, in one form or another, to kiss off. J. Edgar Hoover was only a more notable example of this phenomenon.

There are a number of studies which reveal the weaknesses of pluralism. *Muddy Waters*, a study by Arthur Maass of the Army Corps of Engineers, is an excellent investigation of pluralism in action. The book is somewhat dated, but the basic criticism is still valid. And since it was written at about the time that pluralism, as a normative theory, was capturing the hearts and minds of political scientists, worth noting is the fact that there has always been abundant evidence that bureaucratic responsibility cannot be ensured by the interaction of various groups. We knew even then that the public interest was not served by sitting back and watching the organized interests duke it out.

Maass established an operational definition of responsibility; with that model he weighed the activity of the Corps and found it wanting. If the Corps was responsible, it was only to a very limited clientele, and there is no way one could mistake that clientele with the general interest of all Americans in the area of water resources policy. Only one pressure group had easy access to the Corps. Individual members of Congress, and not the whole body, made water policy through their aggregate demands for a piece of pork to take home to the voters. The President, the Commander in Chief of the Corps as a military unit, was largely powerless to work his will on his subordinates; he could not achieve coordination with other water resources agencies. Broader professional dictates were ignored by the Corps as dams were erected in response to political pressures. In short, the study does not lend support to the thesis that bureaucratic responsibility can be expected by permitting a bureau to operate in a rather unstructured context of political activity.[20]

The Interstate Commerce Commission is generally held up as a bad example of all the bureaucratic excesses. At one time, it was regarded as a model for other governmental agencies. According to Samuel Huntington, it sunk into a stupor once it made the decision to cohabit with the regulated industry. An alliance was struck with the worst possible consequences—a sick regulatory agency overseeing the progressive disintegration of a sick industry, the railroads.[21] The development of a national transportation plan is still something which the American public lacks (along with decent rail service), although the ICC should have been a leader in this area. But the clerks of the Interstate Commerce Omission, as the Nader study group called it, are not easily jarred out of their lethargy, and few outside forces can touch them.

The Corps and the ICC are always trotted out to scare young students of administration, but the deficiencies of pluralism are just as obvious in more recent policy areas. Gary Orfield has detailed how blacks have been shut out of the subsystem which was made responsible for the execution of the civil rights legislation of the 1960s. Minorities won many famous victories in the legislature, but so far they have not penetrated the agencies which are to implement the legislation. The prevalent subsystems within Health, Education and Welfare, Housing and Urban Development, and the Federal Housing Administration are still dominated by the old coalitions. As Orfield concludes, "administrative technicians are far more responsive to detailed, specific comments couched in the appropriate professional jargon and conveyed from one acquaintance to another, than they are to outside indictments or organized general demands."[22]

The pluralist model of administrative responsibility still has its defenders. Lee Fritschler, for example, supports Woll's position that "the existence of a bureaucracy with policymaking power assures a more broadly representative decision-making process than one that relies solely on a legislature."[23] The case he studies is a powerful one since it is a clear case in which the "good guys" won out in a struggle with an entrenched and dangerous subsystem. The tobacco subsystem, composed of members of Congress from tobacco-growing states, the tobacco industry, and the officials from the Department of Agriculture who administer the subsidies for tobacco were able to fight off many attempts to regulate cigarette smoking. In the end, however, the American political system did awaken to the danger and the subsystem is in a much weakened position.

But one can read Fritschler's book and just as well be dismayed by the considerable inaction of the policy structure. The end result is not positive action to eliminate a costly social problem; instead, the tobacco industry has made concessions to the health interests without, apparently, reducing the overall consumption of tobacco. And that took at least ten years after there was reliable information about the harmful effects of smoking—and ten years may turn out to have been a fatally long time for a number of unwitting citizens if the weed is as toxic as the Surgeon General claims.

In the meantime, we are treated to the spectacle of the bureaucracy riding off, on our tax money, in all directions at once. What HEW is trying to stop, the USDA is trying to promote; at one time, bureaucrats on one side of the street were making movies extolling the pleasures of smoking, while on the other side, they were preparing propaganda showing the horrible fate of the addict. In the process, administrators had to perform mental acrobatics to justify the situation. According to Secretary of Agriculture Freeman, tobacco subsidies were a health measure since they kept the price of cigarettes artificially high and therefore reduced consumption. Is that any way to run a government? The pluralists say, "You bet it is!"

UNREPRESENTATIVE BUREAUCRACY

The pluralist thesis regarding the benign effects of bureaucratic participation in policy making requires overlooking basic elements of the administrative mentality. To be sure, I am all in favor of the rich pluralism of interests which characterizes American life, and I am certain that it is something essential for the preservation of the democratic way. I just lack confidence in the ability of the administrative organs to cultivate the true diversity of pluralism. As I hope I have made clear by now, the bureaucrats have sided with rationality over irrationality, with calculation over the incalculable. This perception does not lead to a great deal of optimism about the political capabilities of the bureaucrats.

The pluralists, as we have seen, insist that the bureaucracy is truly representative of all interests of society. In the abstract, it is a terrific argument; when we stop to consider how the bureaucracy functions in the usual case, it looks more dubious. The bureaucracy does not as a matter of course deal with the public in terms of people who just wander in off the street. The people represented must present credentials to prove that they are part of a legitimate interest. Only some interests are identified, classified, and stabilized, which is the same as saying that only some interests deserve representation while new or inarticulate interests may remain outside the calculation. In other words, the bureaucracy still relies on the bounded rationality in determining who should have access to the decision-making process. We can see this when we look more closely at the specific instruments through which representation of the public is supposed to be achieved.

Informal Conferences and Consultations Through this device, administrators are able to feel out important members of the public, to see who will support a proposal and who will resist. They can also learn how a policy can be modified so that its execution will be easier. However, as advocates of this approach admit, the process may be "unrepresentative" in that the choice of sources depends upon the perception of the bureaucrat.[24] For example, does a city planner in urban renewal consult with the realtors or with the tenement dwellers? We can at least hypothesize that administrators will not gladly pick up the phone to talk to people from whom they are sure to catch all sorts of hell. But when used, we are told, this device has great potential for engineering consent, and it does look like participation.

The Commission When a particular policy area is to be administered, it is not uncommon to construct a precisely defined constellation of interests to serve as a combined executive and legislative board. The dismal record of such commissions is so well known that we need not belabor the fact that, logically, the "regulatees" always get identified and eventually wind up doing most of the regulating. The occasional consumer representative will learn, if survival is at all important, that he or she will have to come to grips with the real constituency of the commission. But then not too many general interests earn positions on the board.[25]

Advisory Committees Although the commission has real authority, the typical committee is only advisory. These committees are composed of people who the administrators feel ought to be consulted in a formal way somewhere in the policy-making process. Despite recent attempts to cut down their number, the latest count showed that 1,267 committees are at work in the federal government.[26] They cover a variety of subjects—there is, or was, a Condor Advisory Committee which presumably had something to do with helping that endangered bird—but most are concerned with economic matters.

It is hard to say exactly what they do or how they do it, although the idea is to make available to all interested parties an easy access to government. Not surprisingly, the representatives tend to be friends and patrons of the agency. That is, farmers serve on agriculture committees and businesspersons serve in the Commerce Department. A recent news story reported on the National Petroleum Council of the Interior Department. This panel, which has played a major role in shaping the nation's energy policy, is a 155-person body including the heads of 34 large oil companies, such as Exxon, Standard of California, Mobil, Texaco, and Gulf, as well as executives from the natural gas and petrochemical industries. One wonders how much time this body spends on the problem of dollar-a-gallon gasoline—if indeed they are able to perceive that as a problem.

Lyle Schaller made a very forceful assessment of the operation of such committees in local government, and what he wrote is probably applicable to other levels as well:

> These millions of citizens who are the discards of our urban society—the disinherited, the dispossessed, the despondent, the deprived and the depraved—must be reached and brought into a meaningful relationship with the processes of government which affect their lives. Apparently, this goal requires a form of community organization far more sophisticated than the citizen advisory committee.[27]

In the pluralist model, that is about what one could expect, until such time as there is an American Society of the Deprived and Depraved. With those credentials, the societal rejects could prove that they deserve representation.

Participatory Administration The rhetoric of the 1960s has subsided, and just about everyone has lost enthusiasm for this idea, whatever it was. The maximum feasible participation which was to get the deprived and depraved into the system terrified the powers that be. Bureaucrats were not very helpful in allowing outsiders to interfere with their standard operating procedures. Participation as an idea was fine as protective coloration, but where implemented the result was something like the thoroughly docile PTA in the schools.[28] Also overlooked was the impact of participation on the participants. When they were brought into professional organizations as "paraprofessionals," it was not unusual for the outsiders to begin to aspire to professional status. This may have been good testimony for the upward-mobility part of the American Dream, but it did not make the bureaucracy more representative.

Formal Hearings Many government agencies are required by law to announce in advance that hearings will be held on a proposed change and that interested citizens can testify. Little research has been done in this area, and even if there were studies, they probably would not be too reliable. The observer can go to the hearings, see the hearing examiner with his or her eyes more or less open and apparently listening to aged retirees protest that they will starve if gas and electricity rates are increased. Whether the testimony is making an impression is another question, but one can suspect that the pleas of isolated citizens are not enough to outweigh the imposing mountain of statistics, analyses, and legal briefs supplied by the industries. Only rarely do others complain, as the Justice Department did in an ICC case, about "this basic attitude—that industry sponsored witnesses are all-knowing and wise and that others are naive or ill-informed."[29] But that may be beside the point, since most consumers do not even bother to show up at the hearings.

Decentralization The idea was to submerge the policy makers in the local community and, in its strongest forms, make them directly responsible to the people they serve. Sad to say, there are few, if any, examples in which a large bureaucracy has been completely broken up and returned to the local community. In educational circles, it has been a popular idea; but the horrors raised by the Ocean Hill–Brownsville experiment in New York City in 1968 have made everyone very cautious. In the moves toward school decentralization which have been made, care is taken to ensure that the professionals do not feel that their prerogatives are threatened. As the New York City teachers proved, the professionals, supposedly the object of control, will simply pull out of the operation. The lesson of the 1960s is "that organizations of professionals, particularly those that have only recently achieved power and recognition, will be a continuing and general source of opposition to new community roles."[30]

Representative Bureaucracy When all else fails to prove the pluralist model, fall back on the spooky concept of representative bureaucracy. In its most abstract form, the argument is that there is a natural commonality of interests between citizens and bureaucrats because of the socioeconomic background of administrators. In general, the great majority of Americans are middle-class types, as are the great majority of bureaucrats. Therefore the bureaucracy will automatically represent the interests of the majority. More specifically, doctors are represented by public health departments, teachers by education departments, farmers by the USDA, and veterans by the VA. And following the logic, pacifists are represented by the Defense Department, dopers by their narcotic agents, and the Black Panthers by the Chicago Police Department.

The representative bureaucracy argument, as well as all the other concrete mechanisms for representation, break apart on the shoals of professionalism. If it were not for the professional element, one could conceivably argue that by the judicious shuffling of the membership of committees and commissions it would be possible to keep track of the relevant interests in society. But it will not work when we are talking about representation before bureaucrats who are also card-carrying professionals. Being professionals, the administrators are programmed to reject certain ideas and groups out of hand. Certain people persist in bringing up errors which are patently unprofessional. Thus there is no free competition among groups and individuals before the bureaucracy. Professionals will automatically "ignore messages which do not arrive in the approved form, in the proper way, and from the appropriate sources."[31] Even though democracy may require that all groups will have equal access, the real pro sees some as more equal than others.

If you are taught that the preservation of the forests is a sacred trust and believe that Smokey the Bear lives, how can you sympathize with the lumberjack who wants to clear-cut whole counties? If you are an MD, how can you communicate with the person who believes that eating blueberries will cure cancer? If you are a professional soldier, how can you relate to the person who believes you are a bloody murderer and that your whole life is worthless? If, as a college professor, you believe that a liberal education is the highest good, how can you appreciate a group of parents who want to replace Latin with body-and-fender repair solely for vocational reasons? In short, how can professionals fail to admire the wisdom, the good sense, the expertise of a fellow professional in a friendly interest group? And how can they fail to be appalled by the uninformed nonsense preached by laypersons? They can do otherwise only by denying the basic tenets of their chosen profession, which is to say, by rejecting their whole reason for being.

The pluralist model does not mean the politicization of the bureaucracy; it means the bureaucratization of politics. It means the fixing of permissible values within an iron framework. Within the limits of a single issue, everyone more or less agrees anyway, and that is not politics at all. It is administration, the pursuit of the rational. Even if the representative organs contain a token freak, can we really be sure that freakish values are represented? Professionally, some values have easier access simply because the brain of the bureaucrat has been hermetically sealed against error.

SECRECY AND PUBLICITY

Before we leave the national government, one topic, while of concern at other levels, is especially relevant to the growing fears about the bureaucracy in Washington. The Pentagon papers, the Watergate tapes, and a number of lesser outrages, such as the capers of the CIA and FBI, have just about killed that notion from a simpler time of "an informed public opinion." The problem is that of the manipulation of communications (or non-communications) for the benefit of the governors, and especially of the bureaucracy. So, assuming that public-spirited citizens want to find out what is happening, how can they be sure that they are actually receiving the pertinent information and that they are not being fed carefully fabricated statements which, when it suits the needs of those in power, will be declared "inoperative"? Is it not possible that the government occasionally softens us up by giving us just enough information to make their schemes look good to us?

Some observers have argued that the manipulation of information is narrowing the gap between totalitarian and democratic governments; both are forsaking outright coercion and are relying upon persuasion to modify people's behavior.[32] The words of the government are more and more a part of the environment to which we respond, and so the officials can actually control our perception of reality. If that is the case, who is controlling whom? Unfortunately, the problem is not solved by any extreme position, and every argument has its opposite. Every discussion fades away into a bold "maybe."

Secrecy It is understandable that administrators are not too enthusiastic about working in the hot glare of publicity. No one can perform very well if the public is kibbitzing even before the final decision is made. Furthermore, the bureaucratic culture encourages a secretive manner. It is not healthy to have around an accurate count of all the errors one makes—and in any good bureaucracy, it is almost impossible to keep from violating some regulations.

At the same time, the most rabid democrat should be able to accept the need for some governmental secrecy, even beyond those areas of national security and international relations. Revealing the probable location of public facilities, for example, might drive up land prices at the expense of the taxpayers. An identified Mafia informer would soon be sleeping with the fishes rather than serving the police. A while ago, an underground paper published the names and addresses of all the narcotic agents in a certain city; no good purpose was served when the families were subjected to abuse in their homes. And a final example which everyone should relate to: one's own personnel file. Should any stranger be able to bop into a public office to paw through your tax returns, social security data, employment records, or any of the other dossiers we accumulate?

Granted then, democracy requires some governmental secrecy. Where do we start drawing lines? Or more important, who will do the drawing? There is ultimately no way to avoid the conclusion that it will depend upon the discretion of the people we want to learn about. In matters of secrecy, possession is all ten points of the law. The bureaucrats must decide whether a certain piece of information, insofar as it is a real secret known only to them, is fit for consumption by the public. As Francis Rourke, a keen student of government secrecy, has noted, this gives the bureaucrats a dual-purpose weapon: they can conceal embarrassing facts and they can release their secrets selectively in order to mold public opinion.[33]

But the secretive bureaucrats are not always schemers. It is probably worse when they are quite righteous in their belief that they need to lie to the public. There are all those wrongthinkers out there who only want to destroy a valuable program, it can be argued. The classic illustration involved the Rural Electrification Administration and an anti-New Deal politician. An official concluded that the Congressman was on a "fishing expedition" for information to use against the agency; thus he took it upon himself to juggle some important figures just to protect what he was sure was a program beneficial to the whole public.[34]

Of course, when the bureaucrat becomes obsessed with secrecy as a way to hide everything, the situation becomes intolerable. The military has provided us with numerous examples here. Rather than take a chance on releasing important state secrets, just stamp everything classified; it is much easier to do than to explain why a secret got out. Eventually, it makes sense to stamp SECRET on one's copy of a large daily newspaper as the Air Force did not too long ago. And the public is left out in the dark.

But no more, it is said. We are free at last because of the Freedom of Information Act of 1966. The act states that identifiable documents, unless covered by one of the nine types of exemptions, shall be provided when demanded by a citizen. It also states that the burden of proof for denial rests with the government. It was a significant act, and with its recent amendments, it probably takes us as far as the law can go in this area. The real deficiency of the act, or of any other, is its presumption that the citizen really knows about the existence of a secret—in which case it is not so secret. That is, until the recent startling revelations, it would not have occurred to many of us to ask the CIA about their files on assassinating foreign leaders, or to ask the FBI how its harassment of Martin Luther King was coming along, or to ask the President's close associate if he had planned any interesting illegal entries lately. The law alone can never let the sun shine into every corner of government. And it is in the dark that creepy, crawly things thrive.

Publicity The public relations function has grown rapidly in government, and when an agency such as HEW tries to cut back, there are cynics who dismiss it as another public relations gimmick. The public information officer (PIO) has become an important member of many government agencies, with major implications for the shaping of public opinion.

Again, it is not a one-sided proposition. Some publicity is essential. Indeed, the sole purpose of some government agencies is to produce and disseminate information. The work of almost all government agencies is much easier if the public can be convinced to cooperate. Also, government agencies must be allowed to make known to the public that their services are available. For example, it is estimated that there is still a large number of needy people who simply do not know about the welfare programs for which they might be eligible.

The problem is that publicity may become harmful propaganda; within the bureaucratic setting, such a transmogrification is probably inevitable. There is a cracker-barrel school of administration which says, "don't you fret none—a good job is the best form of advertisement," while no amount of press agentry will conceal the fact you are doing a crummy job. If you are a good manager, it is claimed, you are also a good publicist.

But do the realities of the organization permit such a passive approach? The manager has other things to worry about, and if public relations is so important, a single individual ought to be given responsibility for it. A PIO must be hired—the organizational Pollyanna who is not going to get too many raises by telling the brutal truth. The PIO's reason for being is the improvement of the "image" of the organization, and that image may not always be enhanced by candor. It is probably wiser to take some snappy photos of Miss Series-E Savings Bonds or concoct some story which will require the public to enter into the state of the "willing suspension of disbelief." Anyone who has read a house organ, public or private, has to suspect that a great deal of the really juicy stuff is not getting out.

A more important fact is that in the bureaucratic jungle, one may be out of a job if it is thought that virtue is its own reward. Tooting one's horn seems to be a valuable device, particularly in the budgetary process. That is, if you are doing a good job, it does not hurt to tell people about it, but more, if you are not doing a good job, it is even more critical to tell the public that you are. We are learning now, much to our dismay, just how well this philosophy worked for J. Edgar Hoover and the FBI. It is still incredible that Efrem Zimbalist, Jr., could have engaged in all that shoddy, and not particularly effective, activity. Past a certain point, publicity can also detract from the ability of the citizen to come to an independent decision about government. As with secrecy, no magic means exists for identifying what is "just enough."

IN THE PUBLIC INTEREST

And so the question remains, who is in charge here? Where and how is the political element to survive? Or is policy to be the result of the war of all groups against all as manifested through the bureaus? In my view, the fourth branch does not allow for much divergence from established routines; the system is stacked in favor of the maintenance of the bounded rationalities of the separate bureaus. Where then does the consideration of the totality, of the "public interest," come into all of this?

Just like everyone else, I have thrown around rather loosely the term "public interest," as if I really knew what it meant. We are forced now to consider its significance for democratic administration. I could drink, with everyone else, to the proposition that administration should be in the public interest so that we citizens may be assured that government is actually doing something substantively rational. To use a quaint phrase, government should promote the common weal.

But what about the possibility that there is no such thing, at least not in the sense of an operational standard against which specific administrative acts can be measured before the fact? It should be quite clear that on the bureaucrat's first day on the job, the orientation officer is not able to say, "There's the washroom, there's the water cooler, and over there in the corner is the public interest." Many students of administration have wrestled with the problem, trying to find a keystone for the structure of democratic administration. Twenty years ago, Glendon Schubert reviewed the best thought on the subject and came to the conclusion that there were no certain guidelines; not much has changed in the intervening years.[35]

So what clues about the public interest can be offered to help an administrator when confronted with a political decision? It would be deadly if the administrators should turn their backs on the question, as so many have already done. Most of our brightest administrators know full well that they are up to their necks in politics, without having been told by academics. They like it, they thrive in it, and they have developed an almost uncanny ability to survive. They are proud, and rightly so, of their political skill and agility. But for what end? Is it only a game? If so, how is it scored and how does one know when he or she has won? I would feel much more comfortable if these administrators were always concerned with using their political resources to assist the rest of us, the public, in participating in a democratic system.

Although I am far from confident that it answers all the questions, my approach remains that of the radical democrat. There is no public interest—not in the sense of an identifiable, enduring "thing." The closest one can come to it is the will of the majority of voters at any particular time. If administrators accept this (and what else is there to accept?), they must look to the majority for guides to action. But it is not enough to conjure up one's own majority or interpret what the majority really wants through some mysterious rite. Instead, one can look to the physical embodiment of the majority in the elected officials.

Admittedly, it is not a perfect solution. But it is probably the best one can do in order to remain a practicing democrat in an age when most decisions are made by people who are not directly responsible to the electorate. It is, I confess, a world that looks very much like the one pictured by Peter Woll and the other pluralists, but I am not content to allow the bureaucracy to remain as an independent force. I do not believe that it is too late in the day for the traditional branches to provide a head for the headless branch.

I am not convinced that the Constitution is so far out of date in terms of administration. It still has a number of good things going for it, not the least of which is its basically democratic character. Moreover, as the courts have held, it is a document not overly concerned with efficiency; it is designed to make the job of the administrator harder rather than easier, and so it can serve as an impediment to the perfection of the administrative state. Therefore, I recommend the rehabilitation of the Constitution in order to cope with a massive administrative structure. I am in agreement with the thoughtful analysis of John Millett:

> Our constitutional system possesses the instrumentalities for adequate political control of bureaucracy. So long as the structure of political power encourages the effective operation of the political institutions of our society, and so long as the political institutions lead and encourage as well as direct and supervise the administrative work of government, that long shall we continue to have a politically responsible bureaucracy in a democratic polity and a free society.[36]

My modest contribution to the rejuvenation of the Constitution will not be in the realm of grand principles. My aim is to provide the bearer of a different standard of rationality—the representative of the majority—with ideas about how the retreat of the politicians from government can be stemmed. When I get to the subareas of public administration, my main concern will not be the establishment of elaborate reforms, but rather I will warn about the further rationalization of administration at the expense of politics. In all areas of administration, moves are afoot to eliminate politics, either through removing politicians or by domesticating the citizens. I would like all participants, and especially present and future administrators, to devote a little sober reflection to the situation.

REFERENCES

1 See Everett Hughes, "Professions," in Kenneth Lynn (ed.), *The Professions in America* (Boston: Beacon Press, 1967).

2 Jethro Lieberman, *The Tyranny of the Experts* (New York: Walker, 1970), p. 61.

3 Corinne Gilb, *Hidden Hierarchies* (New York: Harper & Row, 1966).

4 Frederick Mosher, *Democracy and the Public Service* (New York: Oxford University Press, 1968), p. 109.

5 S. A. Lawrence, "The Battery Additive Controversy," in *Inter-University Case Program* (University: University of Alabama Press, 1962).

6 Robert Lane, "The Decline of Politics and Ideology in a Knowledgeable Society," *American Sociological Review*, 31 (1966), p. 657.

7 Eugene Kruszynski, "Professionals and 'The Strike,' " *The Voice of the Faculties* (Sept. 1968), p. 12.

8 Nathan Glazer, "Towards an Imperial Judiciary?" *Public Interest*, no. 41 (Fall 1975), pp. 108–110.

9 Harold Seidman, *Politics, Position, and Power*, 2d ed. (New York: Oxford University Press, 1975), chap. 2.

10 Peter Woll, *American Bureaucracy*, 2d ed. (New York: Norton, 1977), p. 249. See also Peter Woll and Rochelle Jones, "The Bureaucracy as a Check upon the President," *The Bureaucrat*, 3 (April 1974), pp. 8–20.

11 Robert Fellmeth, *The Interstate Commerce Omission* (New York: Grossman, 1970), p. 33.
12 Thedore Lowi, *The End of Liberalism* (New York: Norton, 1969).
13 Henry Kariel, *The Decline of American Pluralism* (Stanford, Calif.: Stanford University Press, 1961), p. 112.
14 Robert Paul Wolff, *The Poverty of Liberalism* (Boston: Beacon Press, 1968), p. 154.
15 Paul Goodman, *Like a Conquered Province* (New York: Random House, 1967), p. 129.
16 J. Lieper Freeman, *The Political Process* (New York: Random House, 1965).
17 Douglass Cater, *Power in Washington* (New York: Vintage Books, 1965), p. 17.
18 Barry Goldwater, "The Federal Government Establishment," *Congressional Record*, 116 (July 14, 1970), p. 24104.
19 Quoted in Richard Neustadt, *Presidential Power* (New York: Wiley, 1960), p. 9.
20 Arthur Maass, *Muddy Waters* (Cambridge, Mass.: Harvard University Press, 1951).
21 Samuel Huntington, "The Marasmus of the ICC," in Francis Rourke (ed.), *Bureaucratic Power in National Politics*, lst ed. (Boston: Little, Brown, 1965).
22 Gary Orfield, "The Politics of Civil Rights Enforcement," in Michael Smith (ed.), *Politics in America* (New York: Random House, 1974), p. 79.
23 Lee Fritschler, *Smoking and Politics*, 2d ed. (Englewood Cliffs, N.J.: Prentice-Hall, 1975), pp. 155–156.
24 William Boyer, *Bureaucracy on Trial* (Indianapolis: Bobbs-Merrill, 1964), p. 70.
25 U.S. House of Representatives, Committee on Interstate and Foreign Commerce, *Regulatory Reform: Quality of Regulators* (Washington: GPO, 1976).
26 Dom Bonafede, "The PRTAIAOB&ST and Friends," *National Journal*, 8 (1976), p. 524.
27 Lyle Schaller, "Is the Citizen Advisory Committee a Threat to Representative Government?" *Public Administration Review*, 24 (1964), p. 179.
28 Elliot Krause, "Functions of a Bureaucratic Ideology: 'Citizen Participation,' " *Social Problems*, 16 (1968), pp. 129–142.
29 Quoted in Fellmeth, op. cit., p. 86.
30 Mario Fantini and Marilyn Gittell, *Decentralization* (New York: Praeger, 1973), p. 123.
31 Philip Beach, "Public Access to Policymaking in the United States," *University Programs Modular Studies* (Morristown, N.J.: General Learning Press, 1974), p. 18.
32 Francis Rourke, *Secrecy and Publicity* (Baltimore: Johns Hopkins, 1961), p. vii.
33 Francis Rourke, "Bureaucratic Secrecy and Its Constituents," *The Bureaucrat*, 1 (1972), pp. 116–121.
34 Winifred McCulloch, "The REA Personnel Report: A Case Study," in R. Golembiewski (ed.), *Perspectives on Public Management* (Itasca, Ill.: F. E. Peacock, 1968).
35 Glendon Schubert, " 'The Public Interest' in Administrative Decision-making: Theorem, Theosophy, or Theory?" *American Political Science Review*, 51 (1957), pp. 346–368.
36 John Millett, *Government and Public Administration* (New York: McGraw-Hill, 1959), p. 477.

Chapter 4

Politics and Administration in a Federal System

It is evident that a central government acquires immense power when united to administrative centralization. Thus combined, it accustoms men to set their own will habitually and completely aside; to submit, not only for once, or upon one point, but in every respect, and at all times. Not only, therefore, does this union of power subdue them compulsorily, but it affects them in the ordinary habits of life, and influences each individual, first separately and then collectively.

Alexis de Tocqueville
Democracy in America

Our attention so far has been directed toward the interplay of politics and administration at the national level. Washington, however, represents only one government among many. After all, ours is a federal system, and it might be argued that all sorts of bureaucratic maladies could be expected to afflict an overgrown system so far removed from the people it governs. Our Founding Fathers feared that possibility and therefore they placed restrictions upon the power of the central government so that a variety of forms could flourish at the local level. Politics is alive and well, it may be felt, in Waco, Texas; Downey, California; and Burwell, Nebraska.

On the surface, that appears to be true. We are a much governed people. Every five years, the Census Bureau counts as best it can the units of government in the United States. After checking all the states, counties, municipalities, townships, special districts, and school districts, the Bureau found that there were 78,268 units of government in 1972. That figure has been steadily decreasing, primarily because of the consolidation of school districts. Even so, there is probably enough government to go around, and all citizens are members of several of these units at the same time.

If we define very crudely a bureaucrat as someone who draws a government paycheck, it is clear that the great majority of them live among us. Of the nearly 15 million government employees in the United States, about 80 percent are working for state and local units. These employees are heavily engaged in such critical public services as education, highways, health services, and police protection. State and local governments spend almost half the several billions of dollars collected in taxes. The percentage would be much higher if we excluded functions related to the national government's monopoly in defense and foreign relations.

Equally important, there are approximately a half million elected officials in the United States. That is *prima facie* evidence of a hearty political life. If one is unhappy with the existing political reality, there would seem to be ample opportunity to take the classic democratic route to change—become a decision maker through the electoral process. Of course, many of these positions are not as powerful and glamorous as those at the national level; there is little pomp and circumstance attached to being director of a noxious weed control district or, unless one is concerned about the ragweed issue, much room for creativity. But then not everyone can be President. At the same time, I feel that there are enough chances for everyone to participate effectively in the political process at some level. The question is whether state and local politicians have any more real control over their bureaucracies than national leaders have over theirs.

In an important contribution to the literature of public administration, Vincent Ostrom (in far more scholarly language, of course) suggests that we blew it. Our nation was founded on the idea of popular administration, which rejected a preoccupation with "simplicity, neatness, and symmetry" and stressed "diversity, variety, and responsiveness to the preferences of constituents." More than that, he indicts the discipline of public administration for contributing to the "contemporary malaise in American society" because of its insistence on a style of administration hostile to more democratic forms. In reviewing some aspects of the federal system, we may see that there is much to this charge.[1]

THE CITY

We shall concentrate first on the most important general-purpose unit of government at the local level, the city. Students of the city are not unanimous in their definition of the very thing they are to study. Therefore, I feel free to take one perspective on the subject and to pursue its implications for our theme of politics and administration. In my view, the city is an excellent observation post for the consideration of the contest between rationality and irrationality.

The modern city, as a possible arena for political life, is a unique combination of collective rationality and individual freedom. The distinctive mark of the city, according to Leonard Reissman, is its "order without planning, the controlled chaos."[2] Anyone who has observed the activity in the downtown area of a large city during the rush hour has witnessed this paradox. The thousands of individuals bustling to and from multiple centers of activity—that so many people can interact in such a close space is incredible. Yet there are rational patterns involved which no corps of bureaucrats could ever duplicate. There is a rationality which has not been imposed from above by formal means.

The ideal city dweller is the person with a peculiar frame of mind. Here I borrow from the sociologist Louis Wirth's famous article on "Urbanism as a Way of Life."[3] Wirth defined the city as "a relatively large, dense and permanent settlement of socially heterogeneous individuals." From the factors of size, density, and heterogeneity, certain traits develop which make it possible for the individual to deal with the environment. Because city dwellers cannot know personally the individuals with whom they come in contact, they must rely upon objective standards. As many sociologists have pointed out, the city is possible only because of social inventions such as the uniform, money, the clock, and the traffic light; these instruments contribute to the image of the city as a place of great impersonality.

At the same time, the lack of a homogeneous social base as might be found in rural areas prevents the establishment of a completely uniform pattern of behavior. The city is made up of a variety of social, economic, ethnic, and cultural types, all living together in a fairly stable state of coexistence. This heterogeneity, so Wirth argued, leads to a sense of toleration for differences in values and perceptions. The city person is more inclined toward an attitude of live and let live—or die, as is shown by tales about how big city folks ignore cries for help and step over bodies on the sidewalk. In the words of Freddie Prinze, "It's not my job!"

The dichotomy between the rational and the irrational has played a role in a number of concepts which Reissman calls "theories of contrast." These theories, which try to distill the essence of the course of world history, emphasize the contrast between the spontaneous, informal society of rural life and the cold, impersonal, rational world of the city. Ferdinand Tönnies' idea of *Gemeinschaft* and *Gesellschaft*—community versus corporation—is one famous example. The theory of the gloomy historian Oswald Spengler, expressed in *The Decline of the West*, was more emphatic in attaching values to the idea; the city was the natural home of the effete intellectuals who would be overrun periodically by the vigorous folks from the boondocks. Emile Durkheim, Herbert Spencer, and Max Weber also produced versions of the theory of contrast.

In terms less pedantic than those of sociologists, Americans have their own feel for the contrast. Our folklore does not exalt the life of people in the city. Instead, there has always been a feeling that cities are somehow unnatural and that the good life is to be found back on the farm, despite the fact that, until recently, people have been fleeing the farms. The American city dweller apparently yearns for a return to a simpler, rustic life. The businessperson considers a move to the suburbs, the auto worker wants to go back home to Kentucky, and the young person fantasizes about peace and harmony in the commune. There may be some good, objective reasons for people's wanting to escape from Gary or Newark, but certainly much of the flight from the central cities is stimulated by a failure to adjust to the peculiar requirements of the urban mind.

CITY POLITICS

For our purposes, a more significant result of the failure to adjust lies in the contrasting visions of what the city means as a political organization. If this analysis is correct, the city could be the most vital arena for political conflict; it could represent the best example of democratic government. The participants are diverse, the problems to be solved are immediate ones, and the people have direct access to their governors. The American city, it might be thought, should be a laboratory for experiments in self-government. Somewhere among the several thousand municipalities in the United States, there should be numerous examples of the public resolving the basic issues connected with the control of bureaucracy.

The evidence is inconclusive, but I cannot find too much to celebrate in the way Americans have chosen to govern their urban areas. The rational elements of urban life have stood out to such an extent that waves of once and future bureaucrats have felt compelled to factor them out to create an ideal society. The reformers may not be in favor of the creation of antiseptic warrens, but there have been periodic attempts to "do something" in order to control the ordered chaos of the city so that, supposedly, all citizens would be satisfied. Starting with Ebenezer Howard's "garden cities," the movement continues down to the present with Jay Forrester's lifeless printouts showing the futility of political solutions to what are simply technical problems.[4] The most sustained efforts at rationalizing the city have come from the city-planning profession, that group so severely chastised by Jane Jacobs for wanting to turn the city into some sort of an ant heap.[5]

In the sphere of administration, the major developments occurred as a reaction against that uniquely American form of local politics—the boss and the political machine. Whatever its excesses, the machine was necessarily responsive to public demands and, through the manipulation of public jobs, it was representative. Most of all, the machine was a bulwark against the rationalization of administration. Max Weber saw this in his visit to America in 1904; at that time, he found the prospects for democracy and individualism to be bleak in the face of bureaucratization. As he wrote, "Those American workers who were against 'Civil Service Reform' knew what they were about. They wished to be governed by parvenus of doubtful morals rather than by a certified caste of mandarins."[6] The workers, however, protested in vain and lost control of their local government to depoliticized bureaucrats.

Reforming the bosses out of business was a necessary condition for the further rationalization of government at the local level. According to Edward Banfield and James Wilson, the reformers, in their death struggle with the professional politicians, believed that the operation of the city should be "businesslike" and that the "task of discovering the content of the public interest was therefore a technical rather than a political one."[7] The "best qualified" in the city should be assured of the leadership in policy making, and the decisions should be carried out by trained professionals. The reform mentality was expressed most forcefully in 1890 as a matter of returning the control of the city, as a piece of property, to those with the greatest interest in its prosperity and eliminating from participation "a crowd of illiterate peasants, freshly raked in from the Irish bogs, or Bohemian mines, or Italian robber nests. . . ."[8]

The city, in short, was not seen as a proper sphere for many of the great public issues. It was to provide certain community services—you either have water, lights, and streets or you don't. And if you decide to have them, there is only one way to provide them, namely, in the one best way. The model city with clean streets, happy children in lovely schools, prosperous merchants in pleasant surroundings cannot be achieved through political means. The achievement of the ideal takes expertise. The city was perceived as a mass of technical questions to be solved by apolitical guardians.

To accomplish reform, the first step was to take politics away from the politicians. This was accomplished in a number of ways:

1 Make it possible for the public to assert its will without politicians. Devices such as nominations by petition, the initiative, referendum, and recall were instituted, with the assumption that the masses would all be struck with the same insight into the truth at the same time.

2 Simplify the voter's task. Give voters more information while decreasing the number of candidates and issues they would be asked to vote on. The short ballot became the goal of a major branch of the reform movement.

3 Separate the city from state and national concerns. Nonpartisan elections in the off-years were necessary in order to implement the slogan: "There is no Republican or Democratic way to pave a street!"

4 Weaken the power of special interests within the city. This was done through at-large elections and by reducing the size of the city council.

Once the politicians had been removed from government, affairs could be handed over to the experts. Civil service reform, i.e., the awarding of government jobs on the basis of "merit" rather than political connections, was a prime requisite. Secondly, the chief executive must be given control of a rationalized government hierarchy. If this had to be done through the strong mayor form, fine, although mayors tended to be politicians even in the nicest of cities. The preferable answer was the city-manager invention. In that form, the professional manager would take broad policy guidelines from a small city council and implement them in the most efficient manner.

The whole reform package was based on the concept of an atomized citizen who, as an individual, would join with fellow citizens in the pursuit of the public interest. However, being a layperson, the citizen would realize that the achievement of any goals would depend upon the assistance of a group of trained bureaucrats. All would somehow come together in a durable consensus about the best way to run the city. It was a breathtaking political concept, assuming that one can believe that the truth is floating around out there just waiting to be discovered.

Like most antipoliticians, armed with the righteousness in the belief that theirs is the only way, the reformers were very effective politicians. But not quite good enough, and in recent years we have become aware of the existence of different values and modes of perceptions, especially in the cities with large concentrations of ethnic minorities. As city services deteriorate, we have also become disenchanted with the image of the civil servant as an expert who can solve all our problems. All this had led to a questioning of the premises of the reformers and to a search for governmental forms that are more conducive to an open political style.

Political science, sad to say, has not been a leader in the revisionist approach to local government. In 1957, Lawrence Herson wrote a devastating critique of the "lost world of municipal government." Textbooks on municipal government, he found, were public administration manuals, and outdated public administration at that. The discipline was still dispensing the traditional reform nostrums in the form of recommendations about the application of the eternal verities to all cities. As Herson wrote, "it is no exaggeration to say that the text in municipal government has turned its back upon a great range of functions performed by the city in order to elevate the administrative function to a position of first importance."[9] Political science has only recently begun to regard the city as a political arena.

Despite our new awareness of politics in local government, the fact remains that monuments to the reform impulse are all around us and reformed structures are turning out important public policy. Oddly enough (or perhaps not so oddly), political scientists have not devoted much research to the question of whether the reforms they confidently advocated not so long ago really have had any impact on the real world. What research has been done is not conclusive, but one investigation did imply that the reformers had fulfilled their goals since the reform package is "associated with a lessened responsiveness of cities to the enduring conflicts of political life."[10] Although moves have been made to reconquer the city for politics, there is as yet no clear-cut method which promises to be as effective in "unreforming" as the reformers were in their movement.

The city-manager form of government, for example, cannot be revamped overnight to accommodate more political activity. The original model was sold on the basis of a nonpolitical administrator who would be a neutral instrument for the implementation of community desires, as expressed by elected council members. At one time, there may have been managers naïve enough to believe that they would not be involved in politics. Today's managers, insofar as they plan on unpacking their bags in any one town, know that they will be up to their necks in the political struggle from the first day, whether the issue is the dog-leash law, civil service unions, or issuing a permit for a rock concert. Yet very few managers are going to blow into town proclaiming, "I am the most powerful politician around here and you clowns had better believe it!" Their whole approach must necessarily be very circumspect. A catechism put out by the International City Manager's Association does not do much to resolve the confusion of a concerned citizen. In response to the question, "Does the council-manager plan make adequate provision for political leadership?" the ICMA states:

> Political leadership in a council-manager city is vested in the councilmen and mayor. They represent the citizens in all policies and decisions. In a democracy the citizens elect their political leaders; under the council-manager plan the councilmen and mayor are the responsible political leaders. They carry the responsibility for the policies and decisions which control the manager.[11]

But as President Nixon instructed us, locating the responsibility may not be the same as finding someone to blame.

In reality, the manager's position is filled with stress, as is indicated by Ronald Loveridge's research into the political activity of city managers in Northern California. He found that managers were ready and willing to take an active part in policy making, even though they were reluctant to get involved in electoral politics, i.e., supporting or opposing candidates for the council. The council members, on the other hand, regarded the manager as their staff aide and not as an independent political actor. Under such constraints, Loveridge argues, the manager is limited to "consensus politics." That is, he or she can be a leader only in the safe areas which already have the tacit consent of the council. Thus it is concluded: "The data we have examined raises doubts as to the probability of the success of the manager in areas of social conflict and economic progress and more generally the quality of city life."[12] Who, then, is in charge of the city in the most important and complex policy areas?

But then, who cares? The role of the city manager or any other executive is only important insofar as the entire administrative structure is under the control of anyone. Even outside those cities such as Los Angeles where the mayor was consciously reformed out of the picture altogether, it is problematic whether the urban bureaucracy is controllable. The bureaucrats possess those attributes which make them so formidable at the national level. In addition, they have learned in the past few years the benefits of concerted action on their own behalf. Unionized city employees are a major new political force, and an anxious urban electorate can only dread what is happening to the political process in their city.

But then anyone who has watched the agony of New York City knows what is in store. In 1971, in a very perceptive article, Norton Long detailed exactly the fate which awaited the Big Apple. The American city has lost its potential for resolving political issues, despite the remnants of democratic trappings. The mayor in most cities is a "transient bird of passage" who, with any ambition at all, is more interested in playing to a national audience. The void is filled by the civil service unions and other bureaucrats who "find it more profitable to milk the city through disinvestment, running down its plant, and wasteful public projects than strive to make the city a profitable, going concern."[13] The end result, according to Long, will be "reservation-cities" filled with problem citizens to be cared for by a bureaucracy with little incentive to eradicate the problems. The cost of such an arrangement, as we shall see, is gladly borne by fellow professionals at higher levels of government.

Theodore Lowi is equally disillusioned with the legacy of the reform movement. The large cities, he writes, have become "well-run but ungoverned." Just as happened at the national level, the resistance of the administrative mentality to politics has only driven that form of human activity underground. The real locus of political power is in the functionally independent bureaucracies which the mayor is unable to control. We have, Lowi concludes, a new and more powerful kind of machine in city politics, supported by "tradition, and the slavish loyalty of the newspapers, the educated masses, the dedicated civic groups, and, most of all, by the organized clientele groups enjoying access under existing arrangements."[14]

In short, the defects of the pluralist approach are just as evident at the local level as at the national, and pluralism has become, according to Todd Gitlin, the ideology of "welfare-state bureaucrats and their academic apologists who find comfort in insisting that an urban system so dispersed makes sweeping change impossible."[15] Despite the objective signs of imminent collapse, we are told not to worry about reviving politics because the city is being run in a thoroughly professional manner. So professional, in fact, that the administrators will not be too embarrassed to demand another pay raise.

The American city, then, does not offer us a system of administration that we might wish to recommend to other levels. This is not to say that all our cities are mismanaged. There are a number of places in which a homogeneous population is satisfied that a city manager can be trusted to solve the burning issue of the day, such as chuckholes and messy front yards. Administrators and citizens are of one mind and there the classic reform measures work to perfection. Particularly in the newer communities which were deliberately designed to deny the diversity of the city—"suburbia as a gadget" in Sidney Slomich's phrase—the political aspect is a carefully programmed part of the whole machine.[16] But where the conflicts between administrators and citizens are intense—so intense in some cases as to lead to costly riots—political leaders are hard-pressed to come up with anything more novel than gimmicks.

FEDERALISM

Even if Americans had not reformed themselves out of an effective local government, there would be pressure to check the impact of politics. The existence of a powerful administrative system at the national level is in itself a threat to the freedom of other levels. The urge of the bureaucrats to bring everything within their bounded rationality compels them to engage in search-and-destroy missions against independent pockets of decision making.

But it might be argued that the surest guard against the maturation of the administrative state is the federal structure of our government. The several million bureaucrats are scattered among a variety of governments and are accountable to politicians elected by all sorts of constituencies. Instead of having all decisions emanating from offices in Washington, federalism makes it possible for citizens to work with officials in their states and communities. Federalism, the truly American contribution to statescraft, will prevent the creation of a bureaucratic caste which could unite in riding roughshod over our liberties.

The Founding Fathers were confident that they had built well in this area. Madison was sure that "ambitious encroachments of the federal government on the authority of State governments" would trigger massive resistance on the part of the citizens. But then, "what degree of madness could ever drive the federal government to such an extremity?"[17] Hamilton was also unable to conceive of the national government overstepping its bounds:

> Allowing the utmost latitude to the love of power which any reasonable man can require, I confess I am at a loss to discover what temptation the persons intrusted with the administration of the general government could ever feel to

> divest the States of the authorities of that description. The regulation of the mere domestic police of a State appears to me to hold out slender allurements to ambition. . . . The administration of private justice between the citizens of the same State, the supervision of agriculture and other concerns of a similar nature, all those things in short, which are proper to be provided for by local legislation, can never be desirable cares of a general jurisdiction.[18]

Poor dear innocent Hamilton: he was as good a student of administration as he was a duelist.

Or perhaps he and the other engineers of the Constitution were too keen in their understanding of the baser motives of humanity. They designed a system which could prevent any single person, inspired by an individual "love of power," from consolidating a dangerous amount of authority. They also diverted the attention of later generations toward vigilance against personal ambition. But it is dangerously misleading to regard bureaucrats as power-hungry tyrants. They are only doing what the administrative mentality tells them comes naturally. Against such pressure the constitutional mechanisms of federalism are inadequate defenses, as recent developments indicate.

Only as a student of administration can one understand anything about the nature of federalism. There is not, it must be kept in mind, any institution charged with the operation of federalism. The President and the governors seldom get together; the legislators at various levels are usually strangers to one another; the courts take care to insulate themselves. The day-to-day operation of federalism is in the hands of the administrators at the several levels. Senator Edmund Muskie used the "fourth branch" language to describe the situation:

> The field of intergovernmental relations might be categorized as the hidden dimension of government. . . . Performing as almost a fourth branch of government in meeting the needs of our people, it nonetheless has no direct electorate, operates from no set perspective, is under no special control, and moves in no particular direction.[19]

The main movers and shakers in this operation, however, are obviously the cadres of permanent officials in Washington, the state capitals, and the cities. The practice of federalism is administrative.[20]

Properly understood, federalism must be seen as the clearest alternative to the classic bureaucratic hierarchy. Bureaucratic structures require that power be precisely distributed so that the decisions flow smoothly from top to bottom; a number of bureaucratic elements, including the power to replace resisting subordinates, are designed to ensure that there is no conflict among the ranks. Federalism means that the lower levels have a built-in source of independent action. As an administrative structure, federalism means that irrationality is intended to enter at various levels, and there is nothing any other level can do about it. Necessarily then, federalism encourages conflict and disharmony, those very things so dreaded by the model bureaucrat.

How well has the federalist model of administration stood up against pressures for further bureaucratization? For some time, the basic arguments against federalism have been administrative ones. Federalism is inefficient, it is pointed out, despite the fact that the writers of the Constitution intended inefficiency to be the consequence of the areal separation of power. It is further stated that federalism is obsolete because only a centralized government can deal with the problems of mass society, simply because the subjects of public policy are nationwide. States and cities, their size and shape the result of historical accidents, are poor administrative subunits for the implementation of a rational policy for the entire nation. But most of the changes in the federal system have not come about after an open debate. The system has been modified in the doing.

The administrative infrastructure of federalism is the real center of action. It is here that the future of our form of government will be decided and not by some publicity-seeking politician standing in the schoolhouse door. To be sure, there is a variety of sources of strength for federalism; but the administrators are in charge of implementation, of modifying our collective environment, and their decisions are the ones which tend to affect us most. Federal, state, and local officials are combining to make general policy; on the surface, it is hard to tell who is in charge.

The language favored by current students of federalism is deceptive. The apologists for the present situation are downright "newthinkish." They speak now of "cooperative federalism" or "creative federalism." They promote the idea that the Founding Fathers expected and that we should relish the idea of all our bureaucrats' being members of one big, happy family. The notion of inherent conflict is played down; for in the administrative mentality, there is something unwholesome about conflict. People should cooperate and not wrangle.

The late Morton Grodzins was a most persuasive advocate of the "new federalism," particularly with his analogies from the cookbook. Federalism, he argued, was not intended to be based on the conflict-filled "layer cake" model in which three separate levels of government regard one another with a considerable degree of hostility. Instead, the United States has always been governed according to the "marble cake" model, with the mixing and blending of resources and personnel from all levels in attacks on common problems. Grodzins, and his protégé Daniel Elazar, have been quite seductive in their praise of the pleasant way in which federalism works itself out.[21] Anyone who does not like marble cake would probably knock apple pie too.

For example, take Grodzins' discussion of recreation policy in the United States. Surely this is federalism at its best. There are several federal agencies and a countless number of state, county, and municipal units involved in providing recreational opportunities for their common citizenry. Beyond the public agencies, all sorts of private groups, composed of the friends and patrons of one form or another of recreation, are involved. There is little order or central control here, and yet it works. Grodzins warned us not to tamper with the system in the name of efficiency:

> Many governments doing one job may appear inefficient and wasteful. Neither charge except for units of small population has been effectively demonstrated. The situation does lack neatness and thus is difficult to comprehend fully. In healthy institutions, ambiguities of this sort must be tolerated. In government . . . the absence of complete direction from above disperses initiative and releases energies. . . . Lack of neatness in the allocation of government functions is a good thing.[22]

His version sounds very much like the sort of open government I have been advocating in this book.

But is this a good illustration of modern federalism? Grodzins took an atypical case because recreation policy, at least when he wrote, had not been greatly affected by the active ingredient of federalism, the categorical grant-in-aid. According to the feds, "A Federal grant-in-aid may be defined as a payment of funds by the National Government to a state government for a specified purpose, usually on a matching basis and in accordance with prescribed standards and requirements." In practice, once Congress approves a grant for a specific purpose, it becomes the sole property of the federal and state officials who are to carry it out. Who, then, is in charge? In the words of Inspector Clouseau, I suspect no one and I suspect everyone. Whatever the case, it does not appear to be terribly democratic and is becoming even less so.

Although the number of categorical grants are not increasing as rapidly as they did during the 1960s, they are still being approved by Congress. This is happening despite an emphasis on General Revenue Sharing and the block grant (the consolidation of related categorical grants into a coherent program). Counts vary, but there is general agreement that there are nearly 500 categorical grants at this time. Altogether, federal aid accounts for more than a quarter of state and local revenue.[23] Without a doubt, that is a handsome chunk of cash.

The point is that the power of the purse, itself a result of the far superior fiscal resources of the federal government, is a most impressive one for bureaucrats at all levels of government. And being impressed, they are happy to participate in the spreading of the defects of the Washington bureaucracies throughout the rest of the United States. We ought not to be misled by the rhetoric of cooperative federalism. Desperate governors and mayors are interested in cooperating with anyone with money. Some officials would probably cooperate with Fidel Castro if the price were right. They are willing to sell out, and as a result the administrative hierarchy fills in more of those awkward interstices left over from the pure federalist form.

To emphasize the point, permit me some poetic license in drawing a caricature of the policy-making process in "cooperative federalism." Let us imagine a group of senators in committee, marking up the HEW appropriations bill. The members wake up the senior senator to ask him if he has any ideas. He remembers hearing that a constituent was killed by botulism, and so he rouses himself to orate on the peril of the botulists and the danger to the American Way of Life of all those radical "isms." His embarrassed colleagues, not wishing to anger him, provide money for a botulism control program. Thus a Bureau of Botulism pops up within an already uncontrollable department. The bureau chief will be a professional, probably someone with a Ph.D. in intestinal disorders. She and her staff will use their expertise in the construction of the guidelines—the regulations which will spell out to officials in other jurisdictions exactly what it is they must do to get the money.

BOB can then announce to the states, "Look here, we've got some money for you." Even the most cautious governor will be reluctant to think the state can afford to reject it. Nor can consideration be given to taking the money to devote to some more pressing state need. Indeed not, for politicians are totally unreliable—irrational—and would no doubt squander the money on something not in keeping with national policy. In fact, the governor is so untrustworthy that the conditions under which the grant is to be administered must be dictated, including the sort of personnel to be hired. Nonprofessionals must not get their hands on the money; therefore, the State Office of Botulism must be staffed with carefully credentialed members of the right profession.

For further implementation of the grant, it might be felt that a special district should be established at the local level. Federal administrators have been rather fond of the special-district form of government since it provides further insulation from the general political activity of the community. It makes it easier for the bureau to ensure uniformity of thought and action. As a result, we now have three levels pursuing a standard policy, since bureaucrats at all levels are pretty much in agreement with one another about the nature of their program. They communicate furiously with each other, but only about the details of a policy they are committed to protecting from meddlesome politicians and members of the public.

And so, while out for a night of elegant dining at Burger Biggie, an official declares your meal unfit for human consumption. On your way out you may bump into bureaucrats who are operating independently of anyone else in the administration of grants for ptomaine and for training baboons as fast-food franchise managers. If you write to your representative, governor, and mayor complaining that "people with bad taste have got rights too," you will probably receive a form letter explaining how the whole situation is really out of their hands. The only real alternative is to eliminate the whole program; but since the elements of the triple alliance have already begun to coagulate around the grant and the bureau, the chances of that's happening are slim.

How much do I exaggerate here? I think it is a fair description of what the Advisory Commission on Intergovernmental Relations (ACIR) called "the major imbalance in federalism today"—"the growing gap between program specialists with their supporting interest groups on the one hand, and elected legislators and executive officials on the other."[24] It is the "vertical functional autocracy" which has resulted from the system of categorical grants.[25] Harold Seidman calls it "cooperative feudalism" in which the technocrats guard their turf against all outsiders—lay administrators, other professionals, and, most of all, the elected representatives at all levels; the administrators up and down the line strive to become "self-governing professional guilds."[26] As good bureaucrats, they see as their main function the preservation of their narrow goals from the forces of irrationality.

A powerful piece of evidence was provided by Senator Muskie's Subcommittee on Intergovernmental Relations in a 1965 document entitled *The Federal System as Seen by Federal Aid Officials*.[27] The study concentrated on "middle management": the bureau chiefs, division heads, and other officials who are normally in charge of the day-to-day administration of grant programs. These are the professionals, the technically trained manipulators of government routines.

As does most legislation in the United States, a categorical grant usually emerges in response to a specific problem as identified by an interest group. The subcommittee found that there was little inclination among grant officials to broaden the scope of the grant or to relate it to similar programs. And indeed, why should they be so interested? In their thinking, the most important thing is to ""protect the integrity of the program." Translated from bureaucratese, that means eliminating everybody with silly ideas, such as politicians, citizens, and other nonprofessionals.

The subcommittee painted an unflattering portrait of these middle-management types. Their character was delineated in terms of four "behavioral themes" and, if my argument has been followed to this point in the book, these traits will come as no surprise:

1 *Functionalism.* The managers were preoccupied with individual programs, especially in terms of keeping lower levels pure and unblemished. They resisted mixing state units within larger departments and found the special district an attractive device.

2 *Professionalism.* The managers were trained in the function they were to oversee. They were natural advocates of upgrading the professionals at the state and local levels, i.e., getting rid of unreliable administrators.

3 *Standpatism.* The managers were not about to upset the cozy routines they had established. The system worked, nobody was getting killed, so what was the problem?

4 *Indifference.* The managers were not really concerned with something so abstract as the operation of the government of the United States. They had their little universe in order, and all other people could look out for themselves.

In short, the managers, the people with the money and the guidelines, are not great and good friends of the messiness which characterizes the democratic political style. Their mortal enemies are those politicians who would try to introduce conflict by opposing the conventional wisdom, who would thwart the erection of a regular bureaucratic hierarchy within the framework of what was once a federal system.

Later in this chapter, we shall consider the attributes of an administrative structure in which local autonomy can be preserved. The key elements in such a structure are trust and toleration. A federal structure mandates trust and toleration because of the independence of the several levels; if one's working partners can tell everyone to go to hell, what option is there but to trust, tolerate, and hope for the best? "Cooperative federalism" is a contradiction in terms, for cooperation—the belief that everyone will get along just fine—is against the federalist tradition. What we do have should be called by its proper name: a national administrative machine which is increasing its strength through the incorporation of previously autonomous units at the state and local levels.

The categorical grant-in-aid has been the catalyst which fuses formerly independent units, the epoxy which forms the bond between federal bureaucrats and their provincial counterparts. It is no longer worth their while to defend the federalist principle. Federalism, it must be recognized, is not in the nature of things. Furthermore, it is not an end in itself, but rather a device for the accomplishment of substantive goals. That is, people do not defend or attack the principle for its own sake. The same is true of the administrator in whose care federalism now rests. What reasons would the modern administrator have for preserving or subverting the idea?

Edward Weidner suggests that there are two possible values which might influence administrative attitudes toward federalism. First, there are the expediency values. These concern the desire for power for its own sake, for freedom from supervision by other organizations. In brief, it is better to be a big frog in a small pond. Administrators so influenced are the parochials who accept their jurisdiction as the universe within which they will live and die, and from which they will receive an adequate reward. They will defend federalism because it does promise freedom from control.

The other set of values can be called programmatic. The major emphasis is on adequate standards of professional performance. The professional program is the main thing, and the individuals look to the profession for guidance and rewards. One must be allowed to achieve professional goals regardless of the expendable organizational structure. These bureaucrats are cosmopolitan in that they identify with the national scene. As Weidner notes, "professional employees do not feel strongly about defending the unit of government for which they work."[28] As various levels of government become more dominated by programmatic types, conflict in a vertical line is decreased, while conflict with outside forces at each level is increased. The continued professionalization of the public service, despite its other benefits for society, is not necessarily healthy for federalism.

The future of federalism has become the subject of a relatively lively debate. Many politicians, especially governors during the Johnson years, expressed alarm at the proliferation of categorical grants and the subsequent growth of agencies free of executive control. The general public heard most often about the New Federalism, with its emphasis on curtailing categorical grants by General and Special Revenue Sharing. However, even if the architects of the New Federalism were not now in disgrace, the more bureaucratically inspired solutions to the problem would have prevailed. The trend now is toward the centralization of state and local units so that "viable" governments can more effectively administer a general range of programs according to professional standards.

The feds have lost patience with the interminable politicking of autonomous local units and are pressuring for the establishment of various types of "umbrella" arrangements to ensure uniformity. A couple of suspicious sociologists viewed such devices as "the control point in an all-embracing bureaucratic system."[29] The ACIR prefers to call it "upgrading the management capabilities of local governments."[30] Upgraded management means that the federal bureaucrats will have more reliable allies at the local level. It is the judgment of at least one scholar that the end result is "an administrative decentralization where the state and local governments dance to music written and choreographed in Washington and checked by a regional office to make sure no essential steps are missed."[31] The linkages among bureaucrats at the different levels are about complete.

DECENTRALIZATION

The realization that federalism is a dead issue may account for the renewed interest in decentralization; *de*centralization implies that we are doing something with a structure that has already been centralized. The perception that the grass may be greener on the decentralized side of the fence is a concession that there is only one administrative structure in the United States. We must shift our perception from the interaction of separate units to the problem of cooperation within a basically unitary organization.

The idea of decentralization is presently muddied by the introduction of all sorts of social scientific jargon and just plain ballyhoo. It has become everyone's favorite solution to whatever ails society, with political types from militant blacks to reactionary state's righters demanding that government be brought closer to the people. Only a very foolish candidate would propose more centralization to the voters. The talk now is of democratic administration, self-determination, community control, neighborhood government, individual initiative, or participatory this and that. All this may be very nice, if we can achieve it. But how far can any move toward decentralization really go?

What does decentralization mean? It is much more than the mere geographical distribution of employees, although geography can play an important role. The U.S. Postal Service has an office and agent in every obscure corner of the country. Yet it has always been the worst example of a highly centralized organization, with even the most trivial decisions filtering up and down the hierarchy. A case was reported from a post office in Wisconsin. A new building had been constructed, with one minor flaw. The men's latrine was right off the lunchroom, and no partition had been provided to keep the luncheon crowd from checking out the guys at their business in the john. The employees requested some sort of screen and even offered to buy the material themselves. Getting approval for this simple request, however, was a major fight which eventually required the intervention of a member of Congress.[32]

Conversely, a decentralized organization can exist within the confines of a single office building. Most university professors like to believe that their departments are fairly autonomous units of the larger organization, although fewer administrators hold this quaint view, much to the dismay of the academics.

All that decentralization requires is that people in subordinate units have some degree of independent decision-making authority, that they have some amount of power delegated to them from higher levels. The authority may come in several forms: the power to hire personnel, to spend money (budgetary flexibility), to make purchases, and, most of all, to adapt general guidelines to specific conditions in the lower offices.[33] In theory, the decentralized model has two basic levels: first, the executive who would devote time to the establishment of broad goals and policy for the organization; and second, the subordinates who would accept the responsibility for meeting the goals, the precise means of attaining them being left to their discretion.

But calling something decentralized does not make it so. The key difference between a federal and a decentralized unitary system is in the final resting place of power. In a decentralized organization, subordinates derive their power solely from the superiors, and their mandate can be withdrawn at any time. Therefore, the most important element in the establishment of decentralization is the success of the subdivisions, as defined by the superiors. If the subdivision fouls up early and often, it will not be given as much discretion in the future.

In essence, decentralization is based on the philosophy of the superiors. The philosophy relates to the question of whether top management trusts people or not. Real decentralization demands that people have the right to make mistakes, the freedom to make an irrational decision. Otherwise, we have only that perverse idea of "the freedom to do right." Considering the nature of the organization, can any executive afford that kind of trust? Before the idea became wrapped in hypes about democratic administration, two leading management experts put it bluntly: "To state the matter practically, the indoctrinated man is the only man who can safely be trusted with that relative freedom of action which is essential in a decentralized organization. . . . "[34]

Executives are not deliberately deceitful in their lip service to decentralization. It must be small comfort to them, however, with their bosses and the politicians breathing down their necks, to think that they are trusting human beings. It must surely occur to them that if you could really trust people to do what is right, you would not need an organization and its executives in the first place. The organization is a loud statement that people cannot be trusted.

I do not see that it is possible to encourage the leaders themselves into assuming a placid state of forebearance. They cannot be expected to sit back and relax while their subordinates are apparently running amuck. It is only a matter of time before the gods will have to descend from Olympus to set things right. The way to ensure decentralization is to build a source of power into the lower levels, to make it possible for subordinates to tell anxious bosses to stick it in their ears. In that case, as we have seen, you do not have a decentralized bureaucracy; you have a federal structure.

No matter how much we preach the idea of decentralization, we are probably moving away from its implementation. The managerial machinery and techniques for interfering in the acts of subordinates are proliferating at an amazing rate. In fact, the major purpose of administrative science seems to be the elimination of decentralization except in name. In those areas apparently most susceptible to decentralization, we have now almost complete control from above. Military commanders in the field who receive their orders from the basement of the Pentagon complain of "electronic despotism." State Department personnel feel that they are nothing more than dignified messengers. Most of all, there is the monumental achievement in centralization in our flights to the moon. No people have ever been so physically removed from central headquarters; yet because of the monitoring devices stuffed into every body orifice, the astronauts might just as well have been sitting on the laps of the controllers in Houston.

I am so giddy in my confidence about the inevitability of the move toward greater centralization that I dare to posit the Law of Centralization:

Given the means, executives will deprive their subordinates of any meaningful decision-making power. A corollary to that law says that, boy, are they ever being given the means. That point will be brought out in the remaining chapters.

ADMINISTRATION IN THE FIELD

I wish to consider the implications of decentralization by concentrating on the geographical division of the organization. The argument for field decentralization, as an alternative to an incoherent system of local governments or as a way of reforming unitary structures, is very simple. Authority for a function is given to a central unit; some authority is then returned to agents in the field. For example, many argue that in most metropolitan areas it would be sensible to establish a single police department; precincts could then be set up in each distinctive community. The central headquarters could handle specialized functions beyond the means of any single locality, and the precincts could tailor their performance to the needs of the community.

How well does the field-decentralization model work in practice? If the organization is the coordination of collective efforts for the rational accomplishment of goals, what does decentralization do to that idea? Or conversely, what do the requirements of the organization do to the idea of decentralization? Two interesting studies indicate that decentralization, if ever put into practice, may cause the organization to foresake its goals; the group may become so tangled up in the grass roots that the general purpose is overlooked.

In his *TVA and the Grass Roots*, Philip Selznick investigated the great political experiment of the New Deal. The Tennessee Valley Authority was to be a brand new approach to the operation of government outside of Washington. An entire region was to be developed along natural lines, and the people would be able to participate since everything would be run from a local office. TVA was, according to one leader, "democracy on the march." It was not going to become an alien force, but instead it would work through existing local institutions.

But the first requirement is that the organization protect itself. There are a number of devices one can use to ensure survival, especially if, as was the case with TVA, the organization is operating within a fairly hostile environment. As Selznick saw it, the TVA selected the approach of cooptation which, in his words, "is the process of absorbing new elements into the leadership or policy-making structure of an organization as a means of averting threats to its ability or existence." All good politicians indulge in the practice of cooptation when they invite real or imagined enemies into their councils. The assumption is that if a person is on your payroll, he or she cannot criticize your actions. Or in the earthy language of Lyndon Johnson, used when reflecting on whether to dismiss J. Edgar Hoover, "it's better to have him inside the tent pissing out than outside pissing in."

Cooptation is quite useful for strangers in an environment which is not very friendly. All successful colonial powers used it to good advantage. Rather than send in the troops to beat the natives into submission, a rather costly and messy affair, it is easier to make the local chieftains your agents, thus ensuring the compliance of the local leadership. However, cooptation is an unreliable instrument since, obviously, you are inviting enemies into your camp where they will have to be listened to and where they may corrupt the minds of the organization's members.

In order to win the consent of the local leaders, TVA incorporated the most powerful interests within the organization. They gained support and, just as important, staved off attacks from the defenders of the status quo. They also created a right wing within the decision-making process. This ultimately caused TVA to give up some of its more controversial goals, since those who, in terms of long-range change, should have been the subject of administration were now sitting among and advising the administrators. From this privileged position, the local elites were able to thwart the implementation of obnoxious policies. The introduction of local elements, in short, can prevent the attainment of goals which are really national in scope.[35]

The Forest Ranger, by Herbert Kaufman, is a report on the more likely outcome of decentralization. The problem for the U.S. Forest Service is "how to devise and operate an agency which will operate consistently, in the sense of reducing to the minimum variations from established organization-wide norms, while at the same time preserving individuality and stimulating creative thinking and action on the part of its members."

The USFS is faced with a number of centrifugal forces. Each district has its unique flora and fauna and a distinct set of economic interests revolving around the use of natural resources. From the Chief Forester in Washington to the local ranger, several hundred people are involved in making important policy decisions. Moreover, these decisions are often critical ones for the local community. In many of the smaller outposts, the ranger is the most important federal official. Although the USFS does want rangers to make decisions because of their awareness of local conditions, the national leadership is conscious of the pressures on them; they are always in danger of being "captured" by the locality. They may become advocates of the narrow interests represented by their friends and neighbors and may start to think of themselves as hometown boosters. If rangers are captured, one can say good-bye to a national forest policy. Kaufman reports that the insulation of rangers from parochial interests is accomplished by three administrative techniques:

1 *The "preformed" decision.* Through a variety of regulatory and budgetary practices, the central office can remove from the rangers' consideration a wide range of unwanted alternatives. Their thinking is channeled into a certain direction, and any significant deviation can be detected very quickly by higher levels.

2 *Rotation.* To discourage the sinking of roots in any one location, the USFS carefully manages the assignments of its rangers. They seldom stay in any one place long enough to develop a real attachment. Rangers move from district to district or from the field to the central office, so that they are always outsiders no matter where they are living.

3 *Development of an "internal capacity to conform."* More indelicately, we might call this indoctrination or a soft form of brainwashing. In becoming a ranger, one submits to a very subtle type of self-selection. The eventual result is a ranger who looks, thinks, and acts very much like every other ranger.

With these techniques, it is possible for the national leaders to trust the rangers—if trust is the word we want. After all those precautions, what is there not to trust? The same phenomena we saw in our review of the administrative structure of federalism are even stronger here. The same conditions are bound to exist in any organization where professionals are more inclined to regard their colleagues than the local community. The bounded rationality, however enforced, is strong medicine against irrational distempers.[36]

In recent years, the most strenuous attempts at decentralization have been made at the local level. The distinctive communities within large cities have been demanding the same sort of autonomy purchased by their wealthier neighbors who could afford the move to the suburbs. Despite all the excitement, there are not many cases in which decentralization has been more than window dressing, and the success there does not convince me that decentralization is more than a very pallid substitute for federalism. The "major efforts" which Fantini and Gittell argue are necessary to reverse the trend toward centralization have not been made.[37] City executives show the same thinking as their federal counterparts: if field personnel actually begin to take the side of the local citizens, it is a sign that they have "gone native" and should be reassigned.[38]

CONCLUSION

Call the structure federal or decentralized, the fact is that we have lost that trust which makes either form viable. Of course, I admit that many governments have gone out of their way to earn our mistrust. I do not wonder that many blacks mistrust the motives of Southern diplomats or that ecologists feel some smaller communities are indifferent about the impact of their laws on the environment. But such examples stand out because of their ethical content; federalism does not mean that the subunit can oppress minorities or endanger other subunits. The really vitiating source of mistrust is administrative; subunits cannot be trusted because they are likely to do something administratively irrational.

In the 1830s, Alexis de Tocqueville, the great French observer of American politics, found in the United States a vigorous political life outside the national capital. In particular, the state legislatures, representing only the desires of a majority, were free of many outside pressures including, as he put it, impediments from the "empire of reason." Americans had resisted the pernicious effect of a central administration which, as in Europe and China, was fit only to maintain "society in a *status quo* alike secure from improvement and decline."[39] Since that time, the empire of reason, the spirit of rationalization, has made steady inroads into the vitality of our political life. As Jacques Ellul and other critics of technology would argue, the bureaucratic state cannot be divided against itself; it must encompass everything, lest rationality be defied. The decline of federalism and the failure of decentralization, together with the depoliticization of American cities, lends credence to their dismal predictions.[40]

REFERENCES

1 Vincent Ostrom, *The Intellectual Crisis in American Public Administration* (University: University of Alabama Press, 1973).

2 Leonard Reissman, *The Urban Process* (New York: Free Press, 1970), p. 19.

3 Louis Wirth, "Urbanism as a Way of Life," *American Journal of Sociology*, 44 (1938), pp. 1–24.

4 Jay W. Forrester, *Urban Dynamics* (Cambridge, Mass.: M.I.T., 1969).

5 Jane Jacobs, *The Death and Life of Great American Cities* (New York: Random House, 1961).

6 Quoted in H. Gerth and C. Wright Mills (eds.), *From Max Weber* (New York: Oxford University Press, 1946), p. 71.

7 Edward Banfield and James Q. Wilson, *City Politics* (New York: Vintage Books, 1963), p. 139.

8 Andrew D. White, quoted in Edward Banfield (ed.), *Urban Government* (New York: Free Press, 1961), pp. 213–214.

9 Lawrence Herson, "The Lost World of Municipal Government," *American Political Science Review*, 51 (1957), p. 335.

10 Robert Lineberry and Edmund Fowler, "Reformism and Public Policies in American Cities," in James Q. Wilson (ed.), *City Politics and Public Policy* (New York: Wiley, 1968), p. 121.

11 *Questions and Answers* (Chicago: International City Manager's Association, 1968), p. 7.

12 Ronald Loveridge, *City Managers in Legislative Politics* (Indianapolis: Bobbs-Merrill, 1971).

13 Norton Long, "The City as Reservation," *Public Interest*, no. 25 (1971), p. 33.

14 Theodore Lowi, "Machine Politics—Old and New," *Public Interest*, no. 9 (1967), p. 87.

15 Todd Gitlin, "Local Pluralism as Theory and Ideology," in Charles McCoy and John Playford (eds.), *Apolitical Politics* (New York: Thomas Y. Crowell, 1967), p. 125.

16 Sidney Slomich, *The American Nightmare* (New York: Macmillan, 1971), pp. 128–130.

17 James Madison, "No. 46," *The Federalist Papers* (New Rochelle, N.Y.: Arlington House, 1965), p. 298.

18 Alexander Hamilton, "No. 17," *The Federalist Papers* (New Rochelle, N.Y.: Arlington House, 1965), p. 118.

19 U.S. Senate, Subcommittee on Intergovernmental Relations, *The Federal System as Seen by State and Local Officials* (Washington: GPO, 1963), p. 2.

20 Arthur Macmahon, *Administering Federalism in a Democracy* (New York: Oxford University Press, 1972), p. 3.

21 Daniel Elazar, *American Federalism*, 2d ed. (New York: Thomas Y. Crowell, 1972).

22 Morton Grodzins, "The Many American Governments and Outdoor Recreation," in *Trends in American Living and Outdoor Recreation* (Washington: GPO, 1962), pp. 67–68.

23 ACIR, *Intergovernmental Perspective,* 3 (Spring 1977), p. 14.

24 ACIR, *American Federalism into the Third Century* (Washington: GPO, 1974), p. 30.

25 ACIR, *Urban America and the Federal System* (Washington: GPO, 1969), p. 3.

26 Harold Seidman, *Politics, Position, and Power*, 2d ed. (New York: Oxford University Press, 1975), p. 163.

27 U.S. Senate, Subcommittee on Intergovernmental Relations, *The Federal System as Seen by Federal Aid Officials* (Washington: GPO, 1965), chap. 6.

28 Edward Weidner, "Decision-making in a Federal System," in Arthur Macmahon (ed.), *Federalism: Mature and Emergent* (New York: Doubleday, 1955), p. 372.

29 Frances Fox Piven and Richard Cloward, "Black Control of Cities: Heading It Off by Metropolitan Government," *New Republic*, (Sept. 30, 1967), p. 21.

30 ACIR, *Governmental Functions and Processes* (Washington: GPO, 1974), pp. 37–38.

31 Peter Lupsha, "New Federalism: Centralization and Local Control in Perspective," in Louis Masotti and Robert Lineberry (eds.), *The New Urban Politics* (Cambridge, Mass.: Ballinger, 1976), pp. 225–226.

32 Edwin Webber, "Personal Privacy—A Case of High Policy," *Public Administration Review*, 20 (1960), pp. 158–160.

33 Howard Hallman, *Administrative Decentralization and Citizen Control* (Washington: Center for Governmental Studies, 1971).

34 James Mooney and Alan Reiley, *Onward Industry*! (New York: Harper, 1931), p. 513.

35 Philip Selznick, *TVA and the Grass Roots* (Berkeley: University of California Press, 1949).

36 Herbert Kaufman, *The Forest Ranger* (Baltimore: Johns Hopkins, 1960).

37 Mario Fantini and Marilyn Gittell, *Decentralization* (New York: Praeger, 1973).

38 Alan Altshuler, *Community Control* (New York: Pegasus, 1970), p. 16.

39 Alexis de Tocqueville, *Democracy in America* (New Rochelle, N.Y.: Arlington House, 1965), p. 75.

40 See Gregory Daneke, "The Metropolitan Miasma: Administrative Theory, Urban Governance, and the Emergence of Metro-Ethics," *The Bureaucrat*, 5 (1976), pp. 295–326.

Part Two

Problems in Public Administration

Chapter 5

The Life and Hard Times of Bureaucracies

By facing squarely the extinction of his program, he has gained a great bit of Wisdom: that if there is a life force operating in Nature, still there is nothing so analogous in a bureaucracy. Nothing so mystical. It all comes down, as it must, to the desires of individual men. . . . But sheer survival depends on having strong enough desires—on knowing the System better than the other chap, and how to use it.

Thomas Pynchon
Gravity's Rainbow

How does one explain the facts of life to presumably innocent babes, many of whom are just getting over the trauma induced by learning the truth about the tooth fairy? Indeed, how to disabuse anyone of a myth the great majority of adults carry around in their heads for their entire lives?

I have supervised government internship programs in a number of places and settings. These programs allow fresh and idealistic would-be bureaucrats to gain an exposure to the big organization before they graduate. In many cases, the interns express shock at the large amount of pure, unadulterated goofing off which goes on in government bureaus. They are heartbroken at the pointless routines of coffee breaks, paper shuffling, newspaper reading, interrupted occasionally by fits of activity directed to largely meaningless ends. I have trouble shattering this naïveté; it would be cruel to scream, "Why God love you, just what did you expect? What reason is there for any sane person to break his back, doing or dying for the Nebraska Division of Brands Inspection or the Gardena sanitation department?" They will learn.

We all will learn. And to aid in this process, let me try to infect you with a most subversive idea: *Organizations are not instrumental.* Organizations are not supposed to accomplish anything beyond their own existence. Most of us insist that they should accomplish goals, and we become upset with the general level of incompetence in our society. We cry, "Why don't nothing work no more?" (including instruction in English). We are involved in a tacit conspiracy, abetted by the illusions from a tiny number of organizations—the Mormon Church, the Ohio State football team, and the Mafia are examples which come to mind—that do work. Such rare examples of success have sustained our wholly unrealistic devotion to the idea that organizations are a manifestation of the rational accomplishment of specific goals through cooperative human effort.

Although the concepts form the basis of the theory of administration established in Chapter 1, one must admit it is really a strange combination of words: "cooperation," "rationality," "goals." Are there such things? The administrators have staked their livelihood on the existence of these concepts, and public administration as a field of study would evaporate without them. But the individuals within the organization have seldom been heard from on this point. I suspect, however, that few of them write on their job applications that their first consideration is the opportunity which employment gives for the rational accomplishment of goals. Most people sign up with an organization having in mind a fairly clear conception of what it means for Me, Old Number One, El Numero Uno.

To be sure, very often enough of these individual motives coincide so that a significant number agree that it is in their best interest that the organization survive. But organizational survival does not imply that anything is being done; some organizations survive because they go out of their way to do nothing. And in some organizations, through happy accidents, the individuals are all motivated to direct their attention toward the accomplishment of specific goals. This latter case is what stimulates the interest in studying administration. The Ultima Thule of administration is the construction of a system so that, day in, day out, all members contribute their whole being to the goal.

The opposing school of thought, which I will try to insinuate in the remaining chapters, does not yet have the imposing credentials of conventional scholarship. We must borrow our basic terminology from Kurt Vonnegut's zany theology. He describes a collection of people, ostensibly sharing some common features, who in fact respond to quite mysterious forces, as a *granfalloon*.[1] Most organizations today are granfalloons. Robert Kharasch's book on "How to Understand the United States Government and Other Bulky Objects" also adds to our understanding. His Third Axiom of Institutional Actions says, "Whatever the internal machinery does is perceived within the institution as the real purpose of the institution (i.e., function is seen as purpose)."[2] That is, if one is assigned to counting paper clips, then paper-clip counting will be seen as the purpose of the organization. Thus, impartial observers of a bureaucracy's culture may fail to detect what Morton Halperin calls the organization's "essence": the activity which a dominant group of administrators feels is important, regardless of social utility.[3]

It must be realized that there is no evidence that the great majority of organizational members are cynical ripoff artists, consciously wallowing in someone else's trough. If that were so, the explanation of administration would be so simple. Instead, individual and group motives become so hopelessly intermingled that in the workaday world it is difficult to make sense of the totality. Most people, I assume, would be affronted by the implication that their work is irrelevant, and that assumption becomes safer the higher one goes in the hierarchy.

For the time being, let us take only one example, one with which most of us are now, or were, familiar—the educational system. This system devours billions of dollars and occupies the time of millions of people. Yet disturbing questions are being raised about the effectiveness of this tremendous expenditure of money and time. In short, the educational system is being perceived as a granfalloon. At the heart of the matter is a concern about how well the major participants understand the ultimate goal. A couple of years ago, professors felt their deepest secrets had been betrayed when researchers at the University of Southern California reported on "Dr. Fox." Dr. Fox was an actor who earned high teaching evaluations after giving lectures composed of sheer gibberish. On the other side of the lectern, the student whose only goal is a high grade point average is not entirely a figment of the professorial imagination. In an insightful article, James Fallows argues that education is largely a matter of "making it"—giving the appearance of accomplishment—rather than "doing it." He suggests that "life never changes after schooltime, that report cards and admission tests continue to be important to us until we die."[4] For the rest of our lives, we will be trying to psych out the people who can give us A's or F's.

I am not upset by granfalloonery. In fact, I believe it to be far healthier than the concepts posited by classical public administration: the notion that the noble bureaucrats are selfless individuals whose only thoughts are about the rational pursuit of the public good. I agree with William Niskanen that "for a positive theory of bureaucracy . . . the beginning of wisdom is the recognition that bureaucrats are people who are, at least, not entirely motivated by the general welfare or the interests of the state."[5] They are motivated by a complex bundle of things which are tied up in the survival of their organization. When we look at the ways and means of survival, perhaps we will then be able to conceptualize ways through which the public can control administration. The survival urges of bureaucrats must be redirected so that politicians and the general public can play a far larger role in their daily calculations.

Nor am I at all unhappy that people are not objects to be manipulated at will by the managers. We shall see that management science keeps going back to the drawing board for the final invention for the robotization of workers. Average members, however, probably go schlepping through this vale of tears blissfully unaware of the devices designed to ensure their cooperative effort in the organization. People are mighty poor material from which to construct the perfect organization, and for that I am grateful.

ORGANIZATION THEORY

For those eager now to get to the "meat" of administration, I will continue to disappoint. Frankly, if I really knew how to organize and manage, I would probably be out doing so right now. To avoid that invidious sort of thought, I claim that we are interested here in the role of the politician and not in manual arts training. And more than that, I will not recite the "principles" of administration because I do not believe that they exist.

The organizational dilemma runs like the San Andreas Fault through all the subtopics of public administration. Once you try to build on it, you must be prepared to watch it come tumbling down. Any theory of the organization must be founded on the individual, and that is not the most solid bedrock. I only hope that an appreciation of the tension between the rational and the irrational will get the reader through the following chapters—and through life.

The first and last subject in organization theory is integration, the attainment of complete harmony among all the diverse parts. Whether using the mechanical or the more oppressive biological analogies, the end is the same: how to turn several individuals into something resembling a single individual. But whether we call the organization a machine or a living organism, the fact remains that the individual cannot be discounted as a cog or a cell. Several people are never the same as one, and the organization remains an artificial device.

The "foundations of the theory of organization," as expressed by Philip Selznick, are still valid. The formal organization is a concrete expression of the desire for rational action. Sovereigns of organizations, with a formal goal in mind, want an instrument with which to change the environment according to their will. To effect modification in the most expeditious manner, they want a control structure which can allow them to calculate precisely the behavior of subordinates. Since they must depend upon others to express the rational act, they require that certain safeguards exist to ensure compliance. The formal structure is supposedly designed with that in mind.

But as we have already seen, that aim is unattainable because "formal administrative design can never adequately or fully reflect the concrete organization to which it refers, for the obvious reason that no abstract plan or pattern can . . . exhaustively describe an empirical reality." In particular, the structure can relate to its human components only in terms of a formal role occupied by the members. "But in fact individuals have a propensity to resist departmentalization, to spill over the boundaries of their segmentary roles, to participate as *wholes*."[6] The ideal of several fingers coming together to form a mighty fist may be attractive to the rational manager, but as long as the digits are spastic there will be difficulties.

Many writers on administration still preach harmony; although after years of frustration, there is a somewhat greater appreciation of the intractability of the human building blocks. Still there are a number of professors, management consultants, and "blue ribbon" commissions on reorganization who insist that a rational plan can be instituted. In most cases, they are able to make this claim only by suspending themselves outside the life of the organization and its political context.

The simple point is that the organization cannot be seen as a gob of pure rationality. Pfiffner and Sherwood describe the organization as a series of "overlays" on the formally designed structure, each overlay representing an element which detracts from complete calculability.[7] A simpler approach is suggested by John Millett, who identifies the organization in three ways: as a technical problem, as a human relations problem, and as a political problem.[8] We shall consider the organization in this tripartite way, with special reference to the political aspects of the birth, growth, and death of government agencies.

TECHNICAL ASPECTS

By use of the rational dimension only, the arrangement of formal roles can be done very precisely. The One Best Way of accomplishing any mission can be broken down into the individual parts, and all the parts can be recaptured through formal bonds, awaiting only the command from the top to energize the whole operation. All this can be done quite easily on a blank piece of paper—where it is likely to remain, a monument to the tunnel vision of the encapsulated experts. The neat logic is usually chopped up by the illogic of the members and of the political forces outside the organization.

The intense devotion to the cult of economy and efficiency in government has prevented the reformers from seeing the totality of pressures impinging upon the organizational structure. They have never been able to comprehend, for example, why the U.S. Forest Service is in the Department of Agriculture. It should be in the Interior Department, alongside the National Park Service, the Bureau of Land Management, and other agencies with a natural resources function. Gifford Pinchot, the founder of the USFS, was a brilliant politician, and he established his agency in a safe haven. After all these years, so many ties have developed around that original decision that it is almost impossible to modify. It makes for a messy chart, but the demands for change are not great.

As befits a nation of gadgeteers and tinkerers, Americans have had at the machinery of government in a variety of reorganization movements. At least since President Taft's Commission on Economy and Efficiency, the eternal verities of rational organization have clashed with the even more severe realities of politics. Politics still maintains the advantage. Right reason has failed to triumph once and for all because the public organization is more than a rational plan. Our politicians, at least until recently, have never bought the idea that the organization is the neutral instrument for the accomplishment of clear policy objectives. This resistance can probably be attributed more to venality than to leadership; all 535 members of Congress are no doubt in favor of a vigorous overhaul of the Pentagon, just as long as their home districts do not suffer. Whatever the reasons, our public organizations have tended to violate all sorts of formal prescriptions.

When speaking of government reorganization, one must mention the Hoover Commission. The conclusions of the Commission, chaired by the former President, have been honored more in word than in deed. Any realist could have predicted the political impact of the proposed reforms just by looking at the stated goals: the three E's of economy, efficiency, and effectiveness. The recommendations were restatements of the classic principles of administration and as a result the report reads like a description of the Weberian model of bureaucracy.

Hoover, the Great Engineer, was a notoriously poor politician, and his recommendations were engineering feats, not political statements. The desire to create a coherent organizational pyramid would have led to a much stronger Presidency, and Congress was not about to enhance its rival, to say nothing of jeopardizing its ties with individual bureaus. As an example of unreality, to have reorganized units along purely functional lines would have destroyed all the comfortable arrangements between bureaus and interest groups. The creation of the recommended United Medical Administration would have lessened the impact of veterans groups on their very own Veterans Administration. In sum, the Commission dwelt on efficiency and Congress had other things to worry about.[9]

I do not argue that the technical approach is completely without significance. Americans generally subscribe to the idea of efficiency, and any gross violation of that principle would probably confirm what most citizens suspect about their government. It is hard to imagine, moreover, that Americans would hold on to such a relic as Chancellor to the Duchy of Lancaster as in Great Britain. When Theodore White writes the 1976 version of *The Making of the President*, he will certainly comment on reorganization of the federal bureaucracy as an issue. Of course, he may have to prepare a quick sequel on "The Unmaking of President Carter" if reorganization is pursued as a matter of mechanics.

It is possible to get carried away debunking organization charts and other signs of the formal structure. After all, they do represent the essence of the complex organization which could not exist without formal control devices—manuals, job specifications, charts, staffing tables, etc. This is especially true in government where many of these features are backed up by force of law. Organization charts, like any maps, do distort reality; but they also say something important about how things are supposed to happen in organizations, if for no other reason than that people use them as a guide in the search for power. The formal structure is a legitimate norm, and as such modifies the behavior of members. I am only saying here that one should not criticize a structure after a cursory study of an organization chart. Hidden factors may shed a great deal of light on apparent irregularities.

THE PERSONAL ELEMENT

At this point, I do not want to enter into a prolonged discussion of the informal structure of the organization. Obviously such things as work groups and informal patterns of communication will have an impact, but this will be covered in a later chapter. For present purposes, I am interested only in why organizations look as they do; and I want to emphasize that they are seldom clean sheets, so that organizers have to take into account the current incumbents and their peculiarities. The ways in which the personal factor can bend an organization out of shape are so numerous that I can only develop the point by examples.

The business of "kicking upstairs" has a number of ramifications, because it presupposes that one has prepared a safe and harmless landing place for the old-timer who for one reason or another cannot be fired or retired. I know of one governor who recently had this problem. His budget director had done loyal duty as the hatchet man, thereby earning the animosity of just about everyone in the state. By reelection time, he had become a political liability, but it would have been an admission of error to dismiss him. So a second budget office, pretentiously titled the Office of Management and Budget, was created. The former director, the only member of the new unit, never did find out exactly what it was he was supposed to do since the state seldom had enough work for one budget office. From a formal standpoint, it was quite irrational, and it would never have been created had the director been more personable.

The notion that an organization is the lengthened shadow of a single individual is not an idle fancy. The FBI might well have developed along much different lines had J. Edgar Hoover retired in 1932. As it was, he had nearly half a century to put his imprint on the organization. According to Joseph Schott, after all those years the organization reflected even the silliest peccadillo of the Director.[10]

The personal factor is also important when it comes to expanding or contracting the scope of a formal role. The job specifications are only abstract approximations. Moreover, they are abstractions based on the average case. A superior or inferior incumbent will add a new dimension to the single position as well as change the expectations of others who depend upon that role. The role will probably stay in its actual state regardless of what the organizers had anticipated.

The formal structure cannot tell us anything about the energy of the people within. Empire builders may seek out new functions to bring within their sphere, while other divisions may be staffed with listless types who willingly give up functions. University departments yield a number of archeological clues about the power struggles of the past. Indeed, the very location of the department of public administration on most campuses is often more the result of personal factors than of rational thought about how the function could best be performed.

And so it goes. The point is not that complex. The personal factor simply means that some unusual and unpredictable occurence has frozen the organization into a particular mold. The idiosyncratic element cannot be dismissed as "wrong," nor can its real justification be learned through the investigation of the formal side.

THE POLITICAL FACTOR

In public administration, the political is obviously the most important factor, and to appreciate it we will have to attack the problem of the life and death of government organizations. This is not an easy topic, but I must put forth some ideas if we are to deal effectively with the role of bureaucracy in public affairs.

We want to know why and how bureaucracies survive. I reject the myth of bureaucratic indestructibility, the idea that God looks out for children, drunks, and bureaucrats. Bureaucracies do die; in the back of the *U.S. Government Organization Manual* one can find an impressive graveyard of federal agencies which for some reason did not make it. I also reject the idea of spontaneous generation for bureaucracies. If the bureau is as rational as I have made it out to be, there must be some reasonable explanation for its existence. At the same time, I question the belief of the rationalist that any single bureau is a tool which can be eliminated or changed at the will of the executive.

We desperately need a theory of the public organization comparable to the theory governing the nature of private business. In theory, a private company is either solvent or insolvent. If it is insolvent, it dies; society has passed judgment upon the need for this particular organization. The same holds true for the components of the organization; if it is necessary to close down a local Safeway because of a failure to turn a profit, it will be done without a great deal of sentimentality.

The theory of the private firm is very clear. The organization offers its goods or services to the public, and if the public does not respond, that is the end of it. There are obviously a number of defects with this bald statement of the theory (although Lockheed and the Penn Central might not find them to be defects at all); but the high death rate of private organizations, represented by the vacant stores and factories one can see in any city, indicates that it works. Profit, or at least a condition of breaking even in dollars and cents, tells us the whole story. How can we find a similar device for organizations which are not designed to make a profit? On the surface, the problem would seem that we cannot expect to find such a thing, and therefore expansion is the rule. Obsolete public agencies will linger on despite the fact that there is no public need for them. There are many concerned people who do not see the humor in John Kidner's graph which proves that on November 13, 1982, every man, woman, and child in the United States will be a government employee.

To grasp the limits of bureaucratic growth, we must extend the essence of the political style—the clash of values and the making of allocative decisions—into the organization itself. A realistic theory must encompass all the members of the organization and not just the ideal manager of the rationalists. That is, everybody is in the organization for some fathomable reason, and there is an internal political process concerned with the matter of getting and giving.

We must ask, therefore, whether the "budget principle"—the allocation of resources according to nonmarket criteria—is as defective as the classical economists maintain. Ludwig von Mises stated that bureaucratic management, free from the discipline of economic calculations, meant that public officials would set up their own self-serving system; there would be no way for outsiders to influence them. There was no hope; once an organization did not have to conform to the severe requirements of the profit motive, it was all downhill as far as effective performance and public accountability was concerned.[11] Such a gloomy view might be acceptable if the resources available to a bureaucracy were determined on a random basis or if the officials could tap at will an unlimited fountain of wealth. The truth is that a government organization depends upon a very mundane document, the budget. It establishes the level of organizational survival and provides some basis for comparison of worth to outsiders.

Therefore, we must remember how budgets are arrived at. They are not made by God nor are they found in the cabbage patch. Budgets are meaningful human acts; they are political documents, put together after a meeting of agents of conflicting social forces. If we can avoid the misleading idea that there is an abstract science of budget making, we can see that one's position in the budget depends upon an ability to manipulate values important to the holders of political power. Or, if somebody "up there" likes you, your agency may make it through another year. How then do you make people—the right people—like you? By "selling" something, of course.

In other words, there is something like a *quid pro quo* transaction involved in government performance. Administrators must bargain in order to preserve all or part of the organization, although it is far from clear how to bargain, or with whom. Assuredly, it is not the same as opening a taco stand on a busy street and waiting for the hungry crowds to rush in. The only evident point is that if you want a larger share of the budget, somebody else will have to suffer; since people are not prone to suffer in silence, they are likely to extract some price. We can say then that bargaining, wheeling and dealing, can go on, must go on, in government. As one economist put it, the "unseen hand" of Adam Smith still lives.[12] There is some invisible set of pressures which regulates the government in such a way that no unit can go too far.

Beginning with the work of Chester Barnard in the 1930s, some students of administration have tried to make this process a little less mysterious. Barnard helped to undermine the rationalist's blind faith that a signed contract took care of all problems of motivation when he wrote that all individuals must be induced to cooperate or there could be no cooperative effort.[13] When one identifies the people who must be induced to cooperate for any single organization, we come to the model of organizational solvency developed by Simon, Smithburg, and Thompson. They list the several components of the model:

1 *Participants.* The participants of any organization include not only the formal membership, but also the entire network of sustaining relations—politicians, other organizations, interest groups, clients, the general public—which have something to give to or take from the organization.

2 *Inducements.* The organization must offer rewards which are significant to the participants. These inducements may be tangible or intangible.

3 *Contributions.* These are the efforts or supports provided by the participants which further the work of the organization or at least make it possible to offer more inducements.

The contributions are then used by the organization so that inducements may be offered to other participants, in much the same way our taco-stand operator collects money from customers to pay employees and to buy more horse meat to continue in business. "Hence an organization is 'solvent'—and will continue in existence—only so long as the contributions are sufficient to provide inducements in large enough measure to draw forth these contributions."[14]

In the public sphere, this process is worked out through the budget. Some groups are willing to have the government pay for an agency in return for benefits from the agency. Within the organization, the several components are engaged in a continuing struggle to preserve or expand their share of the pie. If, and it is a big if, politicians are heavily involved in the determination of the budget, there should be at least a roundabout way of ensuring that organizational survival is dependent upon the feeling of the public about the output of specific units of government. For any individual beholder, and particularly for one of the rationalist persuasion, this may result in a lot of boondoggles. As long as we subscribe to an equality of values, I do not see how it could be otherwise.

Of course, human values are not so diverse as to defy categorization. To simplify our analysis, we can classify the things which people expect from an organization—the inducements they require before offering their contributions. The Clark and Wilson scheme summarizes quite well the things we know about organizational behavior:

1 *Material incentives.* Here we include money or things of monetary value. This is the superficial reason why most people participate in organizations.

2 *Solidary incentives.* These are the intangible rewards which derive from the process of association with others, such as a sense of identification with the group, prestige, gay camaraderie, and just fun and good times.

3 *Purposive incentives.* There are people who join an organization to achieve some formal goal.[15]

As a rule, people participate in organizations for a combination of all three incentives, even though one may predominate over the others at any one time. The leader of the organization must juggle the resources of the organization in such a way that all the contributors—members, supporters, clients, politicians—are satisfied. Looking at what there is to offer, the executive must chart a course that will keep the organization solvent, a state which will be determined at the next budgetary session. One may now begin to sympathize with executives such as college presidents. They must somehow manage things so that students, faculty, staff, parents, regents, state legislators, the alumni, and the general public are all reasonably content. According to Clark Kerr, a president who did not bring it off, it is a devilishly hard job when the only common area of understanding on most campuses is the parking problem.

As in the title of Barnard's seminal work, this is the "function of the executive." It requires a great deal of dexterity because the coalitions and the values within organizations are constantly changing. Take the hypothetical case of a small-town fire department. First it is volunteer, depending upon solidary inducements; the gang likes to get together to drink some suds and relive childhood fantasies. When the city hall burns down while the fire fighters are on their annual picnic, the citizens will demand a purposive incentive, namely, a fire department which can put out fires. That will mean offering a material inducement to full-time fire fighters, the cost of which may in turn alienate the taxpayers. Because of this resentment, the professional fire fighter may have poor morale. . . . The variations are endless, as is the job of the executive.

If one has followed the rather abstract line of thought thus far, it should be evident that one factor is still unexplained. Our concept of solvency is still not as strong as that found in the economic theory of the firm. We must introduce an element which is central to economic thinking: the attitudes of the participants. The private entrepreneur is highly motivated to stay solvent because the alternative is unemployment, destitution, the whip of starvation. The same sort of explanation does not hold in the public organization since we have nothing comparable to Economic Man with an insatiable obsession for profits or an awful fear of failure. The bureaucrat by definition is on a fixed income and in most situations probably has a fairly safe guarantee of job security. Why should bureaucrats care about the survival of their organization? If the Bureau of Widget Inspection goes under, they will be transferred to another bureau and wind up doing the same thing as before. Or they will be pensioned off. It is most unlikely that they will starve to death under a bridge. Why then is it not recorded that any bureaucrat, when informed of the imminent demise of his or her agency, has ever given a little giggle and said, "Yeah! Wow man, like, who cares?" Why not pack it in, right there?

An interesting case, which can be duplicated in any part of the country, has just arisen in Nebraska. Peru State College is a small school with declining enrollment in a state which already has too many institutions of higher education. But when a state legislator recently spoke the truth that "We're carrying Peru today because of nostalgia. There's no reason for Peru to exist," a storm was unleashed. One is hard-pressed to understand the resistance. The president and his fifty-four faculty and staff members could be absorbed into the rest of the state college system, the students could get better education without traveling too far, and the townspeople were assured that a more useful public facility would replace the college. It is not that simple, however, and in the end the state of Nebraska, by no means rich, will continue to pay on the order of 2 million dollars a year for this organization. It is a puzzlement.

BUREAUCRATIC TYPES

Before we can make sense of this and thousands of similar cases, we must be a little more sophisticated about bureaucratic motivation. So far, I have not stressed the obvious differences among public administrators, but instead have implied that all bureaucrats think alike. We will have to play the popular game of identifying behavior types. In their separate discussions, Robert Presthus[16] and Anthony Downs[17] cover most of the primary motivations of bureaucrats:

Indifferents. According to Presthus, this is the largest group in most organizations. They are held to the job only by the cash nexus, and they derive their real satisfactions from off-the-job activities. They have no gut commitment to the organization, but stay at work only as long as they are paid to do so. They are not so significant for our purposes here since they seldom make it to a position where they can shape the organization's overall character. They do form the background against which other types can fight their battles.

Ambivalents. Another of Presthus's types, the ambivalent is split between the need for independence and the realization that the organization is necessary. The strain imposed by organizational restrictions makes the ambivalent so unstable, Presthus suggests, that he or she will probably wind up teaching in college.

Climbers. Presthus calls this same type "upward-mobiles." These people are concerned with their personal value system and the maximization thereof. A person on the make, interested in prestige, power, and income for their own sake, the climber is preoccupied with watching the main chance.

Conservers. According to Downs, these people are, like climbers, "purely self-interested officials." They are content with things the way they are and, unlike climbers, are dedicated to maintaining the status quo instead of expansion.

Downs also identifies three types of "mixed-motive officials" who are drawn by both personal and purposive incentives:

Zealots are the true believers who have some very narrow conception of the public good; they are quite intense in their pursuit of their limited goal.

Advocates take a middle-range approach. They are the pragmatic types who will compromise in order to promote the single bureaus of which they are members.

Statesmen are terminally altruistic. They are bureaucrats who suffer from substantive rationality. They can see the place of their bureau within a larger context and are able to comprehend that their organization is expendable. There are few statesmen.

With this typology, we are in a better position to see how different bureaucrats view their organization and how they might try to steer their organizations through stormy political seas. We can then inquire why, for example, did the horse cavalry die while the Marines, an equally obsolete military unit, survived and prospered.

THE BIRTH OF THE BUREAU

In the following analysis of the growth of bureaucracy, I am borrowing and modifying the brilliant book, *Inside Bureaucracy*, by Anthony Downs. His study is so rich in insights into the administrative process that one must read it to capture the full essence of his theory. Here I can do little more than flesh out some points of the many provocative hypotheses he provides.

As it commonly occurs, the creation of a new bureau can be seen as a variation of the split which Max Weber saw between routine and spontaneity, between bureaucracy and charisma. An existing bureau is the concrete expression of an idea, and to challenge it for a place in the sun one needs more than a different idea. Someone is needed who will upset the previous routine, who will expend the energy needed to overcome the inertia, who will dare to fight the powers that be for a piece of the limited resources. Zealots are most effective at this sort of agitation, and many bureaus depend upon such people for their creation. As William Whyte noted, many existing organizations, now staffed by pale and timid clerks, demonstrate their appreciation by keeping a portrait of Our Founder, a vaguely demented-looking character who would have no chance of getting a job there today.

The zealots feel keenly the need for a new idea, and they are willing to fight for its establishment; because of their beliefs, they strive for autonomy and freedom of action, But if zealots tend to predominate at the beginning, they may eventually be forced out. Their enthusiasm is costly; it makes all sorts of enemies, especially among the established leaders of the organization. Indeed, the zealot may be eliminated (or "martyred" as the followers would have it) before a separate bureau is set up.

Evidence of the mortality rates of zealots is hard to obtain since little research is done on the stillborn. But we suspect that many government documents would yield signs of zealotry which did not quite make it. Reading the War Department annual reports, one comes across the case of Chaplain E. G. Mullins. In the 1880s, the Army had a law on the books requiring educational programs for soldiers, but the new idea remained dormant. When Mullins was appointed in charge of the function, things began to happen. He was a zealot who believed that education was a cure for a variety of military and social ills. Unfortunately, he was too energetic in this trespass upon the "turfs" of powerful staff agencies. The line officers were also unimpressed since they did not relish becoming schoolmarms. Mullins seemed oblivious to all of this, and in his reports he asked for more and more, including a separate corps of teachers under his command. The student of administration wants to call out, "Watch it, Padre, they are going to zap you!" Then one year, the chaplain and his education program turned up missing, and Army education returned to its state as an idea.[18]

One can imagine many situations in which the zealot is essential. Let us say that the public school system decides that instruction in dental flossing is a good idea. Coming down in a directive from the superintendent, the idea may just lie there, earning no resentment but still not working its way into the classroom routine. But one teacher has a fanatic's belief in dental floss—good teeth and healthy gums are the American Way and the best defense against atheistic communism. He will then fight, argue, cajole, harangue, whine, connive, lie, cheat, and step on people's feet until the idea is given its proper recognition, including a separate budget line. Or he may make himself such an intolerable nuisance that his fellow teachers will find a way to get rid of him.

Zealots can be fatal, but their absence can be equally fatal. Without them, it may not be possible to overcome the sterility of the bounded rationality. At least since Franklin Roosevelt, who took care that his New Deal programs were set up outside the established line departments, Presidents have tried to protect their pet ideas from the regular bureaucrats. Kennedy kept the Peace Corps free of the State Department, and Johnson made sure that the old-time welfare bureaucrats did not get a chance to manhandle the War on Poverty. From that latter experience, however, we may see that independence alone is not enough. One suspects that the Office of Economic Opportunity was staffed not so much by zealots as by climbers who saw that poverty was, ironically, the place where all the money was.

GROWTH OF THE BUREAU

Once a bureau is established, the primary concern is sheer survival. The early years are the dangerous ones, and there is a "threshold" of survival, according to Downs, before which the sources have not become firmly fixed so that a certain level of existence is not ensured. Anyone who would kill a government bureau should be like King Herod and strike in its infancy.

To be sure, there may be widespread public sentiment that a certain bureau ought to exist. The President may sign the enabling legislation with a great flourish, and the legislative sponsors may orate endlessly on the dawning of a bright new day. But as it happens, the captains and the kings depart, the tumult and the shouting dies. The bureau is then face-to-face with the workaday environment. It will then have to come up with the routine support necessary for survival; one cannot cash in a Gallup poll showing general public support. The bureau, or its leaders, must convince employees, clients, and other supporters that they are all involved in an important function; they have to overcome the "got-along-without-you-before-I-met-you" attitude that can be so fatal.

It is at this point that all sorts of conditions can be attached to the survival of the organization. The ICC survives because it sold out to the regulated industries; other regulatory commissions have made similar accommodations. The antitrust division of the Justice Department survives because it keeps out zealots about trust-busting. After the Santa Barbara oil spill, some Californians wondered why their prestigious and expensive university system had not come up with any great solutions; it was then discovered that the relevant departments had been subsidized by grants from the oil companies. As we saw in Chapter 4, the TVA bought survival by coopting a specific group with which it then had to share its decision-making power. Whatever the exact form of the conditions, it is clear that the original purpose of the bureau can be distorted at the earliest stage.

Once survival is assured, the bureau may then be faced with a major decision about future growth. It must be understood that the decision to expand is a rational one and not a mindless bureaucratic spasm. Some bureaus consciously decide not to expand; the U.S. Weather Bureau, until advancements in meteorological technology could no longer be ignored, showed few expansionist tendencies. For some organizations, or more correctly, for some personality types, growth is not functional. According to William Starbuck, "organizational growth can take place only if increased size is positively related to the achievement of the organization's goals and/or the goals of the individual members of the organization."[19] Starbuck also provides a convenient list of motives for growth:

1 *Organizational self-realization.* To fill out the big picture is an attractive goal for zealots and others.

2 *Adventure and risk.* Some favor expansion because of the possible excitement, or out of sheer boredom with existing routines.

3 *Prestige, power, and job security.* Ordinarily, the larger the organization, the more power and status one has. This is the commonly suspected cause of bureaucratic "empire building," and certainly for climbers it is very important.

4 *Executive salaries.* Many officials cannot but be impressed with the correlation between the number of subordinates and one's salary, especially in government where this is spelled out in the position-classification plan.

5 *Economy of scale.* In many cases, decreased costs and greater productivity may be achieved by increased size, which allows more specialization and the more efficient use of resources.

6 *Monopoly.* Although government agencies are monopolistic to begin with, there may be areas where it is seen as desirable to run out competition before it becomes too dangerous.

7 *Stability.* The larger one is, the greater the chance of imposing order on the environment.

8 *Survival.* The more people caught up in the web, the more sources of support one can rely upon, and thus the greater the chances of survival. Through diversification, one can expand the number of functions, each with a separate set of supporters.

9 *Lack of adequate measures.* Downs adds this reason for growth as one peculiar to bureaucracy. Without a precise measure of what one is doing, it is natural to keep spending more money in order to be sure that something is accomplished.

One could probably conceive of other reasons for growth. I am not so interested in the exact causes; rather, I wish to indicate that the development of a bureau can take a number of directions. Executives will have to consider the needs and desires of the coalitions they head in order to determine if growth is functional.

THE MATURE BUREAU

Many organizations approach their Golden Years in a very stable fashion. They are in equilibrium. The executives are satisfied with the level of performance, even though they may realize that their work is far from perfect. They are not anxious to engage in search activity for increased effectiveness. Conservers rule!

Downs describes a situation which may shake the bureau out of its contented state. Society may impose a new function on the bureau, and the organization is obligated to do something in order to appease its sources of support. Only so much new activity can be accommodated within the existing routines. An entirely new level of activity will set in motion the "accelerator effect." This happened with NASA after Sputnik, the universities after the GI bill, and police departments after the emphasis on "law and order." The fresh flow of outside support attracts climbers and repels the conservers. The climbers will climb and, at the top, will have the power to seek even more functions. These increased opportunities will in turn attract new climbers.

In the Downsian model, there are brakes on acceleration. Growth cannot go on indefinitely. Competition for budgets and functions will lead to jurisdictional disputes with other agencies; e.g., will the schools or the police run the juvenile delinquency program? The results become less impressive; one may pinpoint the decline of NASA beginning on the day when people failed to huddle around a TV set to watch the latest space spectacular. Size leads to mediocrity of personnel, and the overall ability of the bureau will decline. With so many climbers on board, much effort will be devoted to office politics, rather than to the job to be performed.

According to Downs, the "decelerator effect" takes over. Once a new plateau of equilibrium is reached, hardening of the arteries becomes evident. With a slower growth rate, things can be made more routinized. The climbers will bail out or become conservers. They will now be more interested in the red tape necessary to keep things on an even keel. Procedures are the staple of the conservers, and as the conservers become more dominant, actual performance is seen as less important than method.

It is too much to say that some bureaus become senile, but there is an interesting phenomenon associated with old age in an organization. It was brought most forcefully to our attention by C. Northcote Parkinson. He developed his famous "law" after observing that although the number of ships of the line and British colonies had decreased, the Admiralty and Colonial Office had increased the number of employees. More people were needed to do less work.[20] The same thing has been noted in the United States; members of Congress, only half facetiously, propose amendments prohibiting the Department of Agriculture from having more employees than there are farmers. Other students have attacked the problem in a more sober manner and have come to the same conclusion: There is a tendency for an older bureau to become football-shaped. It is not suggested, of course, that we will reach the stage when the President is commanding a single worker, with everyone else in an intervening staff position.

There are understandable reasons for this development. Management tends to have more seniority than the line personnel, so in layoffs the workers get the ax. Production jobs are more amenable to mechanization, or at least the staff people are generally the ones to decide who will be replaced by a machine. The older the bureau, the more functions it performs; more functions require more coordination, which is the specialty of the staff. Whatever the causes, the administrative types tend to be conservers who are more interested in the existing equilibrium than with specific goals. They are managerial experts rather than specialists in productive functions. For example, accounting or personnel work is the same regardless of the organization's formal goals. The power in the organization thus shifts to people with a lessened commitment to a specific type of production.

The shift in power from line to staff encourages the phenomenon of "goal displacement." The organization winds up doing something different from its original goals. The March of Dimes is the classic example. Originally created to conquer polio, the organization worked itself out of a job. Rather than disband, the leaders shifted to a different set of diseases. The Rural Electrification Administration is another suspicious case. The original purpose was to bring electricity to rural America, but with that goal effectively accomplished, the REA shows few signs of stacking arms and going home. An employee related to me the history of a public hospital. The organization started as a tuberculosis sanitorium, but the eradication of that disease removed its purpose. The leaders shifted to the care of the elderly, but disaster struck again with the passage of Medicare. The hospital has now staked its future on alcoholism treatment, but should the supply of drunks run out, I assume they will try something else. The behavior is indicative of the instinct for survival among staff specialists.

THE DEATH OF THE BUREAU

My argument is that bureaus can die, although almost everything after a certain point is slanted in favor of survival. Herbert Kaufman, in a recent study, found that the bureaus are not immortal, although they are a very hardy species.[21] Of course, it is quite true that a bureau will pass from the scene when it no longer fulfills a socially useful function. That judgment, however, is a highly subjective one. A socially useful function is one determined to be such by the people who can offer political support. If one wants to put a bureau out of action, I suggest that one not worry too much about the rational arguments, unlike President Nixon in his futile attempt to convince Americans that they did not need a Tea Tasting Commission. Instead, look at the configuration of contributions and inducements, and most of all, strike early before that network becomes solidified. And finally, since I have no shame, I will leave you with a bit of wisdom stated by a recent student of the Washington bureaucracy: "You can lead bureaucracy to slaughter but you can't make it shrink."[22]

POLITICAL IMPLICATIONS

I have traced the awesome mysteries of the life cycle of the bureau not simply because I find it more intriguing than the dissection of frogs. The important thing is that we have some grasp on the process so that we may assess its impact on the entire society. If, as I have argued, the bureaucracy shapes the nature of our reality, what is the force which shapes the bureaucracy? Or to return to the essential question, who is in charge here? The theory we have reviewed here does not indicate that in every instance the agency of government is a reflection of public will. The bargaining process as now practiced may leave too much initiative to the bureaucrats, while the public and its politicians are seen not as immediate pressures but instead as an amorphous "something" to be manipulated into usable form.

In his powerful, if erratic, book, *American Social Order*, Jack Douglas argues that in the crucially important area of defining social deviance, the public's notion of proper and improper social conduct has been shaped by the officials for their own self-interest. Our everyday reality is monitored by the bureaucracy, beaten into statistical form, and fed back to us as official information about an alarming social problem. As Douglas stresses, the imposition of organizational definitions upon social acts is "nothing more than the creation of an *ad hoc social reality* which contravenes the social realities of the members of society, and thereby, prevents our ever discovering the truth about such social problems."[23] When the data are manipulated by the bureaucracy for either purposive or material incentives, we have a situation in which the public is at the mercy of the internal dynamics of the organization. The final result is a distortion of social reality.

The point may be substantiated by a look at an issue which may be of special interest to some readers—the peril of Arabian hemp, marijuana, the dreaded doodah. A political decision with severe ramifications for a large number of people was made and, according to one authority, "Public opinion and medical opinion had next to nothing to do with it."[24] The substantive merit of the issue is not the point, and I have no objection if the majority wants to outlaw pot, sunflower seeds, catnip, or apple pie, just as long as it is a decision fairly arrived at through an open political discussion. I do not think that such openness was characteristic of the decision to regulate marijuana. Citizens were responding to a reality manufactured by the bureaucracy.

Just as important, I wonder if the public is now free to change the existing policy. A query: If the laws of the United States were to be rewritten from scratch, would a representative body of Americans replace intact the corpus of law now governing the use of marijuana? One can speculate that an accurate reflection of public opinion would demand a less drastic view of the danger involved. But any change that may come—apparently is coming—will have to fight past the established bureaucracies which have a vested interest in the maintenance of a certain definition of deviance.

My argument is that a number of options have been ruled out, largely because the old Bureau of Narcotics rather diligently distorted the facts. That, I hold, is a perversion of the democratic process, regardless whether the Bureau did in fact save us from becoming a nation of spaced-out degenerates. Until the 1930s, there was no widespread public concern about marijuana, and until the Harrison Act of 1914 there was little control over any form of narcotics. The 1914 legislation only intended a small Bureau with an essentially clerical function, as opposed to enforcement. The Bureau went on to become the scourge of the addict, according to Dickson, "by altering a weakly-held public value regarding narcotics use from neutrality or slight opposition to strong opposition, and by persuading the courts that it should have increased power."[25]

There are a couple of reputable interpretations of how the Bureau went into the business of cracking down on marijuana, both of which focus on the motivation of Harry J. Anslinger, the Commissioner during the 1930s. Becker maintains that Anslinger was a "moral entrepreneur," a zealot who was honestly convinced that marijuana was turning the country into a land of depraved dope fiends. As the expert in narcotics, he had a special obligation to purge this abomination.[26] Dickson sees Anslinger as a shrewd bureaucratic manipulator who, by 1936, realized that the Bureau had expanded as much as it could. Budgets had leveled off, and the best justification for more people and money was a larger jurisdiction. Therefore, he agitated for the passage of the Marijuana Tax Act of 1937, which opened up a whole new field of criminal activity for his organization to control.

Today we have a large narcotic establishment whose members have a lively self-interest in preserving a social environment which provides them with a variety of rewards. I do not believe that the narcotic agents are neutral instruments who can be turned around overnight. In fact, it would be terrible if the narks were to admit that they did not really care about their work, that they had deliberately been wallowing in the public trough for the past forty years, and that they had ruined the lives of many people for no good reason. I assume that most of them have a deep commitment to their work and that they believe in its rightness. That attitude, together with the considerable investment in the machinery of enforcement, represents a sunk cost which cannot be ignored when a change in policy is under consideration.

I stress this sort of case because, as Douglas rightly emphasizes, it is particularly deplorable when deviance, with all its negative consequences for the deviant, is established without society's awareness. However, it should be admitted that bureaucratic maneuvering can have positive results. The educational establishment has been readjusting to a fearful statistic: the number of school-age children is decreasing. Educators have shown considerable ingenuity in thinking up new missions for their organizations to perform. "Special education" or the training of the mentally retarded is such a consequence. We do not insinuate that the teachers have no humane interest in this new clientele or that they might just have easily decided to put underemployed teachers to work at making parakeets talk, but is it entirely coincidental that the concern for this group arose at a time when the enrollment of normal children was declining? In higher education, I am sure that more reforms have been caused by the competition for students than by all the sit-ins and mill-ins of the 1960s. Healthy as these moves may be, however, it cannot be argued that they fit within the conscious design of democracy.

I feel that a normative footnote must be attached to the discussion of organizational solvency. So far, I have only indicated that administrators do bargain in order to keep their organization functioning at a desirable level. I do not think we can tell them how lustily to play the game or that we can convince them that they should keep in mind the best interests of society. Obviously this is not a matter of legislation. There is no law capable of telling bureaucrats that they should not preserve their bureau or that they should not be dedicated.

It is ultimately a matter of the administrator's sense of democratic ethics. The present ethic, as we have seen, includes the belief that one ought to deal directly with pressure groups in order to maintain a narrow piece of the political action. Is it not possible to educate the administrator in something "new," namely, to search for that elusive majority? Put another way, who should foreclose on an organization if it is bankrupt according to our definition of insolvency? If it is someone other than an official directly responsible to a majority of the voters, then we do not have democracy. We have only an anonymous group's peculiar set of values imposed on the rest of us.

Ideally, the contributions and inducements should be channeled through the legislative body. It is probably too late in the day to convince many Americans of such a radical departure from present procedures. In fact, it would very likely be impossible to convince many members of Congress that they should assume that responsibility. It would look too much like hard work with a minimal return for them. They have given up on the idea of laws constructed through an open deliberative process. One way to reverse the situation might be to demand more specific legislation. That might take the pressure off the bureaus as mini-legislatures and return it to Congress where it belongs. Congress is not now an effective broker of the contributions and inducements for the bureaus, but we must think in terms of making it accept that obligation.

Any reform can be effective only when we are more aware of the dynamics I have discussed in this chapter. The critical thing to realize is that bureaucrats do have motives which determine their behavior. Anthony Downs, in noting that public officials are as motivated by self-interest as any humans, concludes that "whether or not the public interest will in fact be served depends upon how efficiently social institutions are redesigned to achieve that purpose. Society cannot insure that it will be served merely by assigning someone to serve it."[27] That is a point well worth pondering.[28]

REFERENCES

1 Kurt Vonnegut, *Cat's Cradle* (New York: Dell, 1970), p. 67.

2 Robert Kharasch, *The Institutional Imperative* (New York: Charterhouse Books, 1973), p. 16.

3 Morton Halperin, "The Presidency and Its Interaction with the Culture of Bureaucracy," in Charles Peters and James Fallows (eds.), *The System* (New York: Praeger, 1976).

4 James Fallows, " 'Making It' Revisited: Nader, Podhoretz, and Morris," *Washington Monthly*, 5 (1973), p. 61.

5 William Niskanen, *Bureaucracy and Representative Government* (Chicago: Aldine-Atherton, 1971), p. 36.

6 Philip Selznick, "Foundations of the Theory of Organization," *American Sociological Review*, 13 (1948), pp. 25–35.

7 John Pfiffner and Frank Sherwood, *Administrative Organization* (Englewood Cliffs, N.J.: Prentice-Hall, 1960), chap. 2.

8 John Millett, *Organization for the Public Service* (Princeton, N.J.: Van Nostrand, 1966).

9 *The Hoover Commission Report* (New York: McGraw-Hill, 1949).

10 Joseph Schott, *No Left Turns* (New York: Praeger, 1975).

11 Ludwig von Mises, *Bureaucracy* (New Haven, Conn.: Yale University Press, 1944).

12 Roland McKean, *Public Spending* (New York: McGraw-Hill, 1968).

13 Chester Barnard, *The Functions of the Executive* (Cambridge, Mass.: Harvard University Press, 1938).

14 Herbert Simon, Donald Smithburg, and Victor Thompson, *Public Administration* (New York: Knopf, 1958), pp. 381–383.

15 Peter Clark and James Q. Wilson, "Incentive Systems: A Theory of Organizations," *Administrative Science Quarterly*, 6 (1961), pp. 129–166.

16 Robert Presthus, *The Organizational Society* (New York: Random House, 1962).
17 Anthony Downs, *Inside Bureaucracy* (Boston: Little, Brown, 1967).
18 Robert Miewald, "The Army Post Schools: A Report from the Bureaucratic Wars," *Military Affairs*, 39 (1975), pp. 8–11.
19 William Starbuck, "Organizational Growth and Development," in James March (ed.), *Handbook of Organizations* (Chicago: Rand McNally, 1965).
20 C. Northcote Parkinson, *Parkinson's Law* (Boston: Houghton Mifflin, 1962).
21 Herbert Kaufman, *Are Government Organizations Immortal?* (Washington: Brookings, 1976).
22 Donald Warwick, *A Theory of Public Bureaucracy* (Cambridge, Mass.: Harvard University Press, 1975), p. 210.
23 Jack Douglas, *American Social Order* (New York: Free Press, 1971), p. 131.
24 Isidore Silver (ed.), *The Crime-Control Establishment* (Englewood Cliffs, N.J.: Prentice-Hall, 1974), p. 58.
25 Donald Dickson, "Bureaucracy and Morality: An Organizational Perspective on a Moral Crusade," *Social Problems*, 16 (1968), pp. 143–156.
26 Howard Becker, *Outsiders* (New York: Free Press, 1963), chap. 8.
27 Downs, op. cit., p. 87.
28 "Do governments expand in direct response to the demands of ordinary people for more and better public-service programs? Or do governments operate independently of the people, producing results that may not be related to the wishes of the citizens and which, on balance, do the people more harm than good?" These critical questions are examined in detail in an important contribution to the study of public administration, Thomas Borcherding (ed.), *Budgets and Bureaucrats: The Source of Government Growth* (Durham, N.C.: Duke University Press, 1977).

Chapter 6

The Budget

These were the generations of Budgeting
Budgeting begat Line Items
Line Items begat Performance Budgeting
Performance Budgeting begat Program Budgeting
Program Budgeting begat Planning-Programming-Budgeting
Planning-Programming-Budgeting begat Management-by-Objectives
Management-by-Objectives begat Zero base Budgeting
Zero base Budgeting begat Evaluation
Evaluation begat Experimentation
Experimentation showed that nothing works.

Allen Schick
"Budgeting"

In this chapter, we shall return to several previously established themes. Remember the "law" that, given the means, managers will centralize operations? Here are some of the means. We shall also see the antipolitical thrust of the techniques of public administration; budgetary innovations generally have as an underlying purpose the removal of politicians from the making of allocative decisions. The calculations of individual bureaucrats about managerial rationality play a large role here. Most of all, we shall find a number of persuasive arguments in favor of submission to the tyranny of necessity. Budget techniques aim at bringing order out of a most chaotic activity by making the individual a helpless observer of abstract events rather than a direct participant. Humans will find freedom through surrender to numerical "laws of the situation."

We are members of what John Wilkinson calls the "Quantitative Society."[1] In the United States and other technological societies, the lure of numerical certainty shapes our thinking and, as Jean Meynaud notes, "seems likely to extend the scope of technocratic penetration" further into the political process.[2] Numbers, or at least their abuse, can divert the direction of politics. According to a sociologist:

> Applied indiscriminately to insufficiently understood aspects of society, the notion of numbers has two ideological effects: it promotes a serialized view of social life, and in its extreme form, it conceals and negates the existing social relations between atomized individuals and substitutes abstract statistical relations; and it becomes the basis on which rational tools for social organization and domination—namely, bureaucracies—are constructed.[3]

There is no conspiracy of mathematicians; it is just "progress." The quantification of the items of administration is the only way in which managers can deal with the variables confronting them. Small wonder then that the dominant mentality in many large organizations is that of the accountant. As Abraham Maslow described these people, "they are the ones who force upon the individual situation the concern with numbers, with exchangeable money, with tangibles, rather than intangibles, with exactness, with predictability, with control, with law and order generally, etc."[4]

These are the patrons who have underwritten the numerous experiments with decision-making devices which, ideally, could operate without human intervention, which could provide a politics untouched by human hands. We shall only be able to hit the highlights, such as planning-programming-budgeting, systems analysis, program evaluation and review technique, operations research, program evaluation, and a few others. But keep in mind that, despite a notable lack of success with most of these, they are only first-generation inventions. We can be assured that ever more ambitious attempts will be made in the search for the ultimate in accountancy: A Place for Everything, and Everything in Its Place. The quantifiers are the ones who want to find out where technology is taking us so they can get us there first; they are the people who joyfully collaborate in the treason to speculation by aggressively ruling out anything which cannot be counted.

While the poor citizens yearn for a consideration of the quality of life, the bureaucracy keeps pulling us into a sea of numbers. As we drown, our perspective becomes distorted. Arthur Ross, a former government statistician, warned that officials suffered from a proneness "to take statistics too literally, to ignore their limitations, and to confuse partial truths with the whole truth about complex realities." In 1968, when most sane people were fearful for the survival of the Republic, he found that the bureaucrats were on the verge of declaring the nation to be a *bona fide* utopia. The body count in Vietnam proved a famous victory, poverty had been taken care of as more people moved above an officially determined income level, and unemployment was at an "acceptable level."[5]

Such are the numerical illusions which continue to mesmerize us. It could be argued, for example, that several recent elections have been decided on the basis of some numbers, the meaning of which is quite debatable. As we have been told often enough, we need leaders who will stomp out Crime in the Streets. The issue is not something which the great majority of us have experienced; few voters, I suspect, are able to figure, "I was mugged once under the Democrats and assaulted three times when the Republicans were in power, so I'll vote for Jones." For most of us, the only hard item is the crime index prepared by the federal government.

Even without looking at the well-known deficiencies of that index, one can make a case that there can be various interpretations of those supposedly absolute figures, that in politics there is even a semantics of numbers. Albert Biderman presents a compelling argument that the rise in crime can be seen as a social good. An increasing crime index can mean a more professional police force, a more public-spirited citizenry, more insurance, more automobiles, and a wider distribution of valuable personal property.[6] All these things are good middle-class virtues, and so one might claim that to start a crime wave in a poor part of town is an intelligent policy decision. The establishment of that or any policy on a set of abstract numbers is, more likely, dangerous and foolish.

ECONOMISTS AND THE BUDGET

As pointed out in Chapter 5, the budget is at the heart of the political process in an organizational society. If politics is the struggle for scarce things, I maintain that there is hardly anything more scarce than public funds. Bureaucrats may not be shallow materialists, but most of them would tend to agree that money is the lifeblood of government. Bureaucratic politics is largely a politics in that arena defined by the budget.

Finance is the key, but what do the experts have in store for us? One can get a very clear idea by considering the trials and tribulations involved with the analytical device which was supposed to get politics out of government once and for all—the planning-programming-budgeting system (PPBS). Within a few years in the late 1960s, it became the sexiest thing to hit public administration. Everybody had to go PPB. We were probably saved from a national catastrophe by the simple fact that nobody ever really understood how to make it work. Now the passion is spent, and there is general agreement among the experts that the experiment was not particularly successful. However, we will continue to feel the aftershocks. The spirit which fed PPB is still around, as hearty as ever, and the self-appointed philosopher kings are still scheming how to procure their rightful crown.

In the area of government finance, the economists are the ones who have anointed themselves. More so than other social scientists, they are terribly impatient with human beings who are just not good enough to fit within their cool models of rationality. The history of PPB shows it was an invention of the economists, which is to say, it was proudly nonpolitical, which is to say, given the importance of the budget in politics, it was highly antipolitical. The idea was developed during World War II and came to fruition under the care of the think-tankers at Rand in the new field of weapons systems analysis. The martial origins of PPB are worth noting since wartime is one of those rare times when organizational participants are looking to the outside and are concerned about the impact of their decisions on the real world, since these decisions are, literally, matters of life and death, a condition which, as Samuel Johnson noted, wonderfully concentrates the mind.

A book by two Randites, Charles Hitch and Roland McKean, impressed the model technocrat who was to become Secretary of Defense in 1961.[7] When Robert McNamara took command, he brought Hitch as Comptroller of the Department of Defense, as well as Alain Enthoven and the Whiz Kids in systems analysis. The Pentagon was using PPB to control its mammoth budgets. The system appealed to President Johnson who, by executive order in 1965, extended it to the rest of the federal government. At about the same time, states and cities began implementing PPB. This sort of movement excited the writers who created a vast literature on the subject, leading to the feeling that it was something no sensible person could resist. But the implementation of PPB turned out to be the fatal mistake; and were it not for the fact that it was tried and found wanting, we would probably still be ecstatic about it.

Before we look at PPB and what it was supposed to do, let us try the economists *in absentia*. We must realize that economics as a tool for political analysis has a number of defects. It is not so much that economists take too seriously their position as the Queen of the Social Sciences, especially because of their ability at quantification. The numbers themselves are not bad; we probably should know what the gross national product is. It is only that quantification does not lead directly to any sort of solution of the human condition; indeed, being inhuman, it may acerbate problems. But a lust for numbers is not peculiar to economics, and many political scientists would not find that a negative factor.

The major error of economic analysis is the pretended value neutrality. Since the beginning of the discipline, most outsiders have not been fooled;

that is why economics was once known as the "dismal science." As a practical matter, however, it is very serious when entrants in the political process claim that they have discovered neutral tools for the solution of humanity's woes. Almost every discussion of PPB by economists contained a disclaimer to the effect that "we are not making policy; we are simply presenting a tool with which the decision maker can make better policy." I know better than that, you know better than that, but not the Ph.D. in economics. As an exasperated Aaron Wildavsky inquired, "How could men make so foolish a statement? Perhaps they identify program budgeting with something good and beautiful, and politics with another thing bad and ugly."[8] Whatever the cause, it is all part of the bounded rationality of the profession.

Economists, moreover, despite their protests, have not quite done away with Economic Man, the totally rational calculator who sees the whole world in terms of marginal utilities, the person who broods interminably about spending a penny on cake or ale. There should be an Economic Man because then everything would work out so well. When economists discuss the budget, they tend to become upset if Economic Man is not in control, if all the variables are not assessed in relation to one another, if the whole complex structure of government is not torn apart on a regular basis and subjected to the most intense analysis. That would obviously be a bad scene for our bemused and befuddled Political Man, who is most interested in maintaining a viable constitutional system, and at the same time looking out for number one. Our citizen, the irrational clod, is not much loved by economists.

In short, I question the ability of economists to solve the Great Issues of Our Day. Of course, political scientists are not any closer to solutions, and therein lies our charm. Political science rejects all those absolute answers and continues to thrive on all the unique values which enliven a society. We preach humility, something which other disciplines seem to despise. We cannot accept some gaudy bauble like PPB if it promises to decrease the sphere of open politics or to limit the conflict of values.

It is the continuing contest between the friends of the "ambiguous" and the "unambiguous." Ambiguous means: "doubtful or uncertain, especially from obscurity or indistinctiveness; capable of being understood in two or more possible fashions." Ambiguity is the bane of the economists. Political scientists, on the other hand, find it no crime if a politician is incomprehensible in pursuit of the major function of keeping society together. But we can understand that it is frustrating for those who see the world as sharply divided between truth and error. The economists take as their standard the idea that there is one best way to spend any dollar of tax money and that that way can be discovered through reason. It can be stated unambiguously, in defiance of selfish interests, in spite of the irrational motives of the uninformed.

Ever since political science came to realize that there was more to budgeting than a bunch of techniques, the incalculability of it all has been appreciated. In 1940, V. O. Key asked, "On what basis shall it be decided to allocate *x* dollars to Activity A instead of Activity B?" He traced all the alternatives and came to the only reasonable conclusion: It is finally a matter of political philosophy.[9] For political science, budgeting cannot be a science in which all the quantities are run through a machine and the final decision is spit out. It must be a flexible system if it is to promote politics. If it is not a generally messy, disorderly affair, there is no economic justification for the maintenance of an elaborate political overhead; Congress can be replaced with a good cost accountant.

All that seems an evident proposition. But it is a disappointing commentary on academics that constant attempts are being made to construct the Pure Science of Budgeting. During the height of the excitement over PPB, political scientists, with the notable exception of Wildavsky, were strangely silent. Perhaps we were intimidated by the greater "rigor" of economics; perhaps we did not want to be the first to cry out that the emperor wore no clothes. Whatever the reason, the discipline was given a reprieve by the collapse of PPB, and perhaps we are now better prepared to defend the budgetary process as the heart of politics.

BUDGETING IN THE UNITED STATES

Economists are nearly unanimous in deploring the traditional budgetary practices in the United States. They say that the budget is an inferior way of making allocative decisions, and its defects encourage the defects of bureaucracy. I would agree that there is much in the present process which encourages bureaucrats to be undemocratic, uncontrollable, and irresponsible. I feel, however, that they would be even more so if and when something like PPB ensures government of, by, and for the technocrats. Paradoxically, that is precisely what the economists were proposing as a remedy for the ills of the existing methods.

To see what PPB was all about, we should examine the nature of the system it was designed to replace. To do that, we might well ask, what are the functions to be served by a budget (beyond the primordial function as a political arena)? Or, if it is a tool, what end does it serve? From the American response to that question, we can see how we floundered into a particular mold. That is, the traditional way of budgeting is just that—a tradition and not a well-conceived package of rationality. That is not to say that it can be, or should be, replaced by such a package.

There are many descriptions of the functions of budgets, but I like the short list provided by Charles Schultze, a major economic adviser in both the Johnson and Carter administrations.[10]

1 *Financial control.* This purpose emphasizes the restriction of administrators to officially approved policies and practices; it aims at the elimination of the corrupt and irresponsible use of public funds.

2 *Managerial control.* Here the executive uses the budget as a tool to ensure that government action is carried out in the most efficient manner.

3 *Strategic planning.* This involves the establishment of goals for society and choosing among ways of attaining those goals in a world of limited resources.

If those are the basic functions of a budget, the United States has realized them only very slowly and so far incompletely. The process by which this occurred has determined the character of the political arena.

Until 1921, the federal government did not even have an "executive budget." That is, the President was out of the picture. Bureaus were generally free to submit their requests directly to Congress, and the members of Congress, through their separate subcommittees, dominated the bureaus. Since there was relatively little money involved, the legislators could get a very precise idea of where the funds went (but not what they did). In budget hearings, there would be long discussions of the purchase of a new typewriter for the post office in Sludge, Arkansas. Such detail was made possible by use of the "line-item" budget. Each item—personnel, equipment, supplies, travel, etc.—was a separate budget line for each agency. A legislator might be able to inquire why the postage bill for the cemetery board was increasing. Unfortunately, that sort of inquiry shows nothing about the relationship of the postage bill and the actual work of the board. When one combined all the budget lines, there was something resembling anarchy. Put all the pages together and you get a thing called a budget only because the government printer is told to use that title.

After the Budget and Accounting Act of 1921, the President had a tool which could give him some idea of what his agencies were up to. At the beginning, however, the emphasis in the Bureau of the Budget was on financial control. Account for every last dime to make sure no scoundrels get their hands on government money. Budgeting became the high art of penny-pinching, the state in which it still exists in some jurisdictions. One of the early budget directors reported the discovery of a miscreant who had made a ball of government rubber bands for his puppy dog to play with. His dismissal was a major achievement that year. For many budgeters, this penny-wise, pound-foolish approach was the whole job.

After the Brownlow Committee of 1937 reported that the President needed more help in running his administration, the Bureau of the Budget was moved into a position of greater power. Among the new functions of BOB, the most important were those aimed at assisting the President in his role as manager of the bureaucracy, "all to the end that the work programs of the several agencies of the executive branch of the Government may be coordinated and that the moneys appropriated by the Congress may be expended in the most economical manner possible with the least possible overlapping and duplication of effort."[11]

In recent years, the need for strategic planning has become obvious. For one thing, the federal budget accounts for a third of the gross national product, and that large a sum is sure to have an impact on the total economy. More than that, governmental resources have not kept pace with governmental activity. We see now that our wealth is not unlimited and that some hard choices will have to be made. Decisions cannot continue to be made in the usual ambiguous political manner. President Johnson told us we could have guns and butter, and we are still paying through inflation the cost of that misjudgment. Another clash of issues concerned the space program: Why should we go to lifeless planets when our cities are becoming just as uninhabitable? We cannot have trips to Venus and pleasant cities at the same time. A setting of priorities is needed.

From this brief history, we can see two powerful legacies which are still at work. To cut through the impediments of the past was one of the major goals of PPB. According to Ira Sharkansky, these two continuing features are "contained specialization" and incrementalism.[12]

Contained specialization means that there can be no rational consideration of the whole operation of government, even though realistic resource allocation should be made within the broadest possible context. There is no single budget for the United States government, nor is there a single agency in charge of the construction, approval, and implementation of individual budgets. Instead, in most budgetary decisions, a number of separate and specialized units are involved. In this feudal system, for anything to be achieved each player has to assume a role; as long as everyone plays the proper role, things can run smoothly, even if resources are poorly allocated.

Incrementalism, particularly as articulated by Charles Lindblom, has become a major descriptive and normative theory of decision making. Interest in it arose because of the obvious difficulties of the pure rationality model; that model simply does not describe how administrators in the real world make decisions. In Lindblom's words, we must accept the reality of the "science of muddling through."[13] Unlike the comprehensive rationality of the budget reformers, incrementalism does not demand superhuman efforts from very frail actors, nor does it require that individuals submerge their own set of values within an abstract code of rationality.

Incrementalists say that we live in a fluid, uncertain world, with a number of social forces living together in an uneasy equilibrium. Major change is unlikely, therefore decision makers should focus on the margins of existing policy and be content with incremental modifications. Given the fragility of the social order, it is folly to say, "Our goal is to do X by 2001!" and then barge right on to achieve that goal. Even if you do not cause civil war, you are likely to find that the goal was not the right one in the first place. Indeed, goals are not separable from the means of achieving them; and once one embarks on a plan, the very elements which went into the original calculations are changed. It is wiser to stick close to terra firma and make adjustments as they become necessary.

So in effect, incrementalism advises us to cool it, be mellow, and hang loose. Instead of trying to reform the world according to a rational master plan, settle for what you can get at any one time and place. Follow the line of least resistance, compromise, settle for half a loaf, a slice, even a crumb, in hopes that next time around you will make more progress. As Lindblom writes, "policy making is typically a never-ending process of successive steps in which continual nibbling is a substitute for a good bite."[14]

Incrementalism, according to scholars such as Wildavsky, is the special genius of the American budgetary system. Budgets are formed after discussion about the annual increment to be added to a base which is itself beyond debate. The system serves to minimize overt conflict among groups about general values or the priorities to be attached to government programs. Nobody knows for sure what it is that government is doing. At least it is so uncoordinated that even antagonistic interests can live together. Nobody gets too much and nobody gets too little. The process supports an advocacy system whereby various interests can find access to the budget without having to prove themselves before an all-knowing rational mind. Incrementalism, in short, is a magnificently political way of making decisions. It excludes no one and by moving at the margins of policy, it alienates no one.

As might be expected, incrementalism has its critics. Some say it is not quite that great as descriptive theory, especially in budgetary matters. It tells us little about the unusual but important decision that occasionally comes along. After all, one cannot take the 1976 budget, reduce it by a percentage increment for each year, and come up with an exact replica of the government of the United States in 1876. Some things did happen in that period which are not explicable by looking only at the expansion of an existing policy base.[15]

As part of the pluralist ideology, incrementalism is suspect as normative theory. It says simply, "that which works is best." Although it gives the impression of great vitality, it is conservative in the sense that those who have, regardless of social worth, get to keep, plus the annual 10 percent. It is dangerously shortsighted in its implication that nothing can be done about massive problems looming on the horizon which require drastic change. To some, incrementalism is the philosophy of conservative drift. Do not get upset, the incrementalists purr, if things are bad, if the rich get rich and the poor get poorer, even if the most outrageous services are frozen in the budgets. It is all part of the game.[16]

In any event, contained specialization and incrementalism are anathema to economists. Nobody is concerned with the best allocation of scarce resources. In this twenty-ring circus, nobody has an idea of what is going on, least of all the participants. The incrementalist would reply, "Great! What people don't know won't hurt them—or make them start a riot which would hurt others." But economists become very disturbed when they realize that in Budgetland, "we are here as on a darkling plain, swept by confused alarms of struggles and flight, where ignorant armies clash by night." Public spending has no relation to public needs. Instead, the budget is only a temporary truce in the political wars, and for those who feel the need for guidance from a Cosmic Mind, that sort of awareness can be quite disheartening. PPB is an aggressive resistance to the old political ways of doing business.

PPB

The defects which PPB were designed to correct can be seen in more detail if we look at the problems facing McNamara when he took control of the biggest government organization in the world. The problems are common to most units of government; and since it was assumed that for a while he had enjoyed some success, his testimony is valuable. On January 20, 1961, these were the headaches for a rational manager:[17]

No method of output evaluation. No one could say for sure what the 50 billion-dollar defense budget was buying.

No matching of goals with limited resources. The goal of the Pentagon is national security, but obviously we do not have enough money to ensure absolute protection; e.g., building a Plexiglas dome over the whole country would not be feasible. Where then do we put our money so it will do the most good?

No system of rational decision making for civilians. Traditional budget making was largely a matter of dividing up the pie among the three services, regardless of the job to be performed.

Disunity of execution of what should have been a common defense policy. Each branch insisted on its separate program for everything from rockets to the procurement of belt buckles.

Short time limit. At a time when major weapons systems took decades to research, develop, and operate, the budget was still seen as a year-to-year affair.

The system finally developed to deal with these and other defects was supposed to provide a number of beneficial payoffs for any unit of government. According to Schultze, PPB would accomplish:[18]

1 The identification of goals for all major units of government. Agencies would be required to state explicitly just what it is they are striving to do.

2 The measurement of government output in terms of the stated objectives. Agencies should be able to show how their activity meets the goals they have established.

3 The determination of total program costs. The entire life span of a program must be calculated, as well as the so-called spillover effects, i.e., the subsidiary costs which should be assigned to a program.

4 The extension of programs over a number of years so that annual budget allocations will be part of a long-range plan.

5 The analysis of alternatives for reaching objectives on a continuous basis in order to "replace, at least in part, the pernicious practice of incremental budgeting."

6 The establishment of systematic analytical procedures as an integral part of the budgetary process.

As it eventually developed, PPB came to include more than the steps indicated by the initials. Planning, programming, and budgeting were not sufficient to describe the whole procedure. The first step, often overlooked, was that of policy making. The PPBSers were nominally apolitical types who assumed that there was in fact a policy about which to plan, program, and budget. Furthermore, they sidestepped the persistent question of how far the implementation of a vague policy is actually policy making. As neutral instruments, the advocates started off their discussions with the planning step.

Planning McNamara testified:

> I consider the budget nothing more and nothing less than the quantitative expression of a plan or a policy. So in developing the budget, I propose to start with the plan or the policy and translate it into quantitative terms, terms of benefits and costs.[19]

The planning function has a special meaning for economists since one cannot make a rational allocation of resources until it is known what is intended to happen. This noble goal tends to fall apart in view of the reluctance of American politicians to state precisely where it is they are leading us. Although we talk about planning, it is not altogether clear how much of that commodity the American political system can tolerate. The assumption that somewhere back up the line someone has a plan to be translated into budgetary terms by humble technocrats does not conform to political reality.

The role of planning is even more dubious when PPB demands that priorities be attached to elements of the plan. We can imagine politicians biting the bullet and endorsing the most general plan which includes something for everyone, but few of them would be anxious to turn that plan into a well-publicized shopping list with weights attached to the several possible programs. It asks too much of the masters of ambiguity to allow themselves to be pinned down that way. Besides, where will the executive get the information upon which to build the plan and set the priorities? Why from the loyal and obedient servants, the planners. Politicians would wind up making plans on the basis of information given them by the very same people with a keen feeling for how the plan will be operationalized. Instead of dreaming dreams for society, the politicians would be hit with the negativism of sober-minded analysts who can prove, as experts always do, that QED, everything but the existing reality is impossible.

Programming This is to be the pivot in the system by which plans are translated into budget requests. The program provides a meaningful link between two functions which were hitherto separate. In the words of the federal manual: "A program is a cluster of government activities that are in closer competition with each other than with those outside the program and whose output has a clearly identifiable purpose." As that statement indicates, the construction of programs is an uncertain art. A program is an abstraction which identifies the things done by government, regardless of specific organizational units. Do we have a city to give us police, fire, and welfare departments? Or do we really want security for life and property, welfare services, and other outputs? If the latter, we should think in terms of programs which provide specific amounts of desired output. A recreation program, for example, might spread across departmental boundaries to include physical education classes in the schools or services for the elderly within the welfare department. This total program should be identified, and costs attached to the whole thing.

Budgeting When government is viewed as a collection of programs, the decision maker can then piece together a combination to attain goals according to the predetermined priorities. Through the use of comparable output data, it is possible to decide whether to use a dollar to purchase more of the police program instead of the education program. Policy makers are forced to feel the full impact of their decisions about specific programs: if you do *x*, then you cannot afford *y*, and *z* will cost so much over the next ten years. The mix decided upon can then be given to the legislators for official approval. If planning and programming have been done correctly, budgeting is a fairly technical matter.

Finally, PPB should have an "A" and an "E" attached to it. The A stands for analysis, since throughout the process it is assumed that careful scrutiny of all alternatives is taking place. One does not recommend a budget level in the incremental manner just because it was there last year. The E is for evaluation because it is also assumed that government objectives and outputs can be quantified and progress toward the meeting of goals can be measured. These two topics are of such importance and are probably the things to be salvaged from PPB that we will look more closely at them in Chapters 7 and 8.

TECHNIQUES OF PPB

PPB should not be understood as a coherent process to be accepted or rejected as a whole. Rather, it is a group of distinctive components, each one of which can stand alone as an instrument of rationality. Beyond the two features of systems analysis and evaluation, there are five other basic concepts which deserve mention.

Program Accounting Traditional budgetary accounts are concerned with specific units, e.g., welfare, police, or fire departments. Program accounts were aimed at stimulating inhabitants of the separate agencies to view their work in terms of programs and not institutions. But it soon became clear that information was not enough to transcend institutional parochialism. If programs spill across agency lines, why not reorganize so that agencies and programs are the same? PPB is therefore a centralizing force. One author even saw the need for including other levels of government within program categories; he doubted whether "a program budget will have much impact on government decisions unless authority is centralized."[20]

That is precisely the sort of talk which makes entrenched bureaucrats rather fidgety. One would have to take a low estimate of the survival instincts of our civil servants to believe that they did not see the handwriting on the wall.

Multiyear Costing The idea of multiyear costing has much to recommend it. The annual budget cycle does not facilitate the careful consideration of a complex and unwieldy program. Officials must have a perspective which allows them to see the entire program as a seamless web of time and space. Merewitz and Sosnick argue, however, that a good idea may be overextended. The making of long-range plans may not be essential for every government bureau, and "to incur these costs with respect to ongoing programs is a strange decision when multi-year costing is not likely to increase the rate of rejection for such activities and will divert attention from whether their budget-year expenditures are worthwhile."[21]

Detailed Description PPB requires bales of data. For each program, administrators are expected to describe their objectives, the measures of goal attainment, the choices made, the projected output, and the effectiveness of the output in meeting goals, together with all the alternatives considered in coming up with a recommendation. In reading the requirements of the federal PPB system, it seems incredible that anyone in government was doing more than filling out budget forms. Moreover, all the requested data are usually very squishy. In Chapter 7, we will consider how reliable any of these facts can be.

Cost-Benefit Analysis At the heart of PPB is the heavy analysis which will go into any decision. Before making a public choice, politicians will have spelled out for them exactly what it is they will have to spend and what its return to society will be. A nice idea, but even in theory there are depressing complications, such as, what is a cost? And here one gets immediately into the murky world of welfare economics. The problem of "discounting the cost stream" is no less metaphysical, and economists who write their learned treatises on the subject never seem to realize that politicians tend to set discount rates which improve the chances of their pet projects. Once we find out the cost, then we can ask, what is a benefit? Not surprisingly, bureaus which have used cost-benefit analysis, such as the Corps of Engineers, tend to minimize the cost and maximize the benefits. Little work has been done to follow up these analyses, but there is some evidence to indicate that many analyses have been rather misleading.[22]

Zero-based Budgeting The year 1976 saw some vigorous moves to knock the crutch of incrementalism out from under bureaucracy. Colorado became the first state to pass "sunset legislation," a procedure which requires agencies to justify their existence every few years; the hope is that obsolete bureaus will be put to a merciful death. One of the themes of Jimmy Carter's remarkable run for the Presidency was his promise to bring the terrible swift sword of zero-based budgeting (ZBB) to the Washington bureaucracy.[23]

Under ZBB, agencies are required to present and defend a budget which has no reference to the level of last year's appropriation. There would be no more working from the base, since the base itself would have to be justified. Each year everybody starts from the same budgetary point, namely, zero. As the Governor of Nebraska informed his agency directors:

> . . . the zero base budget assumes that nothing presently exists and that each activity of an agency must be evaluated and stand on its own merits in comparison to other activities within that same agency. It is no longer valid simply to say that an activity has been going on for five or ten or twenty or fifty years and therefore needs to be continued and that to the amount spent for that activity during the preceding years the cost of inflation must be added.

The idea flies in the face of everything we know about organizational behavior. Certainly government is no tabula rasa; bureaucrats exist as part of an ongoing system. ZBB makes impossible demands upon members of the organization and prevents them from using the very information which might be most useful—what did we do last year? The real problem is that all appropriations can be justified or, conversely, nothing is justifiable. It is still a subjective value judgment, no matter how it is viewed. But in this subjectivity, people are told to let loose of the known universe and to consider all the things that might be. Their world is snatched from them, and so it is no wonder they tend to sneak back to home port. Lo and behold, if God were to restructure the federal government, He would want an Immigration and Naturalization Service, and at about the same level as last year. Even though associated with the supposed evils of incrementalism, last year's budget does provide some certainty in the midst of uncertainty.

From a political standpoint, there are incredible costs associated with ZBB and sunset laws. These threaten nothing less than the reopening of every political wound every year. Since nothing can be regarded as settled—just because we had an army or a social security system last year does not mean we need it now—no political question can ever be resolved, even temporarily. I doubt if many politicians can regard the reconsideration of 525 billion dollars' worth of political conflict every year a happy prospect.

THE DECLINE AND FALL OF PPB

After the disenchantment with PPB, there has been a reexamination of its big splash in the Department of Defense. To begin with, it was not universally admired by the military, largely because they are not given to thinking in wholly rationalistic terms. As I argued earlier, their professional being is rooted in caution about the "imponderables." Hyman Rickover, the hero of the nuclear submarine and no reactionary, stated it bluntly: "Frankly, I have no more faith in the ability of social scientists to quantify military effectiveness than I do in numerologists to calculate the future"; the major flaw was that "all the factors of military effectiveness for which the analyst cannot calculate a numerical value have been automatically discarded from consideration."[24]

Furthermore, it is clear now that the Department of Defense was a misleading example for the civilian side of government. The Department had a fairly coherent set of goals, many of which were quantifiable. Officers were familiar with planning. At the time it was initiated, the Pentagon just about possessed a monopoly of expertise in PPB. The military had control of an entire program and did not need to coordinate with other federal departments or with other levels of government. Perhaps most important, PPB was initiated at a time of rapidly growing military budgets because of Vietnam. One can do an awful lot of reforming when you are increasing the base by 50 billion dollars. When extended to civilian agencies facing retrenchment, things happened less easily.

So PPB died a quiet death in the federal government.[25] If one understands the system as the whole package, Wildavsky is right that there is not "a single example of successful implementation of PPBS."[26] Some experts still keep the faith, and I concede that the final assessment may be premature. After all, it is a long-range idea, and perhaps enough seeds have been planted so that something will eventually blossom. I do not believe that things will ever return to the status quo ante PPB, especially as a new generation of budget specialists work their way to the top. PPB did open new vistas on the governmental process, and it will be impossible for anyone to regard the budgetary system as a simple thing. Instead of a complete package, there will continue to be interest in planning, in programming, and in budgeting, but less desire to bring them together.

So what happened on the way to the revolution? Many pro-PPB people argue that it was implemented poorly. This approach is consistent with their deep faith in the potency of the pure light of reason. If PPB did not work, it was largely because the managers and politicians blew it. Specifically, the lack of trained personnel is seen as fatal. There were not enough qualified people to meet all the complex demands of the system, and in any event, Spokane or Toledo could not afford to hire the same caliber of people who made it work in the Pentagon. There was also general disappointment in the level of instruction in the new techniques. Quite often, lower officials were informed by memo from the governor or mayor that their entire universe had been destroyed overnight. They were expected to assume a new way of walking and talking, and little was done to ease the shock. Training in PPB, if available, might be a two-day affair in which an arrogant analyst would state flatly, "This is the way it is going to be!"

The incrementalists can gloat, "I told you so." The budget is the core of the political process, and PPB was really a political revolution attempted by the technocrats. Once the politicians saw what was coming down and what it would mean to their positions, they gave it the quietus. I could accept that argument if it could be demonstrated that PPB ever impressed itself upon the consciousness of many politicians. I am not sure they perceived it as a threat because I am not sure they perceived it at all. Politicians did not have to kill PPB because by the time it reached them it was already stillborn.

There is a third argument that says that PPB was not implemented because it cannot be implemented. It was totally unrealistic in the demands it made upon officials, budget experts, and politicians. If it were done according to the model, the entire government would come to a halt. As Wildavsky concludes, "failure was built into its very nature because it requires ability to perform cognitive operations that are beyond present human (or mechanical) capacities."[27] The circuits were overloaded by the demands for information.

These explanations have some merit, but I would like to suggest something a little different. I maintain that the economists and their reformist allies came to grief because the budgetary "system" is the grandest of granfalloons. It appears to be a system; but when one tries to change it, it becomes obvious that the participants are doing everything except consciously participating in the rational formulation of allocative decisions. One cannot strengthen, one cannot reform something which never existed to begin with. Actual budgetary behavior is often so far removed from the ostensible purposes of the budget that it is even difficult to give it the theoretical gloss of incrementalism. I believe that to be the message of a number of studies which have been done on the practice of budgeting.

Thomas Anton described how the state of Illinois decided to spend 4 billion dollars—if decide is the word we want here. His book is more a picture of zombies going through the steps without any particular appreciation of what it all means. Part of the problem is time; the cost of decision making is avoided by not making any, by the simple expedient of regarding the process as a matter of clerkship.

The detailed budget instructions were not seen as a guide to contructive decision making. They were a bunch of forms to be filled out as quickly as possible without much regard for the dictates of pure rationality. This was especially true since, as is the case with most bureaucratic directives, the implication was that anyone too far out of line was in for a heap of trouble. Anton writes, "the term 'budget' refers to the forms distributed by the Finance Department which, when filled out, will appear in the budget document submitted by the Governor." Budget making, in short, was not an occasion for brooding about the nature of the universe and the framing of a statesmanlike response to perceived problems.

The budget was part of a stable operation, the main purpose of which seemed to be self-maintenance at a constant state. It was by no stretch of the imagination a manifestation of divine rationality come down into the affairs of people. In words that must chill the heart of the PPB people, who have dedicated themselves to devising a means whereby truckloads of data could be generated for every contingency, Anton remarks on the "relative unimportance of information." The facts really do not matter that much.[28]

John Crecine studied the budgetary process in three large cities. He rejected the models of the budget as an optimizing process, i.e., a system for finding the maximum social welfare. Instead, he looked at budgeting as an internal bureaucratic mechanism, using the model derived from Cyert and March's *Behavioral Theory of the Firm*: most organizational behavior is determined by problems of the allocation of scarce resources among organizational participants, that is, how does one pay off the existing membership of a bureaucracy?

When the organization is viewed as a coalition of independent members, resource allocation becomes a means of holding the divergent parts together; the relative position of those within the system must be maintained unless there are extreme circumstances demanding otherwise. The budget, in short, is a way of restraining that murderous war of all against all that has terrified students of the social order since the time of Thomas Hobbes. Everyone signs an uneasy truce agreeing not to wipe out any other participant. In Crecine's cities, decision makers were faced with the essential problem of keeping the peace in face of the inherent complexity in distributing resources.

The handiest way of coping, Crecine found, was "government by precedent," which certainly offered security to the powers that be. This was, as in Illinois, another stable system in which historical experience and precedent set the operating standards. Also as in Illinois, the simplest device was the budget form itself, especially when busy agency heads must take time out of their hectic schedules and, without much staff assistance, make budget requests. According to Crecine, "the physical makeup of the budget form probably has as much influence as anything in determining the department head's response to the request for budget estimates." The forms confine attention to the present funds and focus only on next year.[29]

Donald Gerwin studied the budgetary process in the local school district. Starting with the premise that the lack of a single operational measure for the allocation of money leads to potentially bitter conflict within the organization, he argued that administrators want to reduce conflict rather than promote the reconsideration of all options. Participants are jealous of their share of the budget, which means that existing appropriations will not be reduced without a fight. New appropriations will be determined through a bargaining process, the chief weapon for the bargainers being the ability to make trouble. When a surplus is available, the leaders will tend to pay off the potential agitators first in return for a tacit promise to reduce the tension. The main purpose of the budget is to keep the armistice alive.[30]

Johan Olsen has an interesting description of budgeting in a Norwegian commune, and even at that distance there are familiar themes. He does not see the budget as part of a decision-making process; instead, it is a high ceremony for the community. It is symbolic action, a ritual in which the instrumental nature of the institution is not decisive. He found many people involved in the budgetary process, and most citizens were convinced that budgeting was important. However, few participants had any information or felt much responsibility for what finally happened. There were few situations in which grand alternatives were seriously debated; instead, decisions were made by consensus. Olsen concludes, "Therefore we should not take it as given that budgetary behavior is always primarily concerned with transforming individual and group values and beliefs into policies."

So what is it all about? What is the Hopi's rain dance about? It is a way of convincing ourselves that all is right in the world, that there is a humanly determined order to things. The word "budget" implies that some small part of the chaos has been pushed back. Olsen found that public participation took three forms: (1) the verbalization of beliefs—rhetoric about questions like the role of local government, the clash of bureaucracy and democracy, and other high school debate topics; (2) the "floor-carpet syndrome" in which people latch on to the minor things they can understand, such as the price of carpeting;[31] (3) the "not now but later syndrome." Here we find the "we'll have to do something about that" sort of thing in which discussions are not directed to the problems at hand.

The budget, then, is a community's security blanket, giving the appearance of order and rationality. The political pros are left with "fire station administration," that is, dealing with the day-to-day problems as they emerge. No real planning is possible. But of course, says Olsen, the real purpose of the ceremony is the resolution of conflict and not planning.[32]

G. H. Hofstede looked at the budget as a control device in four Dutch industrial plants. The main issue, as he saw it, was organizational control versus individual autonomy. He took it as given, as I do, that subordinates will strive to maximize the scope of their freedom of action and thus escape from the harness of strict budget controls. Freedom of action is necessary for the well-being of the members, and they will languish under a system which offers no flexibility. As every mother's child knows, and as every rational budgeter denies, the system will be beaten. Writes Hofstede, "people are always smarter than systems and if the system is functioning in such a way that it pays to make figures 'look right' instead of doing something about the underlying causes, this is what will happen." Members will react to the budget in the spirit of play, as something to be used for its own sake, unrelated to external demands on the organization. Members are not obsessed with their impact on the outside world. The work of the moment is critical, and they want to be able to control their immediate work environment.[33]

What do these studies add up to? The common theme seems to be the relative indifference of people within the system to externalities. Those actually involved in budgeting do not spend much time agonizing over marginal utilities or how their performance will affect the course of Western civilization. Their decisions, in fact, are not directly related to the overall goals of the larger organization of which they are part. They want to survive as individuals, which may mean something about the activity of their unit, but the attitude is not immediately translated into a concern over the general welfare.

When relating these findings to the tradition of rational budgetary reform as represented by PPB, one is reminded of the reply of the old farmer to the county agent with all his great new agricultural techniques: "Hell, I ain't farming half as good as I already know how." The reformers are true children of the Enlightenment. Organizational members are living in darkness, fettered by ignorance and confusion. Give them the necessary information and, like any rational human, they will come to the only right conclusion. As long as budget reform is seen as a structural thing, the free flow of information will be advocated as the major means of improvement.

People do not want to budget any better than they are doing already, particularly when reforms threaten all sorts of nasty things. Be honest, and they will cut your funds. Be frank and candid, and you will be out of a job. Reform is a behavioral problem and not a matter of structural readjustment. Members want to avoid conflict because that introduces a truly uncontrollable factor. To suggest that reform is nothing more than adjustments to the structure so that participants can see more clearly the Brave New World is in fact playing into the hands of the members, because the existing structure is already ritualistic. Participants will no doubt be just as successful in modifying the reformed structure to fit their needs. Members may mouth all the pieties of the new method, but they will not commit themselves to greater rationality. Little games will continue, regardless of the precise nature of the rules.

The conclusion is not that there is no urgent need for budgetary reform. I do not believe, however, that the debilitating rationality of the economists is either functional or humane. What we do need is a reform which will permit elected officials to attract the attention of bureaucrats. What members want now is order and security, and politicians will have to be able to convince them that those good things are more likely to be achieved by concentrating on the performance of organization goals than by striving after internal peace.

The real question is: In whose self-interest is budget reform? If administrators are satisfied with what they have, it makes no sense for them to accept a radically different budget system which might jeopardize their position. And PPB was definitely threatening in all of its aspects. No more the safety of the base and its annual increment, but instead only the vision of an exhausting civil war within the organization. The promise of PPB with its cosmic eye peering into every corner of the organization is not attractive to any reasonable person. So, in the words of Don Corleone, how do we make the bureaucrats an offer they can't refuse? How do we make it worth their while to devote public funds toward worthwhile ends and, more than that, put the real power in the hands of the public? There are no easy answers I can think of, but one hopeful move—and it must be admitted that PPB did stimulate thought in this area—concerns program evaluation. It is to that question and the larger issue of the calculability of government output that we now turn.

REFERENCES

1 John Wilkinson, "The Quantitative Society," *Center Magazine*, 2 (1969), pp. 64–71.
2 Jean Meynaud, *Technocracy* (New York: Free Press, 1969), p. 48.
3 Magali Larson, "Notes on Technocracy: Some Problems of Theory, Ideology, and Power," *Berkeley Journal of Sociology*, 17 (1972–73), p. 22.
4 Abraham Maslow, *Eupsychian Management* (Homewood, Ill.: Dorsey, 1965), p. 214.

5 U.S. Senate, Subcommittee on National Security and International Operations, *Planning-Programming-Budgeting: Hearings* (Washington: GPO, 1968), pp. 240–242.

6 Albert Biderman, "Social Indicators and Goals," in Raymond Bauer (ed.), *Social Indicators* (Cambridge, Mass.: M.I.T., 1966), pp. 111–129.

7 Charles Hitch and Roland McKean, *The Economics of Defense in the Nuclear Age* (Cambridge, Mass.: Harvard University Press, 1960).

8 Aaron Wildavsky, *The Politics of the Budgetary Process*, 2d ed. (Boston: Little, Brown, 1974), p. 190.

9 V. O. Key, "The Lack of a Budgetary Theory," *American Political Science Review*, 34 (1940), p. 1138.

10 Charles Schultze, *The Politics and Economics of Public Spending* (Washington: Brookings, 1968), chap. 1.

11 U.S. Senate, Committee on Government Operations, *Financial Management in the Federal Government*, vol. II (Washington: GPO, 1971), p. 142.

12 Ira Sharkansky, *The Politics of Taxing and Spending* (Indianapolis: Bobbs-Merrill, 1969), pp. 38–52.

13 Charles Lindblom, "The Science of Muddling Through," *Public Administration Review*, 19 (1959), pp. 79–88.

14 Charles Lindblom, *The Policy-making Process* (Englewood Cliffs, N.J.: Prentice-Hall, 1968), p. 25.

15 Peter Natchez and Irvin Bupp, "Policy and Priority in the Budgetary Process," *American Political Science Review*, 67 (1973), pp. 951–963.

16 Yehezkel Dror, *Public Policymaking Reexamined* (San Francisco: Chandler, 1968), pp. 144–145.

17 Samuel Tucker (ed.), *A Modern Design for Defense Decision* (Washington: Industrial College of the Armed Forces, 1966).

18 Schultze, op. cit., chap. 2.

19 Tucker, op. cit., p. 9.

20 Werner Hirsch, *Integrating View of Federal Program Budgeting*, Rand Memorandum RM-4799-RC (Santa Monica, Calif.: Rand, 1965), p. vi.

21 Leonard Merewitz and Stephen Sosnick, *The Budget's New Clothes* (Chicago: Markham, 1971), p. 38.

22 See Robert Haveman, *The Economic Performance of Public Investments* (Baltimore: Johns Hopkins, 1972).

23 "Zero-Based Budgeting—A Way to Cut Spending, or a Gimmick?" *U.S. News and World Report*, 81 (Sept. 20, 1976), pp. 79–82.

24 Hyman Rickover, "Cost-Effectiveness Studies," U.S. Senate, Subcommittee on National Security and International Operations, *Planning-Programming-Budgeting: Selected Comment* (Washington: GPO, 1967), pp. 36–38.

25 Allen Schick, "A Death in the Bureaucracy: The Demise of Federal PPB," *Public Administration Review*, 33 (1973), pp. 146–156.

26 Wildavsky, op. cit., p. 200.

27 Ibid., p. 206.

28 Thomas Anton, *The Politics of State Expenditures in Illinois* (Urbana: University of Illinois Press, 1966).

29 John Crecine, *Governmental Problem-solving* (Chicago: Rand McNally, 1969).

30 Donald Gerwin, "Toward a Theory of Public Budgetary Decision Making," *Administrative Science Quarterly*, 14 (1969), pp. 33–46.

31 Parkinson calls this the "Law of Triviality." See "High Finance," in *Parkinson's Law* (Boston: Houghton Mifflin, 1962).

32 Johan Olsen, "Local Budgeting: Decision-making or a Ritual Act?" *Scandinavian Political Studies*, vol. 5 (New York: Columbia University Press, 1970).

33 G. H. Hofstede, *The Game of Budget Control* (London: Tavistock, 1968).

Chapter 7

The Art and Science of Measurement

We believe, as did Lord Kelvin, that when you can measure what you are talking about and express it in numbers your knowledge is much more useful than when you cannot measure it.

Allen V. Astin
Operations Research

Chapter 6 on budgeting was designed to stand alone as a discussion of an important part of the administrative process. But it is also intended to serve as an introduction to a variety of emerging trends in public administration. Because budgeting has been an essential government function for so many years, and because of the availability of a literature on reforms and the behavior of individuals, it provides us with a relatively clear view of the basic issues. PPB may be stone-cold dead, but the questions it raised are very much alive. From the current haze of uncertainty, one can discern the outlines of things to point to with pride or view with alarm.

The theme of this chapter is the future direction of the "quantitative society," although this society tends to go by the less frightening name of "the knowledge society." The idea is that "knowledge" is increasing at an exponential rate as the various scientific disciplines strip away the mysteries of the universe. A major social problem is the management of this knowledge for the benefit of all. However, it is essential that we recognize that the enthusiasts of the knowledge society are epistemologically biased. Not all ways of knowing are considered as contributing to the knowledge base. Knowledge is a very tangible thing, as can be seen by the terms used to describe this "industry": The "production," "processing," "distribution," and "consumption" of knowledge, as if it were the same thing as canned peaches. We are sure that few of the experts would consider Don Juan and his buddy, El Mescalito, to be involved in the production of knowledge. Frightened humans, lying awake at three o'clock in the morning, also do not qualify.

Knowledge is that which has been developed through the scientific method; in its purest form, it is capable of being expressed in numbers. Thus, I still believe that the "quantitative society" is a more accurate description of a society in which only one form of knowledge is accredited. Because knowledge is of a uniform type, a universal standard of rationality is attainable. Authorities such as Etzioni may warn about the statements of science "that their truth is only relative and tentative, but they also do not escape the reduction of reality entailed in selectivity."[1] An admission of such relativity would undercut the administrative reality. Discussion of the nature of knowledge is ended, and the remaining step in the construction of a new society is the institutionalization of knowledge through the proper administrative arrangements.

At the managerial level, that is, within the organization, the search has led to oohs and ahs over the ultimate in cooperative human effort. The inevitable step in management is what Alvin Toffler, in *Future Shock*, described so breathlessly as the movement from bureaucracy to "Ad-hocracy." As all members of the organization become more knowledgeable, i.e., more indoctrinated in the norms of orthodox ways of knowing, the less need there will be for the formal control structure. Highly trained professionals will come together in unstructured patterns of cooperation to perform the jobs which their perfect knowledge tells them must be done. I know it is cruel, but I must point out that the prime example given us by Toffler of this grand new way is Lockheed Aircraft in the construction of the C-5A air transport, an outrage which towers like Everest over the ordinary blunders of military procurement; "Lockheed" and "C-5A" have become synonyms for hitherto unexplored levels of organizational ineptitude.[2]

I believe that there are substantial problems connected with the idea of the "temporary society."[3] As pointed out in an analysis of the "greatly exaggerated death of bureaucracy," the intellectual tradition stretches unbroken from Auguste Comte, through Taylor and Follet, down to Peter Drucker and Warren Bennis. The basic idea is that servitude to an objective "law of the situation" will set people free.[4] But it is freedom only from the tangible bonds of the organization. Instead of being told what to do, members will have been programmed to do it on their own. It is a free will from which all traces of the irrational have been carefully removed. When we take away the external signs of bureaucracy, we are still left with that "rational discipline" which Weber saw as the basis of bureaucratization. A slavery to rationality, even though voluntarily accepted, is perhaps more dangerous to society than one imposed by brutal overseers.

At a higher level, the political theory of the knowledge society looks toward the end of politics. Society in the "postindustrial" era, it is argued, will be a massive self-correcting mechanism. If politicians survive, their function will be to set very general goals which the technicians will achieve by the use of their sophisticated knowledge. More likely, politicians would be quite expendable because there would be almost total agreement on the nature of the good life—full employment, no crime, good health, quality education, clean air. These goals, which surely no one would quibble about, are easily translated into technical problems for the professionals to solve. Through advanced systems for monitoring societal performance, corrective action can be taken automatically whenever threats to the equilibrium are detected.

Allen Schick describes the new polity as the "Cybernetic State." In this state, government functions as a servomechanism, going into action when indicators show a deviation from standards of societal well-being. The old democratic machinery is increasingly irrelevant because the public is less capable of making decisions about the choice of values. Instead, the people who know how things work are far more important.[5] Goerl notes that "the presentations of the self-guiding society discount the importance of full political participation and representation in the process of 'steering.' "[6] I cannot see how it could be otherwise since only the technicians offer the knowledge necessary for the determination of the correct course of action.

ON THE PROBLEM OF GOALS

The attainment of any of the versions of the knowledgeable organization will require an intersubjective standard of performance. It must be possible to measure in an unambiguous way the degree to which the rational organization is accomplishing its tasks. Ideally, one should be able to take the stated goals of any organization and determine precisely to what degree those goals have been realized. Corrective action, determined by the dictates of knowledge, would then be taken by the technocrats. A major theoretical problem concerns the goals of the organization.

There is a distinct school of administrative thought which holds that there is no clear statement of goals and that even the formal charter of an organization can be quite deceptive. The theorists have reacted strongly to the deficiencies of the narrow rationalism of an earlier day which maintained that the organization was a purely instrumental thing. Organizations, we now know, serve a large number of goals for the individual participants. Thus, although an organization may be very ineffective in meeting its formal goals, it may be quite effective in fulfilling the personal needs of the several members. Etzioni declares that "public goals fail to be realized not because of poor planning, unanticipated consequences, or hostile environment. *They are not meant to be realized.*"[7] In another influential article, Yuchtman and Seashore reject the traditional assumptions "(1) that complex organizations have an ultimate goal . . . toward which they are striving and (2) that the ultimate goal can be identified empirically and progress toward it measured."[8] Paul White states emphatically that "individuals have goals but organizations do not."[9]

The theorists are attempting to make manifest the mysteries of granfalloonery. On the one hand, their motives are humane since they are trying to make explicit the larger social purpose of the modern organization. We will all live within these structures, and the cost of reaching formal goals may be detrimental to a workable society. For example, we could probably speed up the delivery of the mail by holding as hostages the families of the letter carriers. That sort of extreme stress, however, would be dysfunctional in a society with any sort of conception of human dignity. Any organization has some obligation to ensure that it is not contributing to the neuroses of its members.

On the other hand, I cannot help but suspect that these models of goal relativity are in fact designed to improve the effectiveness of the organization in the accomplishment of formal goals. As we will see in a later chapter, the business of business administration, the discipline from which we derive these theories, is the improvement of productivity. We are being told, in effect, that the members are much craftier than was suspected; therefore, the clever manager must be more subtle in manipulating the variables of employee performance. The seventeen "multivariate models" and their theoretical foundations identified by one scholar all seem to promise that with further research, the control of the organization over its members can be even more complete.[10] That is, by what means can the manager "de-granfalloonize" the organization and get people with the program?

I agree with Victor Thompson that behavioral legerdemain may serve to trivialize the role of formal goals. It tends to turn the organization from a "tool" into a "thing," a random collection of individuals. It violates common sense to suppose that when one walks into a government bureau in order to pick up a license, there is just as good a chance of winding up with a diploma, a haircut, or a set of steel-belted radials. Formal goals are important, first, because they set the standard of rationality which most of us are socialized to accept; they provide a sense of legitimacy for our participation and give meaning to our lives. Second, they provide the justification for all administrative science; if organizations were pointless gobs, there would be no need for this book. In Thompson's words, an organization without "normative unity," without a goal, would make meaningless the idea of control and the management function of "securing behavior appropriate to the normative unity of organizations."[11]

For a democratic concept of administration, the idea that formal goals are irrelevant is devastating. It would mean that when the public decides on having a police department, for example, it is taking its chances in a costly game of roulette. This is not to say that public goals are being accomplished simply because there is a formal mandate or that the individual members are fanatically committed to the goal. I suggest only that extreme deviation from formal goals is a political problem of the first order since it negates the idea of responsible government and that the first priority of public administration ought to be the delineation of formal goals so that the public can evaluate the performance of their government.

The model of organizational solvency expressed in the previous chapters seems to explore a reasonably moderate approach to the matter of goals. Bargaining does go on in the organization, but in no way can this concept be extended to make the organization into a free marketplace in which everyone competes with equal ability. Organizations are systems of power, and the managers, who are more committed to the instrumental goals, necessarily have more power. This does not mean that all the members are particularly dedicated to formal goals, and certainly not to the exclusion of their personal values. But self-interest is never defined independent of the dominant culture, and in the administrative structure, a major component of the culture is the instrumental goal or at least the functionally rational pattern derived from the pursuit of formal goals. It is one more manifestation of the dual perspective of *homo duplex*. This dualism within the organization was most succinctly described by Kurt Tucholsky in his remarks about the ambivalence of his highly bureaucratized compatriots: "To stand before the counter, that is the German fate. To sit behind the counter, that is the German ideal!"[12] Our own feelings about the goals may be weak, but in the organizational context, we are pleased to attribute rational behavior to others and to sock it to them on that basis.

Whatever model one uses, insofar as there is any desire to approximate reality, there must be an admission that goals are incredibly complex things, and therefore their accomplishment is hard to measure. The individual motives of the members prevent the universal application of a single measure of effectiveness. Moreover, the public organization presents special problems since in many cases there is a deliberate ambiguity about formal goals. I know of a large public university in which the members are told that the primary function is research and that they will be evaluated on the basis of how much they push back the frontiers of knowledge. The legislators and public are told that the function of the university is teaching and service to the state. The university administrators are in fact fearful that the public will learn that there are professors on the payroll doing research on Albanian politics or on the use of iambic pentameter in Milton's early poems. If either the professors or the public were forced to agree on goals, one or the other would probably withdraw their support.

MEASUREMENT IN GOVERNMENT

A variety of currents in public administration are swirling around the problem of the measurement of government effectiveness. The advocates of the cybernetic state, the refugees from the PPB experiment, the management innovators, and the students of public accountability are all convinced that the first step in their respective reforms is the institution of a system whereby the objectives and outputs of government can be stated in quantitative form. All are finding that the measurement problem is a tough nut to crack. Many of the proposals for the future come to grief, as did PPB, in the debate over what can and cannot be measured.

The aim is an objective measure of the impact of government activity; i.e., did an agency make any difference in the course of human events or did it only spin the bureaucratic wheels, using the taxpayer's money for oil? The innocent reader may be unimpressed with the novelty of this movement. Surely administrators have always been curious about what they were doing. Surprise! This most basic step is now the new frontier of public administration. Some worrywarts might warn us against moving too fast. After all, there is always the danger of finding out that government is beyond control and that none of the deckhands on the ship of fools know what is happening. Besides, it is argued, if you can identify units of government production, why not price them in the open market—or at least tell the public who they are subsidizing and at what costs?

There have, of course, been attempts to measure government operations. The traditional methods, however, tend to leave something to be desired. Most measures turn out to be inputs rather than outputs. Tax dollars are converted into inputs such as employees or typewriters which, through a leap of faith, are interpreted to mean that something useful is being accomplished. With the traditional output measures, there is usually a grossness which is not helpful in making adjustments. For example, the recidivism rate is honored among penologists, but few can tell us how that rate is related to the expenditure of funds. The dangers and promises of measurement can best be indicated if we begin with the area in which it has always been around in some form, the problem of internal management control.

TECHNIQUES OF CONTROL

The problems of control faced by managers vis-à-vis their unit are the same as those faced by the public in relation to the whole government. At whatever level, once a decision is made, one must see to it that it is implemented properly. Any decision-making relationship implies the existence of control devices, if decision making is not to be an entirely futile exercise. When the word "frog" is given, there must be a way to find out if the subordinates are hopping in the right direction. Therefore, all organizations have some sort of control system, unless superiors are certain that they are in charge of a group of true believers who can be trusted to carry out perfectly any orders.

One authority put this managerial function this way: "The essence of control is action which adjusts operations to predetermined standards, and its basis is information in the hands of managers."[13] A little reflection on the reciprocal nature of control systems will reveal that the question is at the heart of organizational authority. If workers believe that their actions are being monitored and that they are being rewarded on the basis of that information, they will conform to authority, to the extent that they feel the rewards are worthwhile. If the information compiled by management is incongruent with actual performance, workers may develop an attitude of "What's the use?" when given a formal command. The resultant instability will undermine the effectiveness of the organization.[14]

These problems have existed since the dawn of history, and certainly before the invention of computers and the other hardware of command and control systems. Problems of control, past and present, have always come back to a basic question: How does the manager know what the troops are up to? It is perhaps a minor question in an organization of two people, as long as the boss can keep an eye on the worker; but it takes on a very significant dimension when the organization is large and dispersed. Few managers at any time in history have been able to rely upon the methods of a Haroum al-Rashid by skulking around the bazaar or to place too much faith in the reliability of spies and informers.

Premodern societies developed some ingenious answers to the problem. Wittfogel describes the control devices of Oriental bureaucracies as the creation of, in his rather unfortunate phrase, "a rootless element" within the organization—administrators who are outsiders and therefore dependent upon the prince. Eunuchs were not likely to start their own dynasties by murdering the rulers. The Mamelukes of the Ottoman Empire—kidnapped Christian children—also provided control through personal loyalty.[15] In modern times, there are political systems where the elite relies on ascribed characteristics such as tribalism, nepotism, and cronyism as a way of getting information about internal operations.[16] Since civil service reforms, however, Americans regard as unthinkable the distribution of fellow members of the same party throughout the hierarchy as a way of political control.

Such devices tend to be irregular and unpredictable, and the bureaucratic preference is to regularize things. As the control instrument becomes routinized, there is a danger, first, that the element of surprise so useful in catching people in the act of being themselves may be lost and, second, that the methods will be too unidimensional to do justice to the complexity of the organization. The latter danger is the greater one, especially when we reflect on the organizational dilemma: The subordinates are thinking too. Primarily they are thinking about how to get ahead in the world on their own terms. By telling them that a particular thing will be measured and that success will be based on that measure, one will divert the attention of workers in a certain direction. But unless the measure reflects exactly the goal of the organization, critically important behavior may be discouraged.

Herbert Kaufman says "administrative feedback is a vital element in organizations because subordinate compliance does not automatically follow upon the issuance of orders and instructions by leaders." In his analysis of nine federal agencies, he found an abundance of data supplied to decision makers through five sources: reports, inspections, personal contacts, investigations, and centralized administrative procedures.[17] The first three are the most important, but reports and inspections tend to be subject to regularization while personal contacts remain irregular. As the organization expands, the paradox noted by Ouchi and Maguire emerges: The more regular devices, particularly the objective measures of the reporting system, assume importance in the areas where they are least appropriate—"in the face of complexity, interdependence and lack of expertise."[18]

The report is the most critical measurement device since it is supposed to give a common indication of the accomplishments of the several individuals or units. Efficiency indices, performance ratings, quality measures, and other instruments are concerned with reducing organizational complexity to numbers and with permitting the leaders to operate on the basis of these numbers as the only reality. In government, little thought has been given to the development of the measures. The numbers may provide comfort while yielding little valid information about tangible accomplishments. Among the traditional measures are:

1 *Actual product.* Miles of street paved, criminals apprehended, welfare checks issued, etc., are included here. Whether the products are related to program effectiveness is another matter. Paving, apprehending, and issuing may not really solve the problems of transportation, crime, or welfare. An emphasis on numbers may give the illusion that progress is being made, even though they are the product of a clerical exercise.

2 *Workload measures.* Here one quantifies the input in a variety of fanciful ways. So many worker-hours expended on a certain program are taken as significant. An act of faith is still required if one is to assume that the programs are actually effective.

3 *Standards of service.* In the more professionalized areas, rather arbitrary standards have been set up, and progress is measured by the attainment of the standards. A good library contains so many books and so many librarians; the performance of the library is measured by the acquisition of inputs. This is the way in which universities are evaluated: accreditation agencies count the number of books and Ph.D.'s on the staff.

The intrinsic emptiness of the numbers is not the major danger. Rather, as Ridgway noted, "the motivational and behavioral consequences of performance measurement are inadequately understood."[19] He was dealing with business where one might suppose that output in dollar units is fairly measurable. How much greater the peril of unintended behavior in organizations such as government where there is less agreement about proper performance. Many public products are incalculable in an unambiguous way, and that which is measured, especially if connected to the reward system, may assume a disproportionate part of the total effort.

There is a "Gresham's law" at work in which the measurable factors drive out the immeasurable. In academe, the "publish or perish" syndrome has its roots in the belief that the only measurable facet of teaching is publication productivity. On many campuses, the professors who never have time to see students because they are working on the next book are considered the best teachers, while the instructors who give their all to the mobs are doomed. One university tried to avoid this silly situation by adding other factors such as the number of grants applied for. This led to a wild stampede on the part of professors to apply for grants and awards they knew they had no chance of winning—NSF Fellowships, the Academy Award, the Nobel Peace Prize—just so they could put another item on their evaluation forms.

It might be argued that professors have only a tenuous connection to reality under the best of circumstances, but more sensible workers have also been lured away from actual goals by measurement standards. Peter Blau's famous study of an employment agency whose goal was the matching of the best worker with the best job showed that goals were undermined by an evaluation system which stressed the number of interviews conducted. Naturally, the interviewers followed mass-production techniques by whipping through as many interviews as possible.[20] The same thing can be duplicated in other agencies. What makes a good police officer? Although it is always vehemently denied by the cops, there is reason to believe that most departments have a quota system for arrests, tickets, and so forth. One could argue, however, that the best police officers are ones with a reputation so fearsome that criminals go out of the way not to commit any offense in their precinct. Such people would have a very low productivity record.

In the Soviet Union, with its rather rigorous sanctions for managers who fail to meet their share of the total plan, there are all sorts of horror stories about the distortions caused by quotas. Perhaps there is no truth to the tales of the shoe factory which met its quota for 5,000 shoes by producing them all for the left foot, or of the railroad manager who shuffled empty boxcars back and forth simply because he had to show so much movement. There is at least a mad logic involved. And there are reliable accounts of "storming," in which managers and workers work feverishly at the end of the reporting period to meet the quota, even if it wastes the physical plant and throws other schedules out of joint. Barry Richman found an endless game in Soviet industry as "each enterprise success indicator precipitates its own distortions and unintended effects."[21]

Richman also found the universal bureaucratic response to the realization that standards are being subverted; namely, introduce more reports which eventually overwhelm both superior and subordinates. And with the proliferation of paperwork, people tend to take it all less seriously. Moreover, the wise employee knows that reports are designed to inform superiors of the good news, not the bad. This feature of reporting may account for our killing of 220 percent of the North Vietnamese Army; one probable kill reported by a private may have been inflated severalfold by the time it reached its final destination. It makes sense, however, if the paper report is the reality upon which executives make their decisions, to embroider the figures in such a way to make the most favorable impression. Purists may call that cheating; I call it realism.

I conclude, therefore, that one should be confident of reports only to the extent that one is confident about what is being measured. In government it is not always easy to find a manageable measure for the total operation, no matter how one tortures the indices. In the uncertain situation, which is the essence of administration, one must rely upon the immeasurable response. If it is made known to employees that the most productive act will not be rewarded, then it is almost assured that the act will not be performed. In spite of these defects, it is unlikely that many managers will be able to forgo the unreliable information of their reporting system. The trust that implies is not prevalent in most organizations.

MANAGEMENT BY OBJECTIVES

The frustration over traditional measures of performance for purposes of control has led to the development of more realistic systems. One such system which has received considerable publicity is management by objectives (MBO). It is particularly significant because of the commitment to MBO made by the Office of Management and Budget (OMB). Since 1973, federal administrators have been encouraged to put into effect MBO within their agencies. It is hoped that by this method the optimal mixture of organizational factors can be achieved: "Maintenance of a reasonable balance between requirements for unity and central direction and for situational differentiation and flexibility."[22]

In theory, MBO is very simple. It requires that all members of the organization do some serious thinking about the basic functions they are supposed to perform. The first step is for an agency to state its goal(s); e.g., the purpose of a Division of Traffic Safety is to reduce the number of deaths on the highway. Objectives are then determined to help the agency meet this goal. An objective for traffic safety might be "the training of 2,000 high school students in defensive driving courses." That objective can then be made the responsibility of an individual or a unit. At the end of a certain period, performance can be reviewed in terms of accomplishment of the predetermined objective. The main point of MBO is that organizations will no longer be able to use such wishy-washy statements as "Our objective is to do nice things."

In essence, MBO is designed to get all the participants in the organization to deliberate together about their reason for being there. It seems to have been favorably received by the bureaucrats, or at least it has not caused the same dissent as PPB. That may be the result of the far mellower mood of its sponsors in OMB. Instead of proclaiming that everyone will be doing MBO by such a date (and like it), OMB has stressed flexibility. It has taken care not to pressure participants into coming up with fantastic results, nor by its very nature does MBO have the same frightening implications of the more rigorous PPB. The crucial question is whether this era of good feeling foretells a real change in bureaucratic behavior.

It is doubtful that MBO is the instrument by which to effect a revolution in government administration. After all, it still requires officials to make explicit their objectives which, in the political context, may be impossible. There is no reason to believe that the practitioners of MBO will have more success in establishing output measures.

More damaging to the future of MBO is the way in which it has been burdened with excess baggage; authors tend to get ecstatic about its implications for "participation," "administrative decentralization," "devolution of authority," and all sorts of good things.[23] It is almost as if they cannot see that the key word is "management," with all its implications for control. Frank Sherwood hit the mark when he wrote: "Though proclaimed a participative process, governmentwide MBO should be more properly identified as a strategy for hierarchical control."[24] That seems clear enough; I doubt whether MBO will survive too long if large numbers of workers decide that their objectives are "more pay for less work," something that strikes me as a most reasonable alternative. I agree with Harry Levinson, in his discussion of "management by whose objectives," that "as currently practiced, it is really just industrial engineering with a new name, applied to higher managerial levels, and with the same resistances."[25] The resistance will be the same behavioral patterns which have thwarted management-control devices from the speedup of the assembly line to PPB. I would not be surprised if MBO were to move toward a more structured version of managerial control. By making a few adjustments in MBO and by jettisoning the talk about participation one can change it into something so strenuous as the program evaluation and review technique (PERT).

PERT

The program evaluation and review technique has made a great impact on management thinking since it was introduced in the 1950s during the development of the Polaris submarine. Although not applicable to all spheres of public management, it can be viewed as the most ambitious attempt to date to lock the employees into a control system in which rigorous quantification is the prime requisite. It is a method in which the manager—not the real manager who may have a hard time figuring out what day it is—can assume the role of the rational godhead from whom all decisions emanate and whose will must be translated into an unambiguous act. What is so impressive—or oppressive—about PERT is its massive rationality, which appears to give life to all the banalities of the textbooks. The old principles of organization and management are made flesh.

PERT promises to improve the critical managerial functions of planning, controlling, and scheduling. But before we look at how it is supposed to work, we should note that it is not applicable to all administrative situations. The cases in which it can best be used have three characteristics:

1 They are sequential. That is, they have a beginning, an end, and a number of steps in between. It would be wasteful to devise a way to PERT (let us pretend there is such a verb) the issuing of dog licenses or the typing of letters.

2 They are uncertain. If one knows beforehand how a sequence of events is going to unfold, there is no point in spending the time and effort to prepare a PERT chart. PERT was specifically designed to handle those uncertainties which are the bane of the rational manager.

3 They are complex. A favorite example of a PERT job is changing a tire. For most of us, however, that process is simple enough to figure out in our heads, so we do not have to diagram whether we should jack up the car before removing the tire.

From what I have said so far, it may be obvious that PERT requires a sophisticated system of information handling, including computers. But it is not simply technique, not simply for a virtuoso computer jockey. It is a style of thinking which in one form or another could be adapted to any organization. Or as one advocate enthused, the PERT style is something we unconsciously display in our everyday lives; he gave the example of a couple planning to marry who "will inevitably PERT their task" so that all the distinct acts between the decision to wed and the big day are completed in the proper sequence.[26] Perhaps so, but my personal advice is that anyone who is about to marry a person who can think in such terms should make some excuse about stepping out for a pack of cigarettes—and never come back.

In any event, PERT helps the model managers with their most basic chore in the establishment of objectives. Managers must consider carefully what the overall output is to be and how that can be broken down into manageable units, each one of which has a measurable indicator of completion. Once the so-called work packages are identified, the pieces can be put back together in the form of a plan, a complex document which shows the necessary steps together with their interrelationships. The PERT network is a logic diagram or a flowchart indicating the interfaces, relationships, and constraints in the program; e.g., the roof cannot go on until the walls are up. Through a number of complicated formulas, the manager will be able to measure the movement of the program along the chart and to shift resources around in order to keep the whole thing on schedule.

In the operational stage of program evaluation, the manager can keep constant check on the activity of subordinates and correct improper action. This requires precise information, and so the ideal form of PERT has a constant flow of data to the manager, usually through machine-readable languages. One can envision the manager hunkered over the computer console which provides instantaneous information about the behavior of each subordinate.

PERT is the ultimate managerial tool. No more reliance upon the willy-nilly cooperation of subordinates, no more putting up with the shucking and jiving through bogus figures. PERT demands compliance; you cannot pretend the walls are up when the roof people move in. As the United States government put the first advantage of PERT, "it imposes a more rigid discipline for considering the various elements of efforts required to achieve the desired objectives and the interrelationships among the elements."[27] A local manager also noted that the benefits of PERT "are related to something which . . . may often be what is most needed in any organization: *discipline*."[28] Ah, there is nothing like discipline. The individual is locked into a solid matrix where he or she cannot jump around without upsetting the entire operation. The deviant stands naked before the world—or at least before the manager.

PERT could be a rather heavy set of shackles for the individual and may seem terribly grim for anyone devoted to the old-fashioned virtues of goofing off. It is described here because I do not believe it is too far removed from MBO, with its emphasis on individual participation. I do not feel that too many managers can restrain themselves from moving toward the type of program evaluation represented by PERT with its promise of forcing employees to behave in a more disciplined, i.e., rational, manner. And this theme of discipline, of conformity to the absolute requirements of scientific laws, is important to keep in mind as we turn now to broader versions of program measurement.

PROGRAM EVALUATION

As was indicated, program evaluation seems to be the one component of PPB which has a good chance of making it on its own. PPB emphasized measurement, but its connection with the equally complex problems of planning and budgeting proved to be too much at one time. Program evaluation is more understandable, more common sense, if you will; in fact, it is so basic that one would have assumed that managers have always done it. Undoubtedly some form of evaluation has been done, but nothing like the systematic way demanded by the theorists. It was only in 1971 that an editorial in the major public administration journal could proclaim that "at this time we need explicit recognition of evaluation as an important process of administration."[29]

The rise of evaluation as a self-conscious function of management and indeed as an art practiced by a small but growing hemidemisemi-profession of evaluators is part of the shift from "analysis to evaluation," to use the words of Allen Schick.[30] It is simply more feasible to identify the payoffs in the area of social management after the fact. At the same time, political considerations were at work, and it is no coincidence that evaluation arose after the disillusionment with the wild jumble of War on Poverty programs. A more conservative administration, constrained by a slackening economy, was interested in controlling the impulse to throw money at a wide range of social problems. Evaluation gave the impression of being a noncontroversial way of eliminating obnoxious programs. After all, if the facts proved that they did not work, who could object if they were curtailed?

Program evaluation is best seen as a tool for use at the policy level and not as a method of internal managerial control. The policy makers—whether politicians or technocratic supermanagers—will have reliable information about which programs are working and which are failures. Evaluation promises to deliver the hard facts about the extent to which specific government programs have an impact on the problems they address; are organizations meeting their goals?

One might suppose that such elementary information would be of great interest to the manager, but the truth is that the news that one's organization does no earthly good does not always change managerial behavior. If it does not, it would seem to be the responsibility of the policy maker to take action against the programs which do not meet social needs. Especially in a time of increasing demands upon public funds, it is essential that policy makers have a way of avoiding what Sharkansky calls the "spending-service cliché"—the notion that added expenditures automatically lead to improvements in public services.[31] The cliché may serve to reduce the complexities of the decision-making process, but it is obviously a luxury which few jurisdictions can afford.

Evaluation has its frustrations. The insistence upon the experimental method, of course, is quite necessary if the pitfalls of cruder methods are to be avoided. It is particularly important when an agency is supposed to prevent something from happening; too often evaluation in those areas is about as sophisticated as that of a child who feels that whistling in the dark will keep the man-eating tigers away. For example, a unit charged with keeping drunks off the street may proudly announce its effectiveness when in fact the reduction is due to a grape blight in California which has forced the winos to turn to heroin. Or a highway safety program may appear successful, although accidents have decreased largely because the Arabs raised the price of oil again. The phenomenon can also be noted in more positive programs; are first-graders learning to read because of an expensive new program or because of "Sesame Street"?

The evaluators take their procedures from the classic design of research. First, one must be able to identify the goals of a program in a way which can be translated into a measurable index of goal achievement. Data on the indicators of success are then collected for both those who have been exposed to the program and those who have not. The data for the experimental and control groups are compared to see if the features of the program account for the differences between the two. For example, can the difference in reading ability be explained by the implementation of a new method? If so, then there is support for the extension of the program throughout the entire school system.

Despite all the good things they want to do, evaluators feel they have been abused, primarily by program managers who are not likely to give them a fair shake. Even in the best of situations, the process is so complicated that success in evaluation is hard to achieve. As Carol Weiss describes the several difficulties:[32]

1 Evaluation deals with real people and real programs. As far as the manager is concerned, the program is primary and evaluation is secondary. Evaluators must compromise with reality, which means that the experimental situation cannot be as pure as when one is working in the laboratory with hamsters or college freshmen.

2 As we know, the identification of goals is a tricky matter. Evaluators sometimes suspect that managers are being deliberately deceptive. When told that the program did not help children to spell any better, the teachers can come back to say, "Well, we were really trying to teach them good citizenship anyway." Evaluators keep hoping that Congress will specify desired results in the authorizing legislation.[33] As Congress now operates, however, one should not expect more than statements for number of flags waved, moms kissed, and apple pie eaten.

3 There are problems in finding and maintaining experimental and control groups. The scientific way is to take a large group and divide it up arbitrarily, which brings up the question of who does or does not get the goodies. It raises a number of ethical questions which would be quite evident if we were the ones who had to tell the person in the iron lung that the tests of the Salk vaccine had been a great success. One can certainly understand the anguish of parents who are told that a new government program will pull some children out of poverty while their own children will be condemned to a short and miserable life in the ghetto.

Regrettably, it must also be admitted that scientists can take some grotesque stands on the issue of group purity. That our government is capable of behavior not too dissimilar from the medical experimenters at Buchenwald was demonstrated by the infamous Tuskegee study of venereal disease. In an attempt to determine the effect of syphilis on the human body, 400 blacks with the disease were to be compared with 200 unaffected subjects. Even after penicillin was found to be an effective treatment, the diseased men were left untreated.[34] One can imagine the doctors saying, "Sehr interessant! Charlie's nose just fell off." The experimenters, it is clear, should not be given free rein in their tests on human subjects.

4 The operational program is seldom a pure entity. The personnel vary in style and ability from project to project, and they are often in transit. The program itself may shift emphasis as it copes with the hard realities of the environment. The maintenance of the integrity of the program is a tough job since managers are not above tinkering with things as they proceed. Intuitive fiddling with the program messes up the needs of a purely scientific approach.

5 The final reports have not been notably effective in improving the quality of programs. Managers do resist the findings, but it must be admitted that the fault may also lie with the nature of the conclusions. Evaluation reports seldom result in a black-and-white recommendation. Since they are couched in the bland language of social science, it is possible to read them to mean that there has been little change one way or the other. The manager is not often presented with conclusive evidence of a complete and unqualified failure; and so one can argue that while it did not do any good, the program did not do any harm either. That is usually enough to keep on keeping on.

6 Organizations have been known to ignore evaluations. In May 1976, it was reported that an evaluation showed that the 4.4 billion dollars disbursed by the Law Enforcement Assistance Administration (LEAA) had done little to control crime. The study called for the abolition of LEAA. Immediately the defenders began to rally 'round the sugar teat. No LEAA official was heard to say, "That's a great idea. Let's close it down." I suspect that the report will not kill the program, effective or not.

The basic question is whether managers really want evaluation. Is it all that helpful to know what one is doing? Evaluators assume that there is a huge amount of sheer wrongheadedness among public administrators. After reviewing the "less noble motives" for evaluation, one writer concluded that the selective manipulation of evaluations "are not as rare as one might suppose."[35] I suppose no such thing, and it is surprising to find that the evaluators assumed they would be welcomed with open arms. For managers, evaluators are a big bother. Anyway, the managers are professionals and are probably convinced of the worth of the program; professional theory says it must work, and that is that. If the measures do not indicate success, it is the fault of the evaluators who are a bunch of clods unable to understand the intricacies of the whole program.

Contrary to what the evaluators imply, the issue is not a struggle between the forces of reason and the pigheaded obstructionists. If that were so, the PHO's far outnumber the good guys, and the whole thing is hopeless. The meaningful question is how much measurement is healthy for an organization and how far it helps executives in their job of keeping a coalition together. If the evaluators are seen as knights errant without commitment to the organization or its procedures, Wildavsky's point that evaluation and the organization are contradictory is well taken.[36]

Thus, there are reasons to doubt whether we will ever attain Martin Landau's concept of a "self-correcting organization" which is so devoted to a single standard of rationality that every act is subjected to the most intensive internal scrutiny.[37] If we look at the political issue—whether the public can control those organizations which do no good—the problem would seem to be that we have no regularized way of declaring a program bankrupt. As Alice Rivlin argues, there are "few rewards for those who produce better education or health service, few penalties for those who fail to produce."[38] In a number of new social programs, we can go on spending money forever in hopeless causes, but success means we have worked ourselves out of a job.[39] Ideally, there should be a way by which the public, when made aware of program deficiencies, could tell the bureaucrats, through their politicians, that it would be good to get on the stick.

But before a political philosopher tries to find the missing link between evaluation and the public response, consider that this higher level of organizational measurement is not unlike the situation at the managerial level. If the figures are the political reality, the tendency will be to distort. Supervisors fudging in their reports to their superiors is one thing. It is quite another when high-level executives work on numbers rather than reality. If an organization is told that its survival depends on the number of drunks prowling the streets, it can make good marks by running them out of town, an act far easier than going to the root causes of alcoholism. If schools are told they will be judged on the basis of reading scores, the measures can be hyped by concentrating on reading to the exclusion of everything else. It is not such an obscure point; I assume that every student, when studying for an exam, has had to make a decision whether it is better to stretch one's mind in a painful learning process or simply to cram for the items which are sure to be on the test. Similarly, organizations are likely to be attracted to "making it" rather than "doing it," especially when the standards for making it have been illuminated by evaluators. Evaluation, in short, is not the royal road to adminsitrative responsiveness and accountability.[40]

SOCIAL INDICATORS

The distortive impact of numbers can also be seen in the most ambitious attempt at formulating the political system of the quantitative society. The social-indicators movement may not be as noticeable as it was a few years ago, when scholars, administrators, and legislators were sure it was the only way to fly. Regardless of the passion behind it, it is certain that this is an idea whose time has come. It brings together some of the most powerful concepts about the management of an entire social system. So far, the substantial work has been scanty, with most of the literature in the nature of a call to arms.

The basic model is the Employment Act of 1946, which established the Council of Economic Advisers to monitor the economic indicators such as the gross national product. The Council was to advise the President on the steps necessary to stabilize the economy. The present argument, as put by Bertram Gross, is that reliance upon economic indicators is the "New Philistinism," since the other measures of the quality of life are ignored. Social indicators would complement the picture of society as painted by the economists. According to Mancur Olson's definition:

> A social indicator may be defined to be a statistic of direct normative interest which facilitates concise, comprehensive and balanced judgments about the conditions of major aspects of a society. It is in all cases a direct measure of welfare and is subject to the interpretation that, if it changes in the "right" direction, while other things remain equal, things have gotten better, or people are "better off." Thus statistics on the number of doctors or policemen could not be social indicators, whereas figures on health or crime rates could be.[41]

Our main interest here is with the ideology of social indicators, with a statement of how a political order should operate. Indicators are in the "nature of things" only if one takes a special perspective on human behavior. Michael Springer argues that indicators are essentially apolitical since the basic concepts are derived from "a social science of managerial rationality."[42] In collaboration with Gross, he defines the result as "an emerging politics of relevance" which "entails a political style that eschews rhetoric and traditional ideology"; it is "a politics whose major strengths and most signficant weakness is a general lack of passion."[43] But then what passion can there be when we stare at the thermostat on the wall? When policy making is nothing more than the interpretation of social science data, it loses some excitement. The resulting image of the policy-making process is not that of a committed people having it out in a public forum; rather it is that of sober scientists, dressed in their white laboratory smocks, poring over computer printouts.

When society is viewed as a cybernetic or feedback system, it is wise to allow the people with the proper expertise to make the necessary measurements. But how will those experts know that their interpretations are for the benefit of everyone? It is simply because there is assumed to be a rational consensus about societal goals; the experts' answer is similar to that of B. F. Skinner when he is asked, "Who elected you God?" Rational people will surely conclude that good health is better than disease, work is better than idleness, eating is better than starving, education is better than ignorance. One can measure movement toward the "good" side in these and other areas and suggest scientifically valid ways of improvement if movement is not rapid enough.

Popper identifies three components of the social-indicator ideology. First, it is elitist. It is assumed that scientific measures can be taken of social movement. The rest of us should be in awe of the statistical prowess of the experts. It is pragmatic; the important thing is to get the numbers where they belong, a style of thinking familiar to those who argue that, after all, Hitler did solve the unemployment problem. Finally, it is melioristic. That is, the assumption is that society is in fundamentally good shape, and therefore one need only take remedial moves rather than restructure the whole system. In all of this, the citizen will participate as an item of administration and not as a factor in policy making.[44]

One can hope that the movement will collapse of its own weight. It is clear now that other social scientists are aping only the form and not the substance of the economists. Economic indicators are based on a fairly coherent body of theory which provides clues for corrective action. Although it is obvious that the GNP is not so unambiguous a statement and that the economists are not the masterful pilots they once claimed to be, the original idea assumed that it was possible to know how the economic world functions. Critics of social indicators state, "It is even difficult to locate partial theories or so-called middle-range ones covering any single aspect of society which have convincing explanatory potential."[45] In other words, we are not half as clever as we would like to think.

CONCLUSION

I hope I have made some sense out of a bewildering array of methods, past and future, for measuring government activity. This review has not even touched on such related areas as "futurology" and "technology assessment," but it should still be evident that something is stirring here. The move is on toward the ultimate ideal of public administration (if "public" is the right word since the division between public and private will soon be meaningless). As the standard knowledge drives out other claimants, the contest between truth and error will be confined to the reeducation of the heretics. Everyone else will be tuned into the orthodox knowledge, and therefore the administrative structure, as a control device, will be unnecessary. The same is true of the political overhead. Every person his own organization! Every person his own government!

Try this sci-fi scenario: In the year 2525, the red light on the computer flashes. There is trouble in River City! An alarming number of children have been born out of wedlock in the past year, a sign of deviance which is interpreted as having severe ramifications for the family structure and secondary effects on all social and economic institutions. It is time for what is already called "an intervention." A team of professionals—psychologists, sociologists, recreation administrators, marriage counselors—will descend on the community and, without central direction, proceed to do their respective numbers to bring the negative factors back in line. When the indicators report a more favorable trend, they will saddle up and, with a hearty hi-ho Silver, ride off to meet the next challenge to the good life. No fuss, no muss, because all right-thinking people agree that the facts are indeed facts.

For those philosophers who view modern rationality as a state of mind incapable of reflecting upon its own value premises, the danger is clear. Knowledge has been debased as a methodology of sociotechnical control; it is no longer a source of enlightenment for the individual.[46] The chance for meaningful change will be gone forever when the nation-state is transformed into a superorganization in which citizens are not expected to interfere in the attainment of utopia. We may be a long way from such a possibility, but at least one national commission has suggested that "improvement in our decision-making apparatus might be achieved by the encouragement of an appropriate body of high prestige and distinction which would engage in the study of national goals and the evaluation of our national performance in relation to such goals."[47] Such a thing, if implemented, would make the world safe for technocrats.

The French, apparently, are more comfortable in discussing the full implications of the rational scientific mode of thought, and it is therefore with profit that we turn to a brief summary of these trends by Michel Crozier, a leading French sociologist. The public organization, he wrote, has resisted rational control because of an irrationality protected by the incalculability of performance. The art of public management has been a political process, in the sense that neither the public nor the employees are completely predictable. Thus, "public administrations remain prisoners of their environment and administrative decisions remain political decisions, that is to say decisions based essentially on power relationships." With a more comprehensive information system, the inadequacies of the old hierarchical arrangements will become evident. Freed from the false constraints of irrationality, the public can pursue pure good as a rational information system indicates is the one best way. Crozier finds this a positive development.[48] I am not so sanguine about the definition of rationality which is implicit in the system.

REFERENCES

1 Amitai Etzioni, *The Active Society* (New York: Free Press, 1968), p. 148.

2 Alvin Toffler, *Future Shock* (New York: Random House, 1970), chap. 7.

3 Warren Bennis and Philip Slater, *The Temporary Society* (New York: Harper & Row, 1968).

4 Robert Miewald, "The Greatly Exaggerated Death of Bureaucracy," *California Management Review*, 13 (1970), pp. 129–133.

5 Allen Schick, "Toward the Cybernetic State," in Dwight Waldo (ed.), *Public Administration in a Time of Turbulence* (Scranton, Pa.: Chandler, 1971).

6 George Goerl, "Cybernetics, Professionalization, and Knowledge Management: An Exercise in Assumptive Theory," *Public Administration Review*, 35 (1975), p. 584.

7 Amitai Etzioni, "Two Approaches to Organizational Analysis: A Critique and a Suggestion," *Administrative Science Quarterly*, 5 (1960), p. 260.

8 Ephraim Yuchtman and Stanley Seashore, "A System Resource Approach to Organizational Effectiveness," *American Sociological Review*, 32 (1967), p. 892.

9 Paul White, "Resources as Determinants of Organizational Behavior," *Administrative Science Quarterly*, 19 (1974), p. 375.

10 Richard Steers, "Problems in the Measurement of Organizational Effectiveness," *Administrative Science Quarterly*, 20 (1975), pp. 546–558.

11 Victor Thompson, "The Development of Modern Bureaucracy: Tools out of People," *University Programs Modular Studies* (Morristown, N.J.: General Learning Press, 1974), p. 5.

12 Kurt Tucholsky, *Gesammete Werke* (Hamburg: Rowohlt, 1961), p. 993.

13 Douglas Sherwin, "The Meaning of Control," *Dun's Review and Modern Industry*, 67 (Jan. 1956), p. 46.

14 Richard Scott, S. M. Dornbusch, B. C. Busching, and James Laing, "Organizational Evaluation and Authority," *Administrative Science Quarterly*, 12 (1967), pp. 93–117.

15 Karl Wittfogel, *Oriental Despotism* (New Haven, Conn.: Yale University Press, 1957), pp. 354–363. See also Lewis Coser, *Greedy Institutions* (New York: Free Press, 1974), chap. 2.

16 Anthony Downs, *Inside Bureaucracy* (Boston: Little, Brown, 1967), pp. 156–157.

17 Herbert Kaufman, *Administrative Feedback* (Washington: Brookings, 1973).

18 William Ouchi and Mary Ann Maguire, "Organizational Control: Two Functions," *Administrative Science Quarterly*, 20 (1975), p. 568.

19 V. F. Ridgway, "Dysfunctional Consequences of Performance Measurements," *Administrative Science Quarterly*, 1 (1956), p. 247.

20 Peter Blau, *The Dynamics of Bureaucracy* (Chicago: University of Chicago Press, 1955).

21 Barry Richman, *Soviet Management* (Englewood Cliffs, N.J.: Prentice-Hall, 1965), p. 164.

22 Chester Newland, "MBO Concepts in the Federal Government," *The Bureaucrat*, 2 (1974), p. 361.

23 Jong Jun, "Introduction: Management by Objectives in the Public Sector," *Public Administration Review*, 36 (1976), pp. 1–5.

24 Frank Sherwood and William Page, "MBO and Public Management," *Public Administration Review*, 36 (1976), p. 7.

25 Harry Levinson, "Management by Whose Objectives?" *Harvard Business Review*, 48 (1970), p. 125.

26 Lawrence Steinmetz, "PERT Personnel Practices," *Personnel Journal*, 44 (1965), p. 422.

27 PERT Coordinating Group, *PERT Guide* (Washington: GPO, 1963), p. 9.

28 Richard Wahl, "PERT Controls Budget Preparation," *Public Management*, 46 (1964), p. 33.

29 Orville Pound, "Why Does Public Administration Ignore Evaluation?" *Public Administration Review*, 31 (1971), pp. 201–202.

30 Allen Schick, "From Analysis to Evaluation," *Annals of the American Academy of Political and Social Science*, 394 (1971), pp. 57–71.

31 Ira Sharkansky, *The Routines of Politics* (New York: Van Nostrand, 1970), chap. 7.

32 Carol Weiss, "Evaluating Educational and Social Action Programs: A 'Treefull of Owls,'" in Weiss (ed.), *Evaluating Action Programs* (Boston: Allyn and Bacon, 1972).

33 Herbert Roback, "Program Evaluation by and for the Congress," *The Bureaucrat*, 5 (1976), pp. 11–36.

34 Walter Broadnax, "The Tuskegee Health Experiment: A Question of Bureaucratic Morality?" *The Bureaucrat*, 4 (1975), pp. 45–55.

35 Weiss, op. cit., p. 14.

36 Aaron Wildavsky, "The Self-evaluating Organization," *Public Administration Review*, 32 (1972), pp. 509–520.

37 Martin Landau, "On the Concept of a Self-correcting Organization," *Public Administration Review*, 33 (1973), pp. 533–542.

38 Alice Rivlin, *Systematic Thinking for Social Action* (Washington: Brookings, 1971), p. 121.

39 Eric Lax, "Nothing Fails like Success," *Washington Monthly*, 3 (1972), pp. 31–35.

40 Bruce Rocheleau, "Evaluation, Accountability, and Responsiveness in Administration," *Midwest Review of Public Administration*, 9 (1975), pp. 163–172.

41 HEW, *Toward a Social Report* (Washington: GPO, 1969), p. 97.

42 Michael Springer, "Social Indicators, Reports, and Accounts: Toward the Management of Society," *Annals of the American Academy of Political and Social Science*, 388 (1970), p. 4.

43 Bertram Gross and Michael Springer, "Who Knows Where We're Going?" in Gross and Springer (eds.), *Social Intelligence for America's Future* (Boston: Allyn and Bacon, 1969), p. vii.

44 Frank Popper, "The Social Meaning of Social Accounting," *Polity*, 4 (1971), pp. 77–90.

45 Eleanor Sheldon and Howard Freeman, "Notes on Social Indicators: Promises and Potential," *Policy Sciences*, 1 (1970), p. 103.

46 Jürgen Habermas, *Theory and Practice* (Boston: Beacon Press, 1973), chap. 7.

47 National Commission on Technology, Automation, and Economic Progress, *Technology and the American Economy* (Washington: GPO, 1966), p. 77.

48 Michel Crozier, "The Present Convergence of Public Administration and Large Private Enterprises, and Its Consequences," *International Social Science Journal*, 20 (1968), pp. 7–16.

Chapter 8

Knowledge and Decisions

Yeah. But it's, but for this country and what it is, it's, uh, almost a death wish, isn't it? It's a death wish. They, uh, we, uh, we're afraid to do this or that because of, uh—Well, it's a—as the country gets more and more intelligent, they get, uh, more and more fearful; and that's, and that's what happened to the Greeks, and what happened to the Romans, it's what happened to the British, it's what happened, you know—That's what happened.

Richard M. Nixon
Decision maker

The specific topics of this chapter are not easily separated from those of Chapters 6 and 7; budgets and measurements are decision-making tools. I am also reluctant to call this chapter by its now common title of "decision making." That title connotes a body of "how-to-do-it" knowledge. I assume that anyone whose brain is more or less under control knows how to make a decision, including the one about whether it is worthwhile reading the rest of this chapter. The question raised by administrative science is the degree to which the decisions in and about organizations are rational ones.

The emergence of things such as "decision-making theory" and academic departments of "decision sciences," plus the counterattacks by critics of the ideology of "decisionism," indicate that there is something more involved here than the process we go through deciding whether to hold the pickle, hold the lettuce on our burger orders. Decision theorists do not often work into their models the *I Ching*, tarot cards, or meditation on the belly button. In fact, those and other signs of irrationality are to be purged from the decision-making process. The driving idea is to get the impurities out of the way in which society makes decisions through the establishment of an unambiguous standard of dialogue among all participants. Our major concern here will be to assess the impact of various tools on the political process.

Herbert Simon is largely responsible for the concentration on decision theory. In retrospect, the revolution he wrought does not seem such a big deal since decision making is, as indicated, a human function almost as natural as breathing. If human behavior is not an involuntary spasm, then one has decided to act, and that decision is based upon some view of the environment. Thus, if we study the decision process carefully, we can discover why one does or does not act and ultimately direct decisions in the proper way. In a sense, Simon was only updating Weber's bureaucratic model as a structure for denying the irrationality of life. As I view it, decision theory is the heir to all the traditions of rationalistic approaches to administration. Taylor's scientific management has become management science, but the longing for the reduction of reality to manageable form is just as strong. As Gore and Silander said of the decision theorists, "one has the impression that there are those who look forward to the time when numerical values, representing estimated outcomes, may be substituted for verbal symbols in a formula representing organizational goals, which would then be solved for a decision."[1] As I have stressed, organizations, and least of all public ones, cannot be regarded as mathematical equations just waiting to be solved.

We have arrived, however, at the essence of the quantitative society, where answers spring from the facts. Accumulate a big pile of facts, study them hard enough, and the truth will materialize. A new horde of value-free barbarians from economics, psychology, mathematics, engineering, and business administration have determined that government needs shaping up; the life force of politics, which makes it possible to continue our debate about values, is seen as inefficient. Decision-making tools will squeeze the irrational juices out of government so that the facts can be given their only reasonable interpretation. Decision theory is committed to the discovery of the right way, and it is not hospitable for those who want to encourage the consideration of a plurality of equally valid right ways.

Put another way, Simon and his several collaborators are saying that we need no longer rely so heavily upon the bounded rationality with all its obvious deficiencies. As we have seen, managers depend upon the bounded rationality to give them some security in a world too complex for absolute rationality. But modern methods of handling data plus the techniques for using them in decision making enable managers to push back the frontiers of rationality; we can expand the boundaries of each manager's universe. We no longer have to depend upon the traditional tools of the decision maker—habit, the standard operating procedures, organization structure, judgment, intuition, and other vague "executive skills." Now there is available a methodology for coping with the "dynamic behavior of complex systems" which makes possible the extension of the known world of any organization. Absolute rationality is no longer such a farfetched idea.[2]

I want to discuss a few of the techniques which, we are told, have effected a revolution in private organizations and are now moving into the public sphere. As characterized by the International City Management Association, "the techniques involved all employ rigorous logic, mathematical and statistical approaches, precise definition of objectives and variables in quantified terms, and the calculation of results in measurable and comparable terms."[3] Distinguishing among the types is not easy work because, frankly, I am not sure I understand all the mysteries of matrix algebra, Monte Carlo, black-box analysis, linear programming, dynamic programming, econometrics, game theory, stochastic modeling, or any of the other glittering gizmos. I am not too ashamed of my ignorance because it is seldom completely clear that the advocates of this or that technique really know what they are talking about or at least that they are so sure of their technique that they can distinguish it from the others. Particularly in practice, it seems to be one big lump of applied rationality. Operations researchers, for example, tend to see the other techniques as part of their tool chest. We will look only at two general approaches which have had the greatest impact so far in public administration.

OPERATIONS RESEARCH

Explaining operations research (OR) is a little like describing American religion to a foreigner. Both have all sorts of denominations, with sects of varying militancy, and a number of dogmatic proclaimers of the One True Faith. Members range from the orthodox in the Operations Research Society of America to the people who claim to be in OR because that is what their boss told them to do. The one common element is the commitment to the introduction of science into management decision making: "Application of the scientific attitude and the associated techniques to the study of operations, whether business, government, or military, is what is meant by operations research."[4] This is hard-core science—quantifiable facts—and OR people get nervous if they stray too far from the measurable.

Operations research was born as one of the martial arts during World

War II. A notable example involved submarine warfare. Should subs surface to use their radar and thus increase their sinkings, even though they themselves become easier targets for enemy aircraft? OR indicated that in the long run, it was more effective for the subs to surface, although we do not know if the submarine crews were polled about their preferences in the matter. From such triumphs, OR moved into industry and is now returning to government applications. Among the areas where OR has been successfully applied are transportation systems, health delivery systems, and police work.[5]

Is this new wave in government a good or a bad thing? Of course, OR is not good or bad in itself, but its worth depends upon the ways in which it is used. We have probably all come across examples of government inefficiency which might be remedied by a little scientific thought. Would it not be possible, for example, for OR to devise a way whereby one city crew would not start digging up a street just as soon as it has been covered by another crew? Universities could well use the queuing techniques of OR to prevent students from getting royally queued during registration.

The problem is the recognition of the very definite limits of OR. The OR person will sometimes remove from a case all the immeasurable factors and solve a simplified equation; then there is the temptation to believe that the limited problem is what we were interested in all along. In the trade, this is "suboptimization," which means, simply, solving the hell out of a minor and probably irrelevant part of the overall problem. OR may come up with a very sophisticated schedule for the distribution of police patrol cars, but the implementation of the plan may have serious consequences for the morale of the police or the attitude of the community. Suboptimization is a major administrative evil since it strengthens functional rationality instead of broadening the perspective of the public officials.

In order to see the biases of OR, we must look at the procedures it follows. It generally involves four basic steps. First, a problem is presented for solution. Let us say a city wishes to use its car pool in the most efficient manner. The second step is the construction of a model; usually this is a mathematical model which accounts for all the quantifiable aspects. Thirdly, a measure of effectiveness is identified; e.g., how many miles should a city car be driven before trade-in to keep pool costs at a minimum? Fourth, experimentation with the model is conducted to find the effectiveness of various inputs. The response to the decision maker will probably be in terms of a ratio of costs and outputs. Through this all, OR is terribly scientific. In fact, the example given might be rejected because of such unknown factors as prestige and public opinion. For example, could a powerful department head be assigned a secondhand Toyota or would the public resent seeing the mayor tool around in a Mercedes even if analysis proved that it was cheaper?

In short, OR requires that all nonquantifiable elements be eliminated from consideration. If you cannot measure it, forget it. Obviously, that means that the burning issues will not be subject to OR. Or does it? What about those burning issues which are perceived as phenomena whose causes can be analyzed through scientific means? What happens to the political process when OR moves from the purely technical questions to more imprecise areas such as the major domestic policy areas of an advanced society? We can see the implications more clearly if we move on to the thing called "systems analysis."

SYSTEMS ANALYSIS

In the voluminous literature which has been produced in the past decade, it is often hard to distinguish systems analysis from operations research or, for that matter, anything else. In fact, it is rather difficult to define exactly what it is and how one does it. The irony was noted by Ida Hoos when she wrote that "for a notion to have become the symbol of the 'rational' and the 'scientific' in management circles in business and government and yet be so deficient as to clarity of meaning is truly anomalous."[6] "Systems thinking" has become so popular a concept in our society that almost anyone can and will claim to be doing it. I wager that if the American Society of Phonies were to hold a national convention, nine out of ten of the bright young things would say, "Hi guy! I'm into systems," or "I'm Bruce. I'm an analyst." The basic buzz words—parameter, interface, module, configuration—have become so much a part of everyday usage that their meaning is debased.

One cannot look to the card-carrying analysts for much more clarity. Among Rand analysts, who have as much right as any group to be called the founding fathers, clichés abound. One finds again and again, for example, the banality that systems analysis only "sharpens intuition." What a sloppy concept to use in justifying an awesomely rigorous approach to decision making! What is intuition in the first place and what does it look like after you have whittled a point on it? Another homely phrase used by Rand types says that systems analysis is only "quantified common sense." Again, reasonable people might argue that is a contradiction in terms.

The most ardent supporters do not help much in our understanding of systems analysis. Simon Ramo, pointing to our desire for solutions to complex problems such as urbanization, transportation, air pollution, medical care, and education, argues that we must reject our old "emotional, crisis, chaotic, piecemeal" methods of dealing with them. The answers, in his view, will come only after analysis which is "no more than just doing things right as against wrong, being intelligent rather than stupid, being objective rather than irrational in approaching problems."[7] Systems analysts are the professionals at being right, intelligent, and objective.

Systems analysis is also an ideology which aims at depriving a large number of political participants of their access to government. While still innocent of the political hardball in Washington, former Defense Secretary James Schlesinger claimed that analysts are moving political arguments from the level of ideology to the level of quantitative calculation.[8] Another pair insisted that, "at a minimum," their method "could impose orderly reasoned processes upon previously unstructured problems."[9] The new dialogue, however, would use only the vocabulary of science. To maintain that one could change the ground rules of politics so drastically and still be a neutral instrument is unreal.

In the most comprehensive sense, the strength of systems analysis lies in the establishment of a "mood" to be used in the consideration of public policy. As described by Alain Enthoven, this mood is based on the scientific method. It has four characteristics:[10]

1 *Reliance upon "an open, explicit, verifiable, self-correcting system."* It is important that analysis be replicable by other analysts.

2 *Objectivity.* Personality and other irrationalities have no room in analysis. "The truth of a scientific proposition is established by logical and empirical methods common to the profession a whole."

3 *Proper testing of hypotheses.* There is no one method applicable to problems of both the physical and social sciences.

4 *Appropriate use of quantification.* Enthoven was careful to insist that not all problems are amenable to complete quantification. As he testified:

> Systems analysis is not an attempt to measure the unmeasurable. But one of the opportunities that systems analysis offers for creative work is seeking ways of giving valid measurements to things previously thought to be unmeasurable. A good systems analyst does not leave considerations that cannot be quantified out of the analysis. Inevitably such considerations will be left out of the *calculations,* but a good analyst will and does list and describe such factors.

For the decision maker, the product of this mood, Enthoven argued, "is a set of ground rules for constructive debate." The participants in public policy making now understand one another better because they share the same information base. The real issues are identified and isolated. The ambiguous political aspects are presented more clearly.

In actual application, systems analysis does not provide as handy a kit of analytical tools as operations research. Specific techniques are determined by the problem under study, and the subjects for analysis are varied. Perhaps the best way to explain the "doing" of analysis is to indicate some of the general guidelines provided by the experts at Rand.[11]

1 The goal is the systematic comparison of alternatives. Analysis is used only when choices are to be made. If no alternatives exist, the analyst is responsible for developing some. The decision maker is poorly served if presented only with a blunt statement of what must be done.

2 In the assessment of alternatives, the cost in relation to the benefit, utility, or effectiveness of the alternatives is most important. Therefore, it is critical that the analyst establish at the onset the conceptual framework, which can be either the "fixed utility approach"—a given goal is to be achieved most economically—or the "fixed resources approach"—a given amount of money is to produce as much as possible.

3 The broad context of the environment, both now and in the future, must be taken into account. Therefore, great care must be taken in the design of the system. The analyst must factor out of the total complexity a "construct system," an artificial design, that will permit treatment of the most important variables. The demands upon the analyst are much greater than in OR. For example, if called upon to plan a dam, OR people would suboptimize by designing a structure to retain so much water. The systems analyst would try to relate the dam to its larger environment. What will it do to to the ecology, how will it affect the local economy, and so forth? Perhaps the dam will flood the old swimming hole so that the kids of River City start hanging around the pool hall, thereby picking up vile habits which will in turn cause expensive problems for the police. Analysts seldom attach numbers to these secondary and tertiary effects, preferring to point out a vague entity called "spillover," but even that may permit the decision makers to grasp the broader ramifications of a decision.

4 Uncertainty must be dealt with. Analysts must face the fact that any complex problem will have its uncertainties, but these uncertainties must somehow be included in the final product. Statistical uncertainty can be treated statistically; e.g., what will be the demographic features of the city in fifty years? Other types of uncertainty, resulting from life's irregularities, are not handled so easily. For example, how do we develop a fail-safe system so that no individual can start a nuclear war? It is a question for which our experience is a poor guide, but it is so important that it cannot be ignored. The analyst will ensure that such uncertainty is taken into account.[12]

5 Qualitative supplementation is essential. After the numbers have been massaged, it is still necessary for qualitative dimensions to be discussed in some form of narrative. The analyst does not present just a computer printout. Moreover, recommendations are not stated in the form of one alternative being an itty-bitty bit better than another. Some analysts suggest that reliable recommendations can be made only when one solution is unquestionably better.

The concrete accomplishments of the analysts are hard to identify. The major applications in the Defense Department are no longer revered as they were in the early 1960s, although it is not clear that the analysts were totally responsible for some of the blunders of that era.[13] The analysts probably had their greatest triumphs in the hardware aspects of the space program. Politicians and laypersons for a while were so enthralled by that great achievement that the common cry was, "If we can send a man to the moon, why can't we . . ." with the sentence concluded by the latest thing to steam the speaker. The oratory about applying "space-age" techniques to earthbound problems such as education and welfare has died down. The aerospace industry has had little luck in converting to civilian affairs.

In her critique of the contributions of analysis to public policy, Hoos cannot point to many dramatic accomplishments. Her review of the literature "discloses iteration and reiteration of platitudes and promises, but little improvement in either the state of the art of systems analysis or of government."[14] In some ways, "paralysis by analysis" is a sophisticated way of avoiding decisions. One wonders, for example, whether the money spent on studies of mass transit might not have been better spent in buying buses. Many analysts feel that if they put together great heaps of data, they are doing their job, even if they never get down to the basic question of "So what?" Perhaps being an analyst is a more elegant way of saying, "I shuffle papers for a living." At the very worst, one might feel that analysts are engaged in a new type of confidence game, with impressive space-age scams.

POLITICAL IMPLICATIONS OF SYSTEMS ANALYSIS

I am not about to argue that American government needs less intelligence in the study of pressing public problems, nor do I want scientists taken out and shot. And Curly, Moe, and Shemp are not my models for decision makers. I simply do not like the encapsulation offered to us by the friends of analysis. I am not speaking only of the dogmatic nut who exhibits all the hateful arrogance of a self-appointed savior, who insinuates that he will take a few weeks out of his important work in designing space capsules or other gadgets to save the human race from its own stupidity. Nor am I too concerned with the learned dolts who, as one scientist put it, "have more than average difficulty in coping with the irrational and nonrational."[15] Such people probably have their place in the world, and it is up to more broad-minded leaders to make sure they stay in that place.

What I cannot fathom, what I feel is the most insidious danger, is the assurance from otherwise intelligent men and women that they are not in fact impinging upon the political process. If the political theory of the analysts were to be accepted, there would be no political process since there would be only one standard of truth. Analysis, so the advocates argue, is completely value-free. They seem to have been blinded by the beauty of it all; those who claim to be advancing the cause of "reasoned dialogue" in government must see the rest of us as nincompoops. But even after we are kicked out of government, they would deny that they had aided in our exit; their gift is only a method for organizing information to help officials who are responsible for allocating public resources to make better decisions in accomplishing public objectives.

Now all of us want better allocative decisions; that is why we go into politics. The problem is that there are countless definitions of better, and few of us are pious enough to insist that our stylized ripoffs are only neutral tools. This nonsense about neutrality is the key to criticizing systems analysis. Of course it is not neutral, and before it is adopted one had better be very sure that the inevitable decisions are bearable. Because once one has accepted an adversary's decisional premises, effective political debate for all practical purposes is at an end. As the German radicals say, the answer is then *systemimmanent;* it is a natural consequence of the standard perception.

Systems analysts have simply substituted their "neutrality" for someone else's, a political trick which has been going on from the beginning of time. The rules of the game will change; a new team will have access to the decision maker. The experience in the Department of Defense provides abundant illustration of that. The analysts valued rationality, efficiency, and quantification; but what about those, such as military officers, who have an ambivalent relationship to these qualities? They learned that one did not walk into McNamara's office to talk about hunches, gut feelings, and intuition, sharpened or otherwise. Halberstam reports one especially revealing anecdote from the days of the Pentagon's infatuation with analysis. An experienced CIA man had been briefing McNamara on the Vietnam situation until he made the mistake of confessing that the volumes of statistics just did not smell right. The adviser was never asked to give another briefing.[16]

Systems analysis strives to "demystify" the decision-making process, and if decision makers are bedazzled by the techniques, only a certain type of information will reach their ears. Insofar as other perceptions of reality are excluded, the political process will suffer. In the end, the choice will come down to a matter of being very, very rational and taking the advice of the experts or of going off on one's own to make a silly, damn-fool mistake. Well before the analysts burst upon the scene, Ellul had predicted that "The politician will then find himself obliged to choose between the technician's solution, which is the only reasonable one, and other solutions which he can indeed try out at his own peril. . . ."[17]

Still, the analysts will maintain that it is not their fault. After all, they are only the completely neutral bearers of hard facts; if those facts are bad news, one should not shoot the messengers. The facts are facts, and no amount of wishful thinking will change them. It may be tough, but analysis is value-free. But that argument is simply not true, if for no other reason than that analysis can be used to erode the bases of other values. It can be used to show that our most deep-felt values are irrational and inefficient. That is the punch line to Lewin's joke about the "Report from Iron Mountain."[18] In this superb satire, the analysts determine that peace is not feasible. Policy makers should therefore devote their attention to the maintenance of a tolerable level of violence. And what sort of impact will this argument have on those of us who believe, despite the enumeration of the odds against it, that there is still reason to yearn for peace on earth, goodwill to men? Ought we then be rational and abandon all hope? In another area, Anatol Rapoport once speculated how the analyst might operationalize Jonathan Swift's "modest proposal" for dealing with famine, i.e., feeding children to the parents.[19] The scientists would view this as nothing more than a series of technical problems of inducing people to consume their offspring. Our untutored minds might recoil at the horror of it all, but that is because we are too irrational.

Is nothing sacred then? Of course not, because sanctity is not an item which can be encased within system parameters. Get down to the facts and sanctity evaporates, unless as Herman Kahn once sneered, you prefer a nice, warm, emotional mistake. We say that unless we hold on to the sacred, our self-image is changed and our sense of human dignity is destroyed. Analysts tell us, for example, that by 1970, the Vietnam war had cost the United States more than 11.6 billion dollars. But so what? Whether half or double that figure, we do not know if the action was right or wrong. A. Alan Post, the respected budget analyst for the state of California, was reported as favoring an economy the state might adopt:

> One item in the $365 million category involves $4.28 million which Post said could be saved if the Legislature removed all restrictions on abortions. He explained that 30% of the prospective mothers covered by Medi-Cal probably would have abortions if they could and the cost of a legal therapeutic abortion under the program ($750) is half that of a live birth.

I cannot imagine any "prolife" advocate, any deeply religious person agonizing over the issue, or even any friend of the right of abortion finding much comfort from those statistics. I regard it as a thoroughly inhuman way to approach the matter.

As with PPB, the device with which it was originally connected, much of the passion for systems analysis has been exhausted. We cannot say that it was because of the perceived political threat. Aside from the general lack of success, the reason for the failure of systems analysis was in the nature of the rationality, albeit limited, to which it aspired. Systems are endless, and even with the most advanced techniques, it is impossible to build solid parameters. And if a complete system, with all the relevant components, were identified, what then? Systems ought to be administered as such; but education, welfare, health, and almost every other public program sprawl across legal boundaries. As Simon points out about our renewed interest in ecological systems, knowledge is a stimulus to action: "With this new ability to trace effects, we feel responsible for them in a way we previously did not. The intellectual awakening is also a moral awakening."[20] That is to say, our perception of the consequences has reached a global level. Systems analysis is a strong impetus to centralization and insofar as the universe is of one piece, logic demands that the planet be run as a whole. Otherwise, why bother?

THE COMPUTER

Behind all our previous discussions of quantification, measurement, information, and decision making, there looms the presence of the computer or, as it is generally referred to, electronic data processing (EDP). The ability to process huge amounts of data has been the principal cause of the interest in greater rationality. Before the computer, there was no sense in aspiring to rationality because of the expense in time and money of accumulating and sorting the relevant facts. EDP has changed all that.

Ever since the first "calculating engines" were invented, fearmongers have delighted in dreaming up all sorts of disasters for the human race. I am not terrified by the idea that we have created a Frankenstein monster, and the notion that a genuine electronic brain will outwit humanity in order to impose upon us complete slavery is overblown. It places an unwarranted faith in modern workmanship which cannot even produce an electric can opener capable of functioning for more than a month or two. Anyway, I assume that if events come to such a pretty pass, we could unplug the things. Nor do I share the alarm expressed by some observers who feel that automation will cause all sorts of economic and social dislocation when human workers have been displaced by machines. I would gladly volunteer for experiments by those who feel that too much leisure will bend humanity out of shape. I think I could live with it.

At the same time, I am not persuaded by people such as Buckminster Fuller, Marshal McLuhan, Zbigniew Brzezinski, or Pierre Teilhard de Chardin with their visions of better living through electricity in the "technetronic society" or the "global village." In their clearheaded critique of the "futurist ethos that identifies electricity and electrical power, electronics and cybernetics, with a new birth of community, decentralization, ecological balance and social harmony," Carey and Quirk demolish the "rhetoric of the electronic sublime." As they correctly point out, the trust in electronics must ignore the present reality of greater centralization and more intensive social control. I fail to see how anyone could deny that the speed and comprehension of electronics has "enlarged the possible scale of social organization and greatly enhanced the possibilities of centralization and imperialism in matters of culture and politics."[21]

It is not the unknown aspects of EDP which concern me. Rather, it is the completely predictable consequences. EDP only exaggerates all the presently known tendencies of administration. If we are unhappy with things now, wait until the full potential of automation is realized. We will then have the same problems raised to a new level. The rationalization of the world can proceed at full speed, uninhibited by the limitations of the human mind. The administrative mentality can now be totally dominant. "The computer as metaphor," to use Weizenbaum's phrase, will determine the popular vision of the possible and the impossible.[22]

EDP brings to the existing managerial processes two critical things. First, it enables one to make decisions which would have been too costly for an ordinary mortal. It can approach the ideal of rationality, namely, knowing everything there is to know about a problem. But again, and this is the second point, "knowing everything" is understood in a very limited sense. The machines can understand only a certain type of language. It is impossible to be ambiguous with the computer, which means to engage it in a dialogue one must think in machine terms. That is, a rational discipline is necessarily imposed upon the user. We conform to the logic of the computer if we wish to make effective use of it. As Donald Michael wrote of the "silent conquest" by cybernation:

> In general, the influence of computers will continue to be enhanced if those who use them attend chiefly to those components of reality which can be put into a computer and processed by it, and the important values will become those which are compatible with this approach to analyzing and manipulating the world.[23]

Put another way, the computer can do anything the ordinary bureaucratic structure can, and at less cost in less time. Weber's bureaucracy was only a very crude, first-generation attempt to force reality to manageable units. The computers will do a much "better" job and therefore increase the impact of administration upon society. Recall what Weber wrote of the strengths of bureaucracy: "Precision, speed, unambiguity, knowledge of the files, continuity, discretion, unity, strict subordination, reduction of friction and of material and personal costs." It reads like something out of an IBM sales representative's manual.

Robert Boguslaw, in his critique of the "new Utopians," makes the same point about computers updating the Weberian model. His argument is that the computer, even more than the bureaucracy, must have its information from the environment in a very specific form, and "the world of reality must at some point in time be reduced to binary form."[24] Since we humans have become the environment, we are required to conform so that inputs are digestible. We must become socialized to adapt to the machine, just as we have already been socialized in our relations with bureaucracy. As Weizenbaum, himself a computer expert at M.I.T., warns about a system which permits only certain kinds of data, "such a computing system has effectively closed many doors that were open before it was installed."[25] As we adjust our thought patterns to a form which can be handled in a mechanical method, it is obvious that we become more of an item of administration.

The application of EDP in government has been relatively benign so far—too benign say the advocates. And it must be admitted that one can make a good case in favor of computerization. If help is not provided, government is in danger of collapsing under the weight of its own paperwork. According to an official of the National Archives and Record Service, all attempts at reducing the amount of information consumed by the federal government have not been effective, and in 1972, files were being enlarged by about 7 million cubic feet of new records annually.[26] How much of the increase is the result of a Parkinson's law applied to computers—if we can now handle a certain type of data, let's get it—is uncertain, but it is obvious that some drastic steps must be taken if officials are to cope with the blizzard of information. The computer offers the most logical way for coping.

The constrictive effect of EDP, however, can be seen at the low level where most government applications have taken place. By now most major jurisdictions have automated the routine functions of government—preparing payrolls, checking inventories, sending bills for utilities, etc. Some advocates are sure that government has only purchased an expensive, high-speed printing press and that the full potential of the machines has been overlooked. However, many citizens have already come into contact with the wild bull computer that will not tolerate any sloppy habits in our communications with it. The examples of bills for 1 cent, which common sense would tell us to disregard, are fairly common. The wretch who refuses to pay this penny will be marked as a scofflaw and be hounded forever, unless the computer is reprogrammed. I would not be surprised if most people have concluded that it is not worth the hassle to fight computers with common sense and in apparently trivial matters have capitulated to machine logic; that is, we have decided to behave rationally.

To take the discussion out of the realm of speculative doomsaying, we can turn to the one area of American government in which the potential of the computer has been most thoroughly tested. Judith Merkle's brilliant analysis of military "command and control systems" indicates what other areas may find in EDP. The stimulus to the development of advanced computer programs in defense matters was the ability of individual members to start the first and last thermonuclear war. Modern warfare made imperative the development of a sophisticated computer hardware, and so "the logic of the computer was inextricably woven into the organization theory that grew out of the operation of nuclear forces." That logic required the total centralization of the military unit and the extension of control by the unit over "all contingent governmental, social and psychological factors that might affect the operation of the national C&C system." Every element had to be adapted to the machine or, as Merkle concluded, "technology has not merely merged with organization theory, it has become organization theory."

Organization theory in turn becomes political theory when the insatiable desire for predictability requires that every sign of human irrationality be eliminated. The logic has gone as far as it can. What is the main element of uncertainty in military operations? Why, the enemy itself! Therefore, the logic "grew to incorporate the enemy command structure itself, by including direct communications with the Kremlin in the international information 'system' required by nuclear strategy." Internally, the organization also needs complete predictability, and therefore the new organization theory insists upon forms of human behavior which are capable of being programmed.[27] In computer terms, the real problem in command and control systems is one of "software," i.e., the things that real people might do to screw up the operation. The social environment, with all those dark and threatening areas of irrationality, must be tamed if the system is to be optimally effective. The human actor, in other words, must "get with the program" by becoming programmed.

I would expect, therefore, that the introduction of computers into government would not open up new vistas of opportunity but instead reinforce the power of the status quo, since that is already the most predictable part of the environment. Kenneth Laudon is one of the few researchers to investigate the enthusiastic claims of the computer sales representatives and a new breed of technocrats about the revolution that would result from the introduction of management information systems (MIS). The provision of a new handle on the masses of information did not seem to have a particularly liberating effect upon the users, nor did it result in more substantively rational decisions. In one city, for example, the police used their handsome gadgetry to concentrate on stolen autos, thereby placing an added burden on the criminal justice system. Laudon was led to speculate that, with the new machinery, "the police may succeed in doing with utmost efficiency that which should not be done at all," while failing to explore truly innovative ways of practicing their trade. Finding that conservative tendencies were emphasized within the bureaucracies he studied, Laudon concludes that "the use of computers in the public sector has tended to strengthen the grip of traditional social policies and appears to lessen the perceived need and public demand for fundamental reconception of social policies in diverse areas such as police, welfare, and health."[28] Weizenbaum concurs that the computer arrived at a time to save "social and political structures that otherwise might have been either radically renovated or allowed to totter under the demands that were sure to be made on them."[29]

I do not see why anyone should have expected anything else from the computer. The main effect of EDP is to drive from decision making the very ways of perception which could facilitate change. The views of prophets, poets, and politicians are hardly the sort of thing one can process satisfactorily. Therefore, I regard with dread the notion that the only way for politicians to deal with computer-based societies is to adopt computer technology themselves. The mechanization of the political process brings to mind the image of a capitol building with all the passion and excitement of an Exxon cracking plant. Yet such is apparently meant in the constant calls for the "modernization" of the executive and legislature. John Saloma, a political scientist, points out that the computer "has already demonstrated its capacity to discipline human thought processes," and that it is precisely because of that capacity that it should be welcomed in the legislative chamber. In his view, it is the only way Congress can go if it wishes to keep pace with the rationalization of decision making already in effect in the executive branch.[30] I fail to see what the outcome of such a development could be other than the communication of two computers, one marked "Congress" and the other "President," in a language from which the irrational has been eliminated. What can there be to disagree about, to stimulate the political organs?

In sum, if you like a centralized, unilinear bureaucracy, you will love computers. To those of us who are fighting to retain the few enclaves of the irrational, there is not a great deal to cheer about. It would seem that we must conform to the rational discipline of the machine. That is my view of the future, and the real question is how it can be resisted. The question can be answered only when we have a clearer idea of how much the computer can know about the environment and especially about the human part of it. The crux of the matter lies in the issue of privacy.

PRIVACY

The privacy issue is an excellent place to review the arguments made so far and to look forward to the matters of control specific to the internal operation of the organization. When the technocrats speak of "data," "information," "knowledge," and the desperate need for their manipulation, we may perhaps let these sterile words obscure the fact that the data concern us, the information is about people. It is misleading to speak of inputs from the environment when, on the personal level, those inputs are parts of our total being, "the real of us." But as I have said often enough, the bureaucracy does not deal with total human beings; we are observed by administrators only insofar as, in Thompson's words, we are the "carriers of a class of data."[31] Some single aspect of our existence is modified by administrators to conform to whatever rational design may be driving them. Therefore, the things we communicate to bureaucrats form the raw material of their work.

The bureaucrats have always worked from abstractions about human life contained in their files. In actual fact, the files or dossiers become the object of manipulation instead of the reality they supposedly represent, namely, us. Arnold Zweig captured the character of traditional bureaucratic procedures:

> In blue, white or grey cardboard covers, with strips of paper hanging out of them recording the names of the parties and the nature of the case—human fates sprawl over each other like pressed plants in a herbarium, the dried

> essence of things once alive: momentous actions great and small, strange catastrophes, all the meanness, wickedness, and mistrust of men, pride long trodden underfoot and now turning against the tyrant, human dignity forever worsted in this foul age, naked souls clothed in the arid garment of a legal document, typed or engrossed in the elegant copper-plate of the clerks. Cases concluded, lives that have run their course, lie there tied round with tape and stamped with many seals. It is there that many a conflict ends in victory or defeat, men sicken and pine and die or pass thence free and forgotten. But the documents remain.[32]

In equally graphic terms, Solzhenitsyn describes the millions of little threads we all produce as we give off information about ourselves, a condition which causes us to develop "a respect for the people who manipulate the threads. . . ."[33]

The files create for administrators a manageable identity more real than the wholeness of our existence. Small wonder that bureaucrats have a desire for a uniform system of identification. A piece of paper which would prove who everyone is would enhance efficient administration, and countries with a longer administrative history than us usually have such instruments. Arthur Miller, obviously a maladjusted artist, objected to the proposed "internal passport" as an arrogant attempt on the part of clerks to "freeze and fix forever what in truth is fluid and flowing."[34] Just being classified, repugnant enough to a unique human soul, is not the greatest threat of reduction to paper. At least when one has the papers, one possesses a claim to existence. What happens when the formal identification is taken away? In the novelist's angry words, "They were dead. Without a country. Without birth-certificates with which to prove they had been born of a mother belonging to the human race."[35]

I am not alluding here to an accidental computer blip which erases a social security number, although one can imagine the difficulty of convincing skeptical functionaries that one does in fact exist. More terrifying is the easy possibility of eliminating human beings just by stamping their papers VOID. In her chilling analysis of the phenomenon of "statelessness," Hannah Arendt proved how easy it is to explain the termination of people who have been made "nonpersons" through their lack of papers. The person is then thrown out of the security of the community and is liable to any sort of abuse because, administratively, there is "nothing sacred in the abstract nakedness of being human."[36]

Still, in American society there has been little attention devoted to the appalling consequences of the paper identity, perhaps because the most intensive attempts at learning all about the individual were directed against people who, by their marginal status in society, were expected to put up with any sort of harassment—criminals, subversives, welfare recipients. It is not odd that the most recent proposals for a national identification system were sponsored by the Justice Department and HEW in order to improve law enforcement and to eliminate welfare fraud. The politically dominant classes in America were socialized to accept the demands of efficiency, and they loyally filled out the forms dreamt up by the bureaucrats.

All of a sudden, it dawned on everyone that the "right to privacy" which we had enjoyed, largely by accident, is seriously threatened. We had privacy for thousands of years, in spite of the most intensive snooping by the busiest busybodies, simply because the technology was so deficient. Now we are acutely aware that the technology of surveillance has advanced so rapidly that our primitive defenses have been overwhelmed. There is an incredible arsenal of devices for bugging, tapping, taping, filtering, decoding, analyzing, and probing the physical space we occupy. Authors such as Vance Packard have made notorious the work of the "brain watchers" with their inventions designed to assault the inner person—psychological testing, psychoanalysis, and therapies which tell us to "let it all hang out."

On top of it all, Americans apparently got the message about applied social science. The data were not being collected for aesthetic purposes. Behind it was the intention of improving administration by a more informed control of social behavior. As Alan Westin put it, the concept of privacy is important because of "the power it grants to individuals and institutions to decide when sensitive information about themselves moves into the public sphere. The important thing to note is that when such information does enter the public domain it exerts a regulatory or constricting effect upon us. . . ."[37] David Berlo noted the same effect within the organization when he wrote that "the consequences of prediction in social science is control. When others give us information about them which enables us to predict their responses, we gain some control over their behavior."[38] Remarks like that make one realize it is not all that long to 1984.

But it is a rather confused sort of Big Brother we face. One cannot identify any single group which is promoting the invasion of privacy. It is all part of the irrationality of rational administrators. I agree with George Lane that "mindlessness is the villain, the failure to think seriously about the ultimate purposes and consequences of actions."[39] With the best of intentions, administrators acting individually have brought us to the point where danger is imminent. We failed to heed the warning of Justice Brandeis delivered in a case concerning government's first attack on privacy over fifty years ago:

> Experience should teach us to be most on guard to protect liberty when the Government's purposes are beneficent. Men born to freedom are naturally alert to repel invasions of their liberties by evil-minded rulers. The greatest dangers to liberty lurk in the insidious encroachment of men of zeal, well-meaning but without understanding.[40]

These well-meaning zealots met a collective defeat in the rejection of the proposed National Data Center. This scheme would have brought together in a central location the files of several government agencies. The ultimate goal was the creation of a system which would register a notation whenever an individual came in contact with the government. Instead of the person's privacy being protected by the fact that the files were scattered throughout a number of government offices, the whole story would be readily accessible in one handy location.

Assurances were given that the center would provide only statistical data to interested agencies, but upon reflection one can see that assurance raises even greater problems. The statistics, I assume, would be used to predict and to control. The agency could take "preemptive action" to meet its goals. For example, people with a certain level of education, a police record, and other characteristics might be likely to get a type of disease; the public health agency could provide such people with preventive medicine. All very humane, but what if statistics show that left-handed redheads who have been convicted of purse snatching are likely, by the age of 30, to have committed murder? Should they all be locked up? At least when the files contained a name, there was a chance of proving innocence. Statistical applications of personal data make control of our own destiny exceedingly tenuous. As Stafford Beer wrote of his "image" in the computer:

> The behavior of the image is predictable in statistical terms. Probably I am not. But the strength of the machine image is in its pragmatic validity. There is no confusion here, no loss of history, no rationalization. I am a mess; and I don't know what to do. The machine knows better—in statistical terms. Thus is my reality less real than my mirror image in the store. That fact diminishes me.[41]

In any event, the specific proposal for a data center caused such an uproar that Congress turned it down. But the melody lingers on, and will for as long as administrators cannot control their craving for more information about us. The proposal, after all, was only to bring together already existing data banks, and such banks have continued to proliferate at a rapid rate as more agencies develop a computer capacity. Private industry, particularly in the area of credit ratings, also maintains a vast amount of data about individuals. Even at the federal level, there is a lot known about us. According to the Senate Judiciary Committee, there were, in 1974, some 858 separate data banks, containing more than a billion records on individuals. The idea of merging these various banks is still strong among EDP experts.

That the war is not over yet is indicated by the repeated suggestions for the development of a standard universal identifier (SUI), a number—social security or others—which would be used for the transaction of all government business. Our names are rather flimsy things since many have the same ones and they can be falsified easily. A single unique number for each citizen would simplify things. Persuaded by the argument about cracking down on welfare cheats, Congress was on the verge of ordering every school child to be assigned an SUI. The advocates pussyfooted about the implications, but their basic assurance was that it was a mere technicality. Europeans, who tend to have such numbers, stated more clearly what was up:

> . . . the introduction of personal code numbers, especially for natural persons, is also disputed because it facilitates considerably the building up of *personal dossiers* inside and outside public administration. This is indeed a major step towards potential surveillance of natural persons on a large scale. It is certainly *more* important than, for example, the physical concentration (in one central place) of several registers containing data on persons with different numbering systems.[42]

Beyond the immediate danger, there is also the possibility that our self-images would suffer. It is not only the crank who feels that there is a difference between being Harry Jones on the Madison Exchange in Elmville, Ohio, and 334-07-9945/(213)344-5678/34556.

Things finally reached a point where it was no longer possible to ignore the impotence of the citizen in face of a mindless technology. A thorough investigation by HEW, itself a major user of computer data banks, concluded in favor of the individual:

> It is no wonder that people have come to distrust computer-based record-keeping operations. Even in non-governmental settings, an individual's control over the personal information that he gives to an organization, or that an organization obtains from him, is lessening as the relationship between the giver and the receiver of personal data grows more attenuated, impersonal and diffused. There was a time when information about an individual tended to be elicited in face-to-face contacts involving personal trust and a certain symmetry or balance, between giver and receiver. Nowadays, an individual must increasingly give information about himself to large and relatively faceless institutions, for handling and use by strangers—unknown and all too often, unresponsive. Sometimes the individual does not even know that an organization maintains a record about him. Often he may not see it, much less contest its accuracy, control its dissemination or challenge its use by others.[43]

It was to meet that threat that Congress approved the Privacy Act of 1974. Although there are important exceptions to its coverage—law enforcement, CIA, the Secret Service—it does offer some remedy to the individual who feels that the government is asking too much. It permits people to review their files in federal agencies and to correct or amend the information. Agencies are prevented from giving information collected for a specific purpose to other agencies without the person's consent. Perhaps most gratifying in light of the reports about the number of strange agencies maintaining mysterious files, bureaus are required to disclose the existence of data banks and are prohibited from keeping files which interfere with First Amendment rights.[44] But the effect of this or any other legislation is not ensured as long as we are dependent upon bureaucratic organizations for the provision of so many services. As James Rule warns, "the seductive appeal of mass surveillance makes it all too possible that the public will become dependent on the benefits of these practices before their dangers are apparent."[45] Snooping, it would seem, can become addictive.

The real challenge is the mindlessness with which computer-based information systems, along with the other decision-making tools we have discussed, have extended themselves into improper areas of political life. I do not endorse a Luddite attack on the computers nor do I feel it would solve anything to purge the analysts. As citizens, we are largely responsible for buying too much snake oil in the first place, for being enamored of the metaphor of the computer. We should have known it would have a distortive effect on our perceptions if we went too far too fast. Perhaps now we have regained a more balanced view so that we can utilize the positive aspects of management science. Again, I do not deny the need for improved decision making. My concept of improvement, however, does not include the elimination of anything which cannot be measured.

Our discussion of the development, production, processing, transmitting, or whatever of information culminates in our nervous apprehension about the computer. The devices, from PPB to EDP, are all of a piece. The human actor is viewed as part of a person-machine information processor. I concur with Churchman about those who "are horrified at the suggestion that computers can think, whereas they should be horrified at the suggestion that people are information processors."[46] Therefore, the several means which are suggested to force us to be free, to offer only the freedom to do right, must be viewed with the greatest suspicion.

REFERENCES

1 William Gore and Fred Silander, "A Bibliographical Essay on Decision Making," *Administrative Science Quarterly,* 4 (1959), p. 112.

2 Herbert Simon, *The New Science of Management Decision* (New York: Harper & Row, 1960).

3 *Managing the Modern City* (Chicago: International City Management Association, 1971), p. 271.

4 Cyril Herrmann and John Magee, " 'Operations Research' for Management," in E. Bursk and John Chapman (eds.), *New Decision-making Tools for Managers* (New York: New American Library, 1965), p. 4.

5 Philip Morse (ed.), *Operations Research for Public Systems* (Cambridge, Mass.: M.I.T., 1967).

6 Ida Hoos, *Systems Analysis in Public Policy* (Berkeley: University of California Press, 1972), p. 15.

7 Simon Ramo, *Cure for Chaos* (New York: McKay, 1969), p. viii.

8 James Schlesinger, *Systems Analysis and the Political Process,* Rand Paper P-3464 (Santa Monica, Calif.: Rand, 1967), p. 31.

9 Eric Denardo and Murray Geisler, *Management Science Frontiers: 1970–1980* (Santa Monica, Calif.: Rand, 1967), p. 5.
10 U.S. Senate, Subcommittee on National Security and International Operations, *Planning-Programming-Budgeting: Hearings* (Washington: GPO, 1967).
11 G. H. Fisher, *The World of Program Budgeting* (Santa Monica, Calif.: Rand, 1966), pp. 11–20.
12 E. S. Quade, *Analysis for Public Decisions* (New York: American Elsevier, 1975), pp. 214–215.
13 Alain Enthoven and Wayne Smith, *How Much is Enough?* (New York: Harper & Row, 1971).
14 Ida Hoos, "Systems Techniques for Managing Society: A Critique," *Public Administration Review,* 33 (1973), p. 157.
15 Donald Michael, "Some Factors Tending to Limit the Utility of the Social Scientist in Military Systems Analysis," *Operations Research,* 5 (1957), p. 93.
16 David Halberstam, *The Best and the Brightest* (New York: Random House, 1972), p. 348.
17 Jacques Ellul, *The Technological Society* (New York: Random House, 1964), p. 259.
18 Leonard Lewin, *Report from Iron Mountain on the Possibility and Desirability of Peace* (New York: Dial, 1967).
19 Anatol Rapoport, *Strategy and Conscience* (New York: Harper & Row, 1964), p. xxi.
20 Herbert Simon, "Applying Information Technology to Organization Design," *Public Administration Review,* 33 (1973), p. 277.
21 James Carey and John Quirk, "The Mythos of the Electronic Revolution," *American Scholar,* 39 (1970), pp. 219–241.
22 Joseph Weizenbaum, *Computer Power and Human Reason* (San Francisco: Freeman, 1976), p. 157.
23 Donald Michael, *Cybernation: The Silent Conquest* (Santa Barbara, Calif.: Center for the Study of Democratic Institutions, 1962), p. 37.
24 Robert Boguslaw, *The New Utopians* (Englewood Cliffs, N.J.: Prentice-Hall, 1965), p. 190.
25 Weizenbaum, op. cit., p. 38.
26 Artel Ricks, "Managing Government Paperwork," *The Bureaucrat,* 4 (1975), p. 270.
27 Judith Merkle, "Command and Control: The Social Implication of Nuclear Defense," (New York: General Learning Press, 1971).
28 Kenneth Laudon, *Computers and Bureaucratic Reform* (New York: Wiley, 1974).
29 Weizenbaum, op. cit., p. 31.
30 John Saloma, *Congress and the New Politics* (Boston: Little, Brown, 1969), p. 222.
31 Victor Thompson, *Modern Organization* (New York: Knopf, 1961), p. 17.
32 Arnold Zweig, *The Case of Sergeant Grischa* (New York: Viking, 1928), p. 165.
33 Alexander Solzhenitsyn, *Cancer Ward* (New York: Farrar, Straus & Giroux, 1968), p. 192.
34 Arthur Miller, "On True Identity," *New York Times Magazine,* (April 13, 1975), p. 111.

35 B. Traven, *The Death Ship* (New York: Collier Books, 1962), p. 143.
36 Hannah Arendt, *The Origins of Totalitarianism* (Cleveland: World Publishing, 1958), p. 299.
37 Alan Westin, "Computers and the Protection of Privacy," *Technology Review,* 71 (April 1969), p. 33.
38 David Berlo, "Empathy and Managerial Communication," in Charles Press and Alan Arian (eds.), *Empathy and Ideology* (Chicago: Rand McNally, 1966), p. 142.
39 George Lane, "The Perils of Pushbutton Policymaking," *The Bureaucrat,* 2 (1973), p. 300.
40 *Olmstead v. United States,* 277 U.S. 479 (1928).
41 Stafford Beer, "Managing Modern Complexity," in U.S. House of Representatives, Committee on Science and Astronautics, *The Management of Information and Knowledge* (Washington: GPO, 1970), p. 52.
42 Uwe Thomas, *Computerised Data Banks in Public Administration* (Paris: Organisation for Economic Co-operation and Development, 1971), pp. 22–23.
43 Secretary's Advisory Committee on Automated Personal Data Systems, *Records, Computers, and the Rights of Citizens* (Washington: GPO, 1973), pp. 28–29.
44 For more details, see the symposium on the Privacy Act of 1974 in *The Bureaucrat,* 5 (1976), pp. 131–188.
45 James Rule, *Private Lives and Public Surveillance* (London: Allen Lane, 1973), p. 358.
46 C. West Churchman, *The Systems Approach* (New York: Delacorte, 1968), p. 125.

Chapter 9

Management

If I wanted to get good and useful work out of the prisoners then, contrary to the usual and universal practice in concentration camps, they must be given better treatment. I assumed I would succeed in both housing and feeding them better than in other camps. . . .

I believed that in such conditions I could obtain the willing cooperation of the prisoners in the constructional work that had to be done.

Rudolf Hoess
Commandant of Auschwitz

"I want no surprises" is reported to be one of the favorite bits of wisdom of Harold Geneen, the master manager of ITT. According to Anthony Sampson, he took the desire for predictability to its ultimate; his organization claimed the body and soul of every employee, and the pursuit of rationality, the elimination of surprises, led finally to the Oval Office and into sordid foreign adventures.[1] Geneen, however, seems to have suffered no pangs of conscience over this sort of behavior because, as a good manager, he was only following a rational natural process. He and his subordinates, as well as anyone with whom his giant corporation comes into contact, are only submitting to the laws of nature—and in that there is freedom.

I suspect that lesser managers are equally attracted by the vision of a world with no surprises. How distressing then when they survey the chaos over which they preside. Harlan Cleveland, himself a veteran public administrator, quoted with approval a military officer's description of management:

> The art of management consists of issuing orders based on inaccurate, incomplete, and archaic data, to meet a situation which is dimly understood, and which will not be what the issuer visualizes, orders which will frequently be misinterpreted and often ignored, to accomplish a purpose about which many of the personnel are not enthusiastic.[2]

It would be so much easier if the employees were wooden blocks to be moved around at the pleasure of the manager, but even the poet can perceive the folly of aspiring to great projects through individual members "still used to just being men, not block-parts."[3]

Management deals with people in their relation to the internal processes of the organization. Managers do not do the work of the organization; they see to it that others perform in accordance with the formal goals. Given that assignment, the manager sitting at the peak of the organization cannot be too happy. Even if all the recommendations of the textbook are followed, the vantage point cannot provide too satisfactory a view of the subordinates. One must become heartsick about the individuals composing the organization. If they are not actually stupid, lazy, and disloyal, they certainly are not doing all they could to promote organization goals. Vanity of vanities, all is vanity, must be the lament of managers who thought they would be in control of events.

Although the Slough of Despond runs close by managerial headquarters, students of administration keep their hopes up and continue to issue inspiring messages about improved managerial methods. At best, there is the subtle promise of social science that a world in which surprises do not exist, a world safe for management, is something attainable. Therefore, the rationalization of the internal processes of the organization continues at a busy pace.

It is again to Herbert Simon that we turn for a clarification of the elements of rationalization of management, of ways to ensure that the individual decisions which make up the actual performance of the organization will "also reflect the broader considerations to which it is the function of the organized group to give effect." Since all behavior is based upon a decision, every member is constantly involved in problem solving. The question is not whether workers make decisions, but rather whether those decisions are the right ones in terms of the bounded rationality. Simon mentions five mechanisms by which the manager can be assured of uniformly rational behavior:

1 *Division of labor.* When given an assignment, the workers' attention is concentrated on a specific problem. They can specialize in making decisions about one little piece of the overall goal.

2 *Standardized practices.* The standardization of practices relieves the individual of the responsibility for deciding *de novo* what is to be done. As in the "preformed decisions" of Kaufman's rangers, one has only to decide how a limited number of variables fit into a given form.

3 *Authority structure.* Members agree to accept authority; that is, they use another's decision as a guide to action.

4 *Channels of communication.* The workers receive only that information which will aid them in making a rational decision. They are not overburdened with the knowledge of the universe.

5 *Indoctrination.* In Simon's words, this factor "injects into the very nervous system of the organization members the criteria of decisions that the organization wishes to employ." That sounds a little sinister, as if the workers were shooting up on company doctrine. The most effective injection, however, comes from the training one receives for the job. For example, professional engineers are not likely to make too many decisions which other engineers with similar training would find irrational.[4]

THE STUDY OF MANAGEMENT

If all the managerial mechanisms are working, then organizational behavior should be rational in the bounded sense. Simon has merely updated Weber by pointing out the devices by which the inhabitant of the bureaucracy is enmeshed in the net of rationality. Simon and the rationalist students of management, however, have gone far beyond the simplistic notions of an earlier age of administration. It is no longer a tenable proposition that workers willingly accept their role because of a formal contract. Workers are infinitely tricky but—and this is the "but" that sustains a mass of research in management—they can be figured out. Through scientific investigation, we can learn every person's price and proceed to buy, manipulate, coerce, or seduce his or her compliance.

Basically, I have no objection to such a concept of the worker in the organization. It emphasizes the individual's position as a bargainer in the never-ending conflict with the organization. I feel that it is based upon a healthy awareness of the "organizational dilemma"—the individual and the organization can never be as one. This idea sees workers as having some control over the conditions of the truce which they will sign with the organization. The organization and the individual are involved in an ongoing game, with each pursuing a limited view of rationality.

Those of an existentialist persuasion may find this approach to management offensive since it still takes the individual as a means and not as an end. As long as the organization is expected to accomplish something, I am unable to see how some degree of individual submission to collective ends is avoidable. I only hope that the workers understand the conditions by which their compliance is obtained so that, as individuals, they can determine for themselves if it is worth it or not. But for those who are concerned that the human being has become nothing more than an instrument to be played by sophisticated masters who can calculate every move that the individual may make, Dostoyevsky many years ago described the final escape hatch:

> Now, you may say that this too can be calculated in advance and entered on the timetable—chaos, swearing, and all—and that the very possibility of such a calculation would prevent it, so that sanity would prevail. Oh no! In that case man would go insane on purpose, just to be immune from reason.[5]

One can applaud such heroic defiance, but in a practical sense, there must be a better way of proving one's independence than going mad. Relief lies in the recognition of the organizational dilemma, in the realization that the organization does require some conformity but that conformity must be procured in terms of each individual's set of values. It seems to me a simple point, but the alarming fact is that management science takes as its basic mission the elimination of the line between individual and organization. Somehow the two are to become one, and thereby the manager can be confident that there will be no surprises to prevent the organization from reaching peak efficiency.

The subjugation of the individual within a completely rational scheme is not the most difficult problem. Throughout history, organizations have used an awful inventory of means to break the will and brutalize the body so that workers will respond perfectly to orders. As I said in Chapter 1, however, beating people into a standard shape can be dysfunctional. They will not then be capable of that self-adjustment which is the most important organizational behavior in the uncertain situation. Like robots, they will go through their preprogrammed routines while the world around them collapses. Or worse, they will revolt at the first sign of weakness. That scene from *Dr. Zhivago* when the bonds of control dissolve and the soldiers rather nonchalantly murder their commander must have caused nightmares for many managers. The free and willing contribution of the individual is difficult to obtain. If the capacity for self-adjustment could itself be brought within the calculations of the managers, the organization would perform at the highest levels. Such a happy prospect is the promise of schools of business administration and other havens for management scientists.

Workers are viewed as raw material for the construction of a rational machine, and those free options which I would preserve for them are seen as problems to be solved by the scientists. As in the title of Loren Baritz's history of social science and industry, the scholars have become the "servants of power." Social scientists, from the beginning of their study of management, have taken the manager's side, and "this commitment to management's goals, as opposed to the goals of other groups and classes in American society, did color their research and recommendations."[6] There is little in the serious literature of management which could be construed as a survival manual for the person at the bottom of the heap.

I do not accuse the social scientists of having made a conscious decision to sell out to management, although I suspect that most scholars find more personal satisfaction in being courted by the rich and powerful than by listening to the woes of the poor working stiff. Instead, they have seen themselves as agents of the laws of nature. The organization and its participants are seen as technical problems to be solved in terms of efficiency. There is a startling similarity in the language used by generations of management specialists. They see their task as the identification of the immutable laws which govern the work situation. Once those laws are identified, managers are told, all the potential energy of the organization will be directed to the accomplishment of formal goals.

Scientific management advocates were the first to be sure that their science was based on an understanding of the modification of individuals to conform to the "relative fixity of the non-human elements in a managerial situation."[7] The appropriate laws could be discovered so that the organization could run almost without direction. Mary Parker Follett, writing in an attempt to give a new dimension to scientific management, also felt that a thoroughly depersonalized system of management could be devised if scientists could only discover the "law of the situation" in any human environment to which all participants must conform.[8] More recently, a friend of the knowledge revolution saw a time when all members would be motivated by the "logic of the situation."[9] Even Abraham Maslow, the patron saint of a supposedly more humane school of management thought, was only chasing the elusive laws of the situation.[10]

The perspective of these and other writers is that of adherence to the notion of a science of humanity. The science they have in mind, of course, is the epistemologically limited view of the behavioralist—human behavior is caused by objective factors which can be discovered through empirical research. Once one has found the causes of behavior, it is a relatively simple matter to institute ways of application so that the formal occupational role will be more effectively carried out. Though the specific fads may come and go, every school of management science, as de Grazia notes, "has its own way of asserting that its principles flow from the fount of science; every school, that is, is pseduoscientific."[11]

Even if this pseudoscience is benevolent—and all writers insist that their approach will benefit the whole society—I am not so confident that a pure science of human behavior is attainable. I concur with Chris Argyris, himself a leading scholar in organization behavior, that all social research is normative because the stuff of the science is not a concrete reality but only a convention constructed and maintained by humans. Moreover, in application, "where the non-scholars are uninterested in philosophical speculation about the nature of man, it is almost inevitable that the 'is' statement is transmogrified into an 'ought.' " "Thus," according to Argyris, "the descriptive theory may not take a normative point of view, but in the hands of practitioners, it becomes an important map for designing the future and acculturating our people."[12] In short, it is premature, as I hope it will always be, to pin down the protean nature of humanity. But such stabilization is exactly what is required by management theory since the protean person represents too scary a bundle of surprises. The attempts at the scientific regularization of the individual within organizations can be seen in a review of the ideology of management.

MANAGEMENT IDEOLOGY

More than one writer has made the point that organization theory shares the same territory as political theory and that all political philosophers are management specialists.[13] The basic problem in both areas is the maintenance of order in spite of the variability of individuals. The analogy may be more apt than one would like. Organization theory has usually had one distinctive difference from its general cousin—formal organizations tend to be in the totalitarian mold because their goals are known. The question really is: How can we have order so that we can produce widgets or teach third-graders? In liberal political philosophy, the question has generally been framed in terms of permitting individuals to achieve a number of conflicting values; how do we achieve order when there is no overarching goal to guide individual behavior? Political theory in the democracies has taken on some ominous aspects, with the talk about "goals" and "priorities." As we have seen in an earlier chapter, there is emerging a view of the polity as one big organization that managers instead of politicians can guide toward generally agreed-upon objectives. The management of society, in other words, is not seen as qualitatively different from the management of the Ace Nuts and Bolts Company or the Bureau of Parking Meters. All the more reason then to understand the ideology which has determined management behavior and the sources of what Kaufman calls "the myth of managerial omnipotence."[14]

As I have suggested, an ideology is a fairly coherent body of ideas which explains to the believer how the world ought to operate. Some may feel that ideology is some crackpot idea which leads unstable people to seek foolish goals; the truth is that it is even more significant in the support of any existing social order. It then becomes the reality for the members of the collectivity and explains why things must be as they are. Ideologies are particularly important in power relationships because they justify the subordination of one human to another. As described by Reinhard Bendix, all management ideologies are "attempts by leaders of enterprises to justify the privilege of voluntary action and association for themselves while imposing upon all subordinates the duty of obedience and the obligation to serve their employers to the best of their ability."[15]

The ideologies of management could take a variety of forms and until we know more about the innate need for hierarchy in human affairs, we cannot say that all forms of obedience are the result of a contrived pack of lies. The main point for the study of management in an advanced society is that management science is itself a major ideology. The "is" of the situation, as perceived by researchers, becomes the "ought" which can be used to tie individuals more closely to their work. In a critical examination of organization theory, Sherman Krupp cuts through the scientific verbiage of the theorists to reveal the repressive nature of the message. Organization theory has become organization technology with its aim the control of people. The major aspect of this so-called science is that "it would justify this control by emphasizing the voluntary aspects, by regarding it as consent."[16] Again, submission to law is freedom.

In their study of the impact of management theory on communist society, Frederic and Lou Jean Fleron put the matter very plainly:

> The richness, complexity, and uniqueness of human life cannot be understood by "objective science" and any attempt to "administer" it by reference to so-determined "scientific law" is repression. Repression we take to mean any social order or social force imposed on human beings which prevents them as individuals from realizing their uniquely human potentials, from exercising their human power over their own lives, their desires, and activity.[17]

They go on to stress a point so obvious that we can easily overlook it: "There never has been a revolutionary administration theory—that is not a possibility." Theory, as ideology, must be used to emphasize elements of harmony and play down the factors which lead to disagreement. Conflict is not congenial to the managerial mind; it means that there are surprises and that control is never complete. Of those who claim that there can be more than repression in organization theory, Thompson asks, "Who would design a tool that constantly undid whatever it did?"[18]

In his analysis of "managment creeds," William Scott makes a convincing case that the central concern of management has not changed over the years. On the surface, there appears to be considerable difference between the managers of fifty years ago and their modern counterparts. The common desires of both are so potent that the variations are essentially meaningless. In management thought, there has been little deviation from two themes. First, the goal of management is efficient production, and all the superficial changes in the creeds are ultimately justified in terms of productivity. Second, the emphasis is on the harmony of management and workers because disharmony would be an admission of the divergence of thought, i.e., the possibility of irrational behavior. With that in mind, let us turn to a consideration of the major developments in management ideology.

SCIENTIFIC MANAGEMENT

I have mentioned SM as the first serious attempt to rationalize management according to scientific principles. In the eyes of Frederick Taylor, an engineer, the workers were truly rational calculators, real Economic Men. Even the worker he described as "so stupid and phlegmatic that he more nearly resembles in his mental makeup the ox than any other type" was still motivated by a keen sense of self-interest as calculated in monetary terms.[19] Managers did not fully understand this sort of motivation and so did not take advantage of the most effective way of eliciting cooperation. Through careful analysis, both managers and workers could be united in a harmonious unit which would function for the benefit of both. All that was needed was the identification of the "one best way" to perform any organization job and to attach attractive rewards for those who conformed to the law of the situation.

Scott and Hart found similarities between Taylor and Thomas Hobbes, the gloomy English political philosopher, in their view of humanity. Humans were a sorry lot, infected by all sorts of destructive urges, and the problem of order is how to keep these passions under control. Whether it is the whole society or the factory floor, the life of people without some check on their natural inclinations is "solitary, poor, nasty, brutish, and short." While Hobbes recommended an autocratic state as the best check on a swinish humanity, Taylor was more intrigued by the control possibilities of knowledge itself. Individuals could be taught that it was in their best interests to conform to organization requirements. Through obedience to natural law, both managers and workers could achieve a conflict-free (and quite productive) state of harmony.[20]

The prophets of scientific management, good Americans all, were not very pleased with the autocratic implications of their theory. Therefore, far in advance of George Orwell, they had to argue that slavery is freedom. They could claim, apparently with little embarrassment, that obedience to scientific laws "creates a compensating individual freedom not realized under conditions of apparent absolute independence."[21] Presaging the doctrines of "people's democracy," these stalwart sons of capitalism praised the inherent democracy of their system. Henry Gantt, an early leader in the movement, could proclaim that "the new democracy does not consist in the privilege of doing as one pleases, whether it is right or wrong, but in each man's doing his part in the best way that can be devised from scientific knowledge and experience."[22] As Samuel Haber wrote of this pioneer, "democracy had nothing to do with the control of policy by those affected by it, but rather concerned the method and purpose of managing men."[23]

In application, scientific management was based on the idea that the worker responded to only a few physical stimuli. Therefore, each step in the work process could be broken down into its component parts and rewards related to each step. The so-called efficiency experts placed much emphasis on time and motion studies, trying to learn how many tons of coal a person could shovel in a day and still come back for more. Things like lighting, ventilation, and rest breaks were also thoroughly studied. Piecework was stressed since that made clear to the workers what their efforts were worth.

The error in all this was that the workers did not always calculate according to the organization's rationality. The workplace was still a matter of perception, and perceptions vary. Moreover, perception is not an isolated act for the individual but instead is colored by social forces. As Peabody put it, the motto of SM was "Organizations without People"—at least without real, live, sweaty, confused people.[24] Still, in comparison with later management styles, SM does seem more honest. The system did provide a standard basis of comparison for all members, and everyone knew exactly what the game was. Work hard and you get a reward; "soldier" and you get punished. In most cases, SM did not demand that managers and workers love and understand one another. Outside of the small area of economic calculations, the worker's life was pretty much his or her own. This is in contrast to what replaced scientific management.

HUMAN RELATIONS

And then came the Great Awakening. All of a sudden, it became evident that the worker was more complex than was previously thought. Social scientists found Truth in the Bank Wiring Room of the Hawthorne Plant of Western Electric, although I would agree with Henry Mayo that it is disgraceful that "American academics had to have a scientific experiment . . . to prove that factory workers were human beings."[25] In any event, from that amazing discovery we had the birth of "human relations." The title should not deceive, and in fairness to old-time managers, it must be said that they did not subscribe to "inhuman relations" nor did they idealize Ebenezer Scrooge as the model manager. One can even find in the military literature of the 1920s the same revolutionary ideas which the academics were to express in the 1930s. It is tribute to the power of social science to rewrite history that we now view the Hawthorne experiment as a turning point in management thought.

The experiment is by now an oft-told tale.[26] Actually, it was an experiment that failed. The researchers were trying all the traditional methods of improving productivity when it was realized that the results did not conform to existing theory.[27] The famous Hawthorne women, for example, did not react in the expected way when the physical environment was modified, i.e., when lighting was increased or decreased. It was finally decided that the women were responding to social rather than to physical factors. They were starved for affection and the fact that the company now seemed to be paying attention to them was enough to stimulate higher production. In the Bank Wiring Room, it was learned that the small informal work group could thwart formal control by establishing its own norms.

It became obvious that the organization had to attend to the psychological needs of the worker. The resulting theory encouraged managers to say that "We're all part of one big happy family!" and the organization blundered into the business of carefully dispensing units of "psychic rewards" in order to improve morale, which is to say, to increase the willingness to work harder. The modern manager was expected to view the worker as a complicated organism and to learn all the "how-to-get-along-with-people" techniques of a perverted psychology.

But was there any real change? Not a bit. It may have been one big, happy family, but make no mistake about daddy's authority or what the kids were supposed to do. As Scott says, "Human relations extended the motivational horizons beyond the economic to the social and psychological. It also introduced the small groups (the informal organization) to management thinking."[28] Lewis Coser dismissed the movement as the attempt at "transforming sullen robots into cheerful ones, and to changing the factory into an easily manipulated pseudo-community."[29] Ellul denounced human relations as "characteristic of the fakeries and shams with which men must be provided if the conflicts provoked by life in a technicized environment are to be avoided."[30]

There is now widespread recognition that truly humane relations cannot be programmed. The legacy of the movement, however, is still around us today. In particular, the emphasis on the group continues to characterize several management theories. The operational impact of the group theorists may not be as potent as it was in the 1950s when William Whyte delivered his famous attack on the Organization Man and his manipulation through the "social ethic," or "that contemporary body of thought which makes morally legitimate the pressures of society against the individual."[31] The belief in "belongingness" as a basic need of the individual resulted in a suffocating conformity. The individual was declared obsolete by science.

But what a strange science it is that despises our individuality. Such a science is subsidized by management since the apparent lessons of Hawthorne cannot be ignored. Groups do exist, they do modify employee behavior, and therefore they must be considered another factor of production. I would only ask, why, if there is indeed a science of group dynamics, is that knowledge not used to reinforce individuality? Why are people not taught that the groups are bad influences and that we have to exercise special care to resist group pressure? We are not so informed because it would serve no useful organization purpose. That is, I maintain that social science could serve to liberate us from the group and to enhance our self-image as free actors. That such is not to be the case is indicated by the developments in the latest approach to management.

"HUMANISM" IN ORGANIZATIONS

The latest phase in management ideology developed around the early 1960s. On the one hand, all sorts of data about human behavior in organizations were piling up. On the other hand, there was a feeling even among scholars that the organization had become too efficient and dehumanizing. Thus today one can identify two conflicting themes which, when they appear together in the same management textbooks, can only lead one to conclude that there is uncertainty as to whether the aim of management is to limit or increase human freedom.

Pure management science has regained its confidence that the ultimate motivator for all people can be found through further scientific research. Every person has a breaking point, and a technology must be developed to exploit that point. There may be room for an "applied humanism," but nothing so radical as to reintroduce the possibility of surprise into management calculations. An applied humanism may be a useful therapeutic device to keep the minds of workers occupied and free of "melancholy reveries" which detract from productivity. The meaningful decisions of an organization must still be made according to technical imperatives.

Scott and Hart condemn the line of thought pursued by management science. They find that it is still deeply rooted "within the dominant paradigm of scientific and management rationality." The view of the human actor in this paradigm is that of "administrative nihilism"—humans are seen as infinitely malleable by experts in the techniques of social adjustment. In the most brutal terms, the individual "is by nature nothing. And if he is nothing, he has the potential to be made into anything."[32] The "anything" to be created, of course, is a cog in the machine. There is nothing in modern management doctrine which would prevent managers from taking advantage of the frightening inventions in behavior control now available. Everything would seem to be justified if it meets organizational needs. As Perry London points out, the means of behavior control are based on "the notion that man is a machine."[33] If that is so, then these machinelike characteristics can be treated as any other part of the productive process. A Dostoyevsky screaming "For all that I am still a man" is then rather irrelevant. Such cries come from an inner sanctum which has not yet been breached by science, but that too shall be solved.

The threat, as I see it, is not that the individual will become a robot from which all inefficiencies have been clinically removed. I do not believe that human beings are as plastic as assumed by management science because the behavior-control devices are aimed at only one dimension of the whole person. What I do dread is the continued malaise of the worker in the large organization, a condition which cannot be cured by "more of the same." Management science can be redeemed only when, as Scott and Hart argue, there is a reconsideration of the metaphysical factors of what it is to be human. The philosophical problem is summed up in the concept of "alienation."

I do not refer to the sickly concept of alienation developed by industrial psychologists in studying why auto workers persist in sabotaging assembly lines. In the traditional sense, it is the violence done to the nature of humanity by a deliberate, but ultimately futile, attempt to create life on a single plane. In Fritz Pappenheim's rephrasing of the marxist concept, alienation occurs when the human mind "has become unable to approach the world in inner freedom and therefore cannot experience its fullness and richness."[34] As Erich Fromm characterized the unnatural separation of thought from feeling, "thinking deteriorates into schizoid intellectual activity, and feeling deteriorates into neurotic, life-damaging passions."[35] Only those who really get into necrophilia, the adoration of the morbid, can adjust to such a sterile world. But for the rest of us, the approximation of adjustment is, to use the saddest phrase I can think of, a waste of time. It is a waste of time because, tied up with the frustrations of everyday life, we are prevented from true speculation about our existence. It is a waste of time because it takes our minds off the fact that we are finite creatures with a tragically short time to accomplish anything humane. The alienation from ourselves can be cured only when we are able to live in a world which recognizes a concept of wholeness.

The second current in contemporary management thought purports to confront the problem of alienation. The advocates of what might be called "organizational humanism," such as Rensis Likert, Chris Argyris, Warren Bennis, Douglas McGregor, and Robert Golembiewski, are notable for their talk about "human dignity," "liberation," "authenticity," "self-actualization," "genuine relationships," "the reciprocal transfer of life energy," and other pleasant-sounding terms. Their view of human nature is similar to that of Jean-Jacques Rousseau. People are basically good, or in Rousseau's words, men are born free, free to realize their potential. Society is the evil force which distorts humanity's innate goodness. Just as the state prevents humans from living with others in a harmonious arrangement, so the bureaucratic organization prevents workers from realizing their natural urges to gain satisfaction from their work. The problem is the one which perplexed Rousseau: how to reconstitute the formal structure so that one can realize his or her potential for good.

In recent years, the major theoretician of organizational humanism has been Abraham Maslow. The starting point of most discussions is his "hierarchy of needs."[36] According to Maslow, humans are not motivated by the same thing at all times. Rather, there are levels of needs, and when one level is satisfied, the next level becomes important. The categories of needs begin with the physiological—those things needed to sustain life—and security needs. Higher needs are love and belongingness, self-esteem, and finally, self-actualization. In our affluent society, the lower needs have been met for most people, and our attention has turned to self-actualization. This need is vaguely defined, but it usually refers to the opportunities afforded individuals to develop themselves in their work, to grow and to perform as mature actors and not as a dependent means in the work process.

It is important to realize that, for all the importance attached to the hierarchy of needs, there is little hard evidence to substantiate its existence. Writers intoxicated by it admit as much and then proceed to construct their models of humanity as if it did exist. It all boils down to a matter of faith. In application, we come back to Rousseau: Benighted workers, long under the domination of tyrannical managers, must be forced to be free through self-actualization. It is in their very nature to want liberation, whether they know it or not. The enlightened manager will readily accept the change in attitude when it is realized, just as it was to have been realized under scientific management and human relations, that workers who have actualized themselves will also produce more. The humanists, that is, have not refrained from promoting the idea "that a relationship exists between work performance, variously identified and measured, and the satisfaction of certain human needs, again variously identified and measured."[37] None of the theorists want to tell management, "Look, why not leave people alone and let them enjoy themselves, even if we don't produce as much as before?" Instead, as Golembiewski argues, the organization must develop its people to serve both human values and organizational ends.[38] The message in essence is that through liberation, the worker will become a more reliable part of the system.

The first major weapon in the manufacture of self-actualization was the group-therapy technique known variously as T-group, laboratory, sensitivity, encounter, or human potential training. I do not wish to speculate on the effectiveness of these techniques for modifying individual behavior. I will grant that many people derive much satisfaction from participation in group sessions. The question is: What is the organization up to when it underwrites such experiences for its employees? Argyris says it is for the benefit of both the individual and the organization. People must rid themselves of the crusts they acquire; they must develop a sensitivity to the needs and aspirations of others. In the group situation, with no formal agenda, no armor provided by formal roles, and no authority, people are stripped of their defenses so they can see how their personality affects others. As a result, everyone in the organization appreciates more the humanity of others, and in the work situation there will be a greater chance that all members will join together in a more supportive situation.[39]

My suspicion that organizational humanism is only the latest version of the old managerial ideology is aroused by the fascination of managers with the comprehensive package of training known as organization development (OD). According to Bennis, OD is "a complex educational strategy intended to change the beliefs, attitudes, values and structures of organizations so that they can better adapt to new technologies, markets, and challenges, and the dizzying rate of change itself."[40] It is hard to say what that is supposed to mean, but the fact that organizations, both public and private, are adopting it at considerable expense leads me to believe that efficiency is the bottom line. Therefore, when an expert claims that the expenditures on OD are really signs of a liberated organization, it is touchingly naïve.[41] The payoff which managers have in mind is probably more substantial than the praise of fuzzy-minded theorists.

I do not see why OD should be regarded as anything more than a sophisticated form of technocratic conditioning. Frederick Thayer, certainly one of the least conventional of organization theorists, is correct when he states that "OD, despite the excitement surrounding it, remains open to the charge that it, too, seeks only to manipulate."[42] What else could one expect from a method designed and sold to "develop" the organization? I will feel better about it when the letters stand for "organization destruction" or, at least, "organization derationalization."

The ideological coloration of the humanist style of management is seen most clearly in the literature concerning "democratic participation" within organizations. Worker democracy is inevitably viewed as a means for increasing productivity and not as a way in which workers can effectively shape the overall organization. Stanley Herman notes the "student body government" flavor of various schemes which allow "subordinates the privilege of choosing between equally inconsequential alternatives within the framework of unimportant questions."[43]

The intrinsic absurdity of the claims that a new age is dawning can be seen in one of the more widely acclaimed attempts at worker participation—the Topeka, Kansas, plant of General Foods. According to the company's "manager of organization-development operations," in order to improve operations:

> . . . a style of management which encourages people to participate was adopted. When people feel they are really participating, they are more flexible, responsive to change—both internal and external. Teams establish and change work rules . . . recruit and select . . . have major influence in firing recommendations . . . participate in all important decisions, not just those considered "safe."[44]

But obviously the most "unsafe" decision for any polity is the one regarding ultimate purposes, and the end result of the happy activity is the production of dog food. In the grand end of making Gainesburgers, workers are to find meaning in life, to actualize their potential as members of the human race. When Senator Kennedy inquired whether the workers might indeed decide to get into some less frivolous line of production, the manager of organization-development operations indicated that such a possibility was inconceivable.

I reject the ideologies of management because they all are based upon the false premise that the organization and the individual can be united in such a way that conflict is avoided. The symbiosis of members offends my sense of individual worth, and I am also put off by pseudoscientific theories such as Maslow's which insist that we must submerge ourselves in our work. Most repugnant of all is when the unproved models of humanity are peddled to eager managers, with their particular needs for regularity. I do not fault the managers, for their function is to manage, to get the work of the organization done. However, I do find it unconscionable that the servants of power—the social scientists—have failed to provide equal protection for the subordinates.

MOTIVATION

I would hate to be thought a callous crank. But all I yearn for is a return to common sense as summed up in what Etzioni said of the organization dilemma: The divergence between the formal and informal elements can never be eliminated. Those areas of individual life which are protected by informality, that is, those factors beyond the calculations of management, are indispensable to our well-being. It is within those insulated areas that we can seek true self-actualization, which for me is defined by the self doing the actualizing and not by trained therapists. It may turn out that some of us prefer to get our stuff together with a jug of Ripple in the stockroom and not in a "group grope" with other members who, to tell the truth, are probably a rather unlikable bunch. The point is that the elusiveness of the worker is something to be regarded with reverence. I say that, all the while realizing that collective action requires uniformity of behavior. I do not feel my understanding is contradictory.

The call to "formalize the informal" in order to increase production is an illusory goal even though, as Sexton writes, "the majority of writers who have concerned themselves with an informal organization have concluded that there must be a fusion of the formal and informal organization."[45] That sort of thinking is contradictory and represents the very negation of the human spirit. How can one ever hope to harness the infinite forces of irrationality to the formal goals of the organization through formal means without first breaking the will of the members? There is something like Heisenberg's Uncertainty Principle in organizational matters. When observed for purposes of control, human behavior is no longer quite the same as before. The spontaneity so essential for the work of administration cannot be manufactured at will. The dead hand of bureaucracy can only squeeze out the lively elements through which the individual tries to find whatever satisfaction is obtainable in this far from perfect world.

The modern theories of management are so ethereal, so filled with the insubstantial jargon of a well-meaning but confused humanism, that one can best go directly to the real world of administration in order to see the pressures posed by the dilemma. There we need not be concerned with the "phenomenological administrators" or the executive fresh from postgraduate work at Esalen. We are interested only with the problem of the real managers, sore afraid and appalled by all the strange and threatening behavior of their subordinates. The most hopeful message they are likely to derive from the writings on management is the fact that something called "motivation" is critical. It is a specific function to which they must give adequate attention.

Now of course, only a sadist would argue against humane forms of motivation. Surely it is more pleasant to be seduced into cooperation than zinged by a cattle prod. But what does the logic of the rational organization do to that quite acceptable sentiment? One should try to remember, after imbibing the heady wine of the humanist, that one is not going to be paid as a roving ambassador of goodwill or the company Florence Nightingale. In Thompson's words, "Motivational functions are performed, impersonally, in an indirect and roundabout fashion, through many intermediate links. . . . They are performed through functionaries acting according to rules or instructions."[46] The organization has hired a clerk, not the Messiah, and that person will think and act like a clerk for as long as he or she wants to hold the position.

Managers understand that motivation will be a crucial determinant of production. They know that morale, if defined as a state of mind predisposing the worker toward the accomplishment of goals, is the only thing which can get the organization over the inevitable rough terrain. But if morale is all that important—if it is in fact the only thing determining the eventual effectiveness of the organization—can it be left to chance? Can the manager find peace of mind in the hope that this vital function will occur automatically through the unobserved actions of the several employees?

The logic of the division of labor will come into play. The manager has a host of other things to attend to and cannot afford to play psychologist for several hundred or thousand employees. The thing to do is to delegate the motivational function to a hapless staff specialist, who is charged with the responsibility for the survival of the organization. That person's survival in turn will depend upon the goodwill of the individual employees, and that cannot be a happy prospect since each employee is the bearer of a distinct strain of germs causing bad will. With limited time and money, how does this Vice President in Charge of Tender, Loving Care respond to the variety of individual demands? Naturally, the solution is to bureaucratize the job.

I am saying that in the function of motivating, one must fall back on something which can itself be administered. But through the very act of administration, one is unlikely to touch upon the true sources of good morale. It may end up alienating the employee. We would like to have our bosses think well of us because we are intrinsically worthy of respect and not because they learned from Dale Carnegie that it would improve our disposition to be told sweet little nothings. Take for example the practice of "stroking." We are told by a Ph.D. in psychology that it is an extremely useful device which "often leads to a happier individual and to higher production in the long run."[47] Even though the author insists that the verbal stroke must be sincere, how many of us can believe in sincerity when we saw the use of stroking in the Nixon administration as a step preparatory to letting the poor strokee twist slowly, slowly in the wind?

The inevitable folly of the administration of motivation was best described by Robert Frost in his poem on the funeral practices of ants: "It couldn't be called ungentle, but how thoroughly departmental."[48] The attempts to formalize the informal stink of departmentalization, of the heavy-handed touch of administration. As long as individuals retain their good sense and ability to calculate their own self-interest, the attempts are bound to fail. Unless, that is, individuals are made so insensitive to the human condition that they can in fact be deluded into believing that their motivation is a fit subject for some anonymous clerk.

That possibility, I conclude, is the real danger of the management ideologies. Motivation cannot be administered unless the ultimate organization person is produced, conditioned to respond to a manageable number of stimuli. When that time arrives, it will be true, as Adorno wrote, "that men resign themselves to loving what they have to do, without being aware that they are resigned."[49] All models of behavior, from the economic calculator of scientific management to the self-actualizer of organization humanism, pose the same threat to the options of the individual. We may become programmed to believe that what they offer is what we want. When any one of the models becomes dominant, as models are likely to do because of their endorsement by a supposedly scientific approach to human behavior, we will have bought the farm, will have lost our right to determine for ourselves what it means to be a human. Worse, we will be even more under the control of a mindless technology and incapable of surprising our masters.

POWER, AUTHORITY, AND ALL THAT

The subject of power summarizes what administration is all about. We get to the vital juices of management—getting other people to do something. More than most human relationships, organization behavior is determined by the efforts of one person to modify the actions of another. Because of the centrality of the subject, there is not a great deal I can add. Each generation seems to rediscover that fact of power and to learn to adjust to it, as is indicated by the current popularity of "assertiveness training" and the huge success of books by bush-league Machiavellis such as Robert Ringer and Michael Korda. Making sense of the literature on power, derived from philosophy, political science, sociology, psychology, fiction, and the Sunday supplements, is a difficult job; and I agree with Cartwright that the first concern must be to "keep from getting lost among masses of discrete data and interminable theoretical distinctions, especially since the natives appear to have no common language."[50]

I will simplify my approach to power by taking a normative stance and arguing that everyone has the right to participate in an organization's power struggle. Although it may seem odd to the reader who has progressed this far, I will side with Herbert Simon and the other hard-core management scientists. In an informative debate, Simon and Chris Argyris took different sides on the "rational man issue." Simon said that a science of management could advance based on an image of individual rationality controllable by the formal organization. Argyris came out in favor of making an a priori statement about the nature of humanity and building the organization around the model.[51] Although both probably expect far too much from their theories, I prefer the Simonized version. Management science is very candid; it informs anyone with a lick of sense that "We gonna git you!" Argyris and the other organization humanists accept a model that is inevitably totalitarian, with the emphasis on a compulsory human redemption through submission to the social engineers. I do not relish being confronted with the wild-eyed converts to truth and love who are determined to force me to be free; instead I prefer the impersonal management scientists who know deep down inside that they will never convert me, but only control my behavior. That approach opens up an area of maneuver for the individual.

POWER IN ORGANIZATIONS

Different writers use different terminology, and so I will take the liberty of establishing my own. Power I will call the ability, whether conscious or unconscious, of one person to modify the behavior of another. As such, it is something which we all indulge in every day, either modifying or being modified. Any collection of people will establish certain rules about the use and distribution of power. That is, normative elements naturally adhere to power. The tax collector, the priest, the thief, and the spouse all tell an individual, "Hand over your money!" But there will be wide differences in the reaction of the subject of power to each of these instances. The reactions will depend largely upon the social conventions accepted in the culture.

A formal organization must ensure that the power is arranged in a specific manner so that all activity can be directed toward its goals. Even if it were possible, not everyone in the organization can be allowed to have the same amount of power over everyone else. Therefore, the organization manufactures a type of power which I will call "authority." This is the power which accrues to individuals because of their occupation of a formal position. Indeed, the organization structure is nothing more than a statement of power relationships, all arranged in such a way that maximum effort will be directed toward formal goals. According to the formal regulations, one individual has a right to use power and another has the duty to obey.

For a long time, authority was the essence of organization theory. The hierarchy was to be constructed as a finely tuned system of graded authority, with each individual having the proper amount of power necessary for the accomplishment of his or her assignment. The old principle had it that "authority must be commensurate with responsibility." Because one person was vested with authority, it was assumed that subordinates would perform exactly as required in order to meet rational objectives. Two things shattered this simplistic notion of power.

First, we now know much more about the informal processes within the organization. Countless studies since the Bank Wiring Room experiment have shown the ability of the informal structure to defy formal authority. Workers naturally band together and develop a consensus about what is right and wrong, independent of the orders from management. It is not only the small group which has an impact here. A clerk with candid photos of the boss at the Christmas party may have as much power as his formal superior. A host of accidental features makes a mockery of the most carefully designed hierarchy.

Second and far more important, we have derived from Simon a greater appreciation of the complexity of the decision-making process at lower levels of the organization. We see now that a formal chain of command is a convenient myth as more and more premises for decisions are being supplied by staff experts. The personnel officer says that clerk-typists should earn $2.88 an hour because of the law and the salary survey. When that is implemented, who actually exercised power? Persons in authority are helpless to resist the pressures from the staff specialist and insofar as their function has been divided completely among their staff, they are mere figureheads who might well be replaced by a signature stamp.

The most important contribution of decision theory was to make us realize that the subordinate has to make a decision about compliance with formal authority. It can no longer be assumed by any intelligent manager that there is some Iron Law which holds that people obey simply because the organization chart says that they ought to. The individual is still a free agent who can calculate about "what's in it for me" in the very act of deciding to obey. As Simon puts it, "the individual sets for himself a general rule which permits the communicated decision of another to guide his choices without deliberation on his own part on the expediency of those premises." Further, according to Simon, authority is effective when "a subordinate holds in abeyance his own critical faculties for choosing between alternatives and uses the formal criterion of the receipt of command or signal as his basis for choice."[52] The butchers of My Lai, to put the kindest possible face on it, "held in abeyance their critical abilities" and proceeded to follow formal commands.

This feature of the power problem within organizations can be called the "acceptance theory" of authority. Chester Barnard was the first to bring it to the attention of managers. He wrote of the "zone of indifference." A certain class of orders will be acceptable to subordinates who "are relatively indifferent as to what the order is so far as the question of authority is concerned."[53] Simon describes the feature more positively as the "zone of acceptance."[54] If authority goes beyond the boundary drawn in the mind of the subordinate, disobedience will occur. Within the zone, the worker is saying, in effect, "You're the boss," or "I'll play your silly game."

Both Barnard and Simon maintain that an important job of management is the expansion of the zone through positive or negative sanctions, i.e., rewards or punishments. As Barnard wrote, "the zone of indifference will be wider or narrower depending upon the degree to which the inducements exceed the burdens and sacrifices which determine the individual's adhesion to the organization."[55] That simply means that the managers must make believers out of their subordinates. The job is not so easy since there are always troublemakers who would rather fight than switch. In the extreme case, we have the military where there is often no sanction equal to the order ("Charge up that hill into certain death or spend five years at Leavenworth" is not a real choice). Civilian managers must spend a good deal of time wondering what it is that will gain the compliance of their subordinates.

THE CONDITIONS OF OBEDIENCE

But not nearly enough time is spent on the question of obedience, and, in view of the terrible crimes which organizations can commit, it is not as problematic as it should be. There has been much written about the fearful tools of manipulation now available to management but, sad to say, modern managers do not really need to be so clever since the odds are already on their side. The most insidious means for the implementation of organization power is the force I have been flailing away at throughout the book: the power of ideas which make legitimate people's behavior. There are probably many managers who can repeat the boast of Albert Speer, Hitler's superbureaucrat, that "I exploited the phenomenon of the technician's often blind devotion to his task."[56] There would be some redeeming quality in that course if in fact managers were aware that they were "exploiting" one perception among many. I doubt, however, that managers themselves are conscious of alternatives to obedience to technique.

That the moral indifference of technology can have startling results is borne out by Stanley Milgram's experiments in obedience to authority. In the laboratory setting, he found that a large number of people would inflict pain on their fellows simply because they have been told to do so by technicians who look like they know what they are doing. We have made it depressingly simple for people to assume what Milgram calls the "agentic state"—the condition people are in when they see themselves as agents for carrying out another person's wishes.[57] In that state, as the instrument of a disembodied science, a normally moral person can assist in the perpetration of moral outrages. The phenomenon is most alarming when a entire operation takes place without the conscious effort of any specific "manipulator" or "exploiter." It is all a matter of doing what comes naturally, as defined by the laws of science.

That is the sobering truth behind Simon's identification of indoctrination as a source of managerial control. The nervous systems of workers have been injected with so much "rationality" that they cannot respond to the total problem. Their critical abilities have atrophied so that they are in a permanent condition of abeyance. The rational discipline of the bureaucracy is freely embraced because, in our society, there is no legitimate alternative. The discipline which holds the organization together and eliminates the possibility of the individual perceiving the real sources of power is the product of the entire educational system.

Our growing awareness of this fact accounts for the critique of American education, from kindergarten through graduate school, as a machine for the processing of bureaucratic fodder and not as preparation for inquisitive reasoning. The graduate is certified as being properly docile upon the completion of the standard academic rigamarole. Yet the criticism is not new. Years ago, Lewis Mumford noted that the disciplinary base of technical education and the educational methods for factory workers of 1832—"silence, absence of motion, complete passivity, response only upon application of an outer stimulus, rote learning, verbal parroting, piece-work acquisition of knowledge"—were then as now the style of behavior needed by bureaucracy.[58]

According to Chang, the remarkable stability of the Chinese bureaucracy was based upon a similar system. The allegiance of the intelligentsia was ensured through an elaborate training and examination process which eliminated everything but the bureaucratic reality. One can understand why an emperor could exclaim, "The heroes of the world have fallen within the range of my arrow shot." As Chang comments, "He knew well that through the examination system he had brought under control the free-ranging thought of the leading social group."[59] It sounds awfully familiar.

Ivan Illich, an outspoken critic of a society where "people have been schooled down to size" so that they fit in the bureaucracy, argues that "everywhere the hidden curriculum of schooling initiates the citizen to the myth that bureaucracies guided by scientific knowledge are efficient and benevolent."[60] The programming of the individual, whether as client or member of the organization, is the greatest source of organizational power, all the more effective because it is impalpable. It rules out options; it forecloses on disobedience because obedience is the only rational act for the individual. The only antidote for such calcification of the mind is the reconstitution of the critical abilities of the individual so that there will be less chance of reneging on humanity in those situations where a broader rationality is appropriate. The simple act of thinking is the most revolutionary one an organization member can perform.

SUMMING UP

I have not even scratched the surface of the intriguing topic of power. I have only tried to suggest that it is not a foregone conclusion that the individual will always comply with the formal power arrangements. My hope is that the individuals will play the power game as vigorously as the managers, that they will not forget their perceptions as independent actors in a complicated network of cognitive, motivational, and social structures. I do not presume that there is any equality of power within organizations; power is naturally congruent with the hierarchy. But it must be stressed that the little people do have their share of power.[61]

Members must be encouraged to calculate for their own interest in terms of their view of the world and of what is desirable in that world. Management science is devoted to finding out what the individual's strategy is. And the strategy revealed is no strategy at all. If the enemy is coming through the pass, we can ambush them; managers are in the nature of bushwhackers, trying to find out what each person is up to and formulating an incentive to deflect worker strategies in the right direction. The humanist alternative is to start with a concept of what motivates people and to force the individuals into a single mold. Rather than fighting battles on countless fronts, management can state by fiat that this is what people want and it is what we are offering.

I will stick with the calculative style of the management scientists, as long as it is recognized that workers as well as managers can calculate, rather than buy into the totalitarian ideal of the depoliticized organization suggested by the humanists. It is hard to come out against something called "humanism," but if we regard the organization as a polity it does not seem the sort of thing we need. Politics requires a space between people, whereas the "understanding" of the humanists destroys that space. The bond between citizens is fundamentally different from the bond between lovers or members of a family. If we are to maintain a meaningful degree of freedom within an organization, we must keep a clear head (already no easy task in light of the education we receive). The suffocating atmosphere of the humanists, even when free of the manipulative designs of the managers, does not really provide room for the individuals to live their own life. If people do not have some space, they are not free. And just as importantly, they cannot be held responsible.

REFERENCES

1 Anthony Sampson, *The Sovereign State of ITT* (New York: Fawcett Crest, 1974), p. 70.

2 Harlan Cleveland, "A Philosophy for the Public Executive," in Edmund Falker (ed.), *The Influences of Social, Scientific, and Economic Trends on Government Administration* (Washington: U.S. Department of Agriculture, 1960), p. 7.

3 Stephen Vincent Benet, *John Brown's Body* (New York, Rinehart, 1927), p. 82.

4 Herbert Simon, *Administrative Behavior* (New York: Macmillan, 1960), pp. 102–103.

5 Fyodor Dostoyevsky, *Notes from Underground* (New York: Signet Books, 1961), p. 115.

6 Loren Baritz, *The Servants of Power* (New York: Wiley, 1965), p. 197.

7 Harlow Person, "The New Attitude toward Management," in Person (ed.), *Scientific Management in American Industry* (New York: Harper, 1929), p. 28.

8 Mary Parker Follett, "Constructive Conflict," in Henry Metcalf and L. Urwick (eds.), *Dynamic Administration* (New York: Harper, 1924), p. 58.

9 Peter Drucker, *The Age of Discontinuity* (New York: Harper & Row, 1969), p. 290.

10 Abraham Maslow, *Eupsychian Management* (Homewood, Ill.: Irwin, 1965), p. 10.

11 Alfred de Grazia, "The Science and Values of Administration," *Administrative Science Quarterly,* 5 (1960), p. 568.

12 Chris Argyris, "Some Limits of Rational Man Organizational Theory," *Public Administration Review,* 33 (1973), p. 258.

13 A popularized version of the idea is provided by Anthony Jay, *Managment and Machiavelli* (New York: Holt, 1967).

14 Herbert Kaufman, "The Direction of Organizational Evolution," *Public Administration Review,* 33 (1973), p. 307.

15 Reinhard Bendix, *Work and Authority in Industry* (New York: Harper & Row, 1963), p. xi.

16 Sherman Krupp, *Pattern in Organization Analysis* (New York: Holt, 1961), p. 184.

17 Frederic Fleron and Lou Jean Fleron, "Administration Theory as Repressive Political Theory: The Communist Experience," *Newsletter on Comparative Studies of Communism,* 6 (1972), p. 5.

18 Victor Thompson, "Organizations as Systems," *University Programs Modular Studies* (Morristown, N.J.: General Learning Press, 1973), p. 4.

19 Frederick Taylor, *The Principles of Scientific Management* (New York: Norton, 1967), p. 59.

20 William Scott and David Hart, "The Moral Nature of Man in Organizations: A Comparative Analysis," *Academy of Management Journal,* 14 (1971), pp. 242–246.

21 Person, op cit., p. 31.

22 L. P. Alford, *Henry Lawrence Gantt* (New York: American Society of Mechanical Engineers, 1934), p. 196.

23 Samuel Haber, *Efficiency and Uplift* (Chicago: University of Chicago Press, 1964), p. 48.

24 Robert Peabody, *Organizational Authority* (New York: Atherton, 1964), p. 18.

25 Henry Mayo, *An Introduction to Democratic Theory* (New York: Oxford University Press, 1960), p. 231.

26 F. J. Roethlisberger and William Dickson, *Management and the Worker* (Cambridge, Mass.: Harvard University Press, 1939).

27 Some claim that the results did not conform to the new theory either. See Alex Carey, "The Hawthorne Studies: A Radical Critique," *American Sociological Review,* 32 (1967), pp. 403–416; and H. M. Parsons, "What Happened at Hawthorne?" *Science,* 183 (Mar. 8, 1974), pp. 922–932.

28 William Scott, "Organization Government: The Prospects for a Truly Participative System," *Public Administration Review,* 29 (1969), p. 44.

29 Lewis Coser, "Introduction," in Daniel Bell, *Work and Its Discontents* (New York: League for Industrial Democracy, 1970).

30 Jacques Ellul, *The Technological Society* (New York: Knopf, 1964), p. 356.

31 William Whyte, *The Organization Man* (Garden City, N.Y.: Doubleday, 1956), p. 7.

32 William Scott and David Hart, "Administrative Crisis: The Neglect of Metaphysical Speculation," *Public Administration Review,* 33 (1973), p. 419.

33 Perry London, *Behavior Control* (New York: Harper & Row, 1969), p. 184.

34 Fritz Pappenheim, *The Alienation of Modern Man* (New York: Monthly Review Press, 1959), p. 86.

35 Erich Fromm, *The Revolution of Hope* (New York: Harper & Row, 1968), p. 42.

36 Abraham Maslow, *Motivation and Personality* (New York: Harper & Row, 1954).

37 Frank Gibson and Clyde Teasley, "The Humanistic Model of Organizational Motivation: A Review of Research Support," *Public Administration Review,* 33 (1973), p. 90.

38 Robert Golembiewski, *Men, Management, and Morality* (New York: McGraw-Hill, 1965), p. 23.

39 Chris Argyris, "T-Groups for Organizational Effectiveness," *Harvard Business Review,* 42 (1964), pp. 60–74.

40 Warren Bennis, *Organization Development* (Reading, Mass.: Addison-Wesley, 1969), p. 2.

41 Malcolm Knowles, "Human Resources Development in OD," *Public Administration Review,* 34 (1974), p. 119.

42 Frederick Thayer, *An End to Hierarchy! And End to Competition!* (New York: New Viewpoints, 1973), p. 26.
43 Stanley Herman, *The People Specialists* (New York: Knopf, 1968), p. 251.
44 U.S. Senate, Subcommittee on Employment, Manpower, and Poverty, *Worker Alienation, 1972* (Washington: GPO, 1972), p. 101.
45 William Sexton, *Organization Theories* (Columbus, Ohio: Charles E. Merrill, 1970), p. 189.
46 Thompson, op. cit., p. 6.
47 Thomas Clary, "Motivation through Positive Stroking," *Public Personnel Management,* 2 (1973), p. 113.
48 Robert Frost, "Departmental," *Complete Poems of Robert Frost* (New York: Holt, 1949), pp. 272–273.
49 Theodor Adorno, *Prisms* (London: Neville Spearman, 1967), p. 100.
50 Dorwin Cartwright, "Influence, Leadership, Control," in James March (ed.), *Handbook of Organizations* (Chicago: Rand McNally, 1965), p. 4.
51 Herbert Simon, "Organizational Man: Rational or Self-actualizing?" and Chris Argyris, "Organizational Man: Rational *and* Self-actualizing," *Public Administration Review,* 33 (1973), pp. 346–357.
52 Simon, *Administrative Behavior,* pp. 126–127.
53 Chester Barnard, *The Functions of the Executive* (Cambridge, Mass.: Harvard University Press, 1960), p. 168.
54 Simon, *Administrative Behavior,* p. 12.
55 Barnard, op. cit., p. 169.
56 Albert Speer, *Inside the Third Reich* (New York: Avon, 1971), p. 283.
57 Stanley Milgram, *Obedience to Authority* (New York: Harper & Row, 1974), p. 133.
58 Lewis Mumford, *Technics and Civilization* (New York: Harcourt, Brace, 1934), p. 176.
59 Chung-Li Chang, *The Chinese Gentry* (Seattle: University of Washington Press, 1955), p. 198.
60 Ivan Illich, *Deschooling Society* (New York: Harrow Books, 1972), p. 106.
61 See Michel Crozier, *The Bureaucratic Phenomenon* (Chicago: University of Chicago Press, 1964), chap. 6.

Chapter 10

Public Personnel Administration

The trouble with personnel experts is that they use gimmicks borrowed from manufacturing: inventories, replacement charts, recruiting, selecting, indoctrinating, and training machinery, job rotation, and appraisal programs. And this manufacturing of men is about as effective as Dr. Frankenstein was.

Robert Townsend
Up the Organization

We have now surveyed most of the terrain of the administrative state and in every instance have come to some gloomy conclusions about the prospects for the individual, as a person and as a citizen. By this time, the optimist may wish to fall back on one last hope: These dreaded bureaucrats are, after all, people just like us. That hope, I regret, is misplaced because bureaucrats are not people; they are *personnel* and thus have surrendered some of their claims to humanity.

The word "personnel" has a harsh, metallic ring to it. Apparently it entered our language from French military usage as the counterpart of "materiel"; a military machine was constructed out of so many units of personnel, so many units of materiel. Current terms such as "manpower management" or "human resources development" are not great improvements. They still tend to disguise the fact that the managers are dealing with human beings. But this view of workers as disembodied inputs is a natural consequence of bureaucratization, for today the human animal, with all those whims, passions, and idiosyncrasies, is dysfunctional. Personnel administration has become the procurer for a variety of organizations—business, government, education, and private associations. Its aim is to tool the human component so it will fit into the system, to wrap a precise amount of "manpower" in cellophane for eventual consumption by the organization. Put another way, it is a process of turning something so vital and unique as a "personality" into something so bland as "personnel."

Personnel administration is one more cause of our present discontent; and if our civilization is to regain a more balanced condition, it has to be changed. As the "Port Huron Statement" of the Students for a Democratic Society (SDS) rightly said, our sense of estrangement and isolation "cannot be overcome by better personnel management" but rather by the establishment of a society in which people are not managed as personnel.[1] The radicals of the 1960s were wrong, however, to call for a violent confrontation with this system, for the personnel process is almost immune to revolution. Open resistance can be labeled maladjustment and, in many ways, personnel administration is little more than a set of techniques for neutralizing the maladjusted. But it can do little about the person who, deep down inside, is not a true believer in the empty purposes of personnel procedures.

Personnel administration, particularly in the public sphere, has never been a progressive field. There are probably still many civil service commissions where the cry is, "If it was good enough for Grover Cleveland, it's good enough for us!" But if enough intelligent people within the organization ask questions about the operation, perhaps the atmosphere of complacency will evaporate. There is one question which, if asked early and often, would topple the edifice of functional rationality now supporting personnel administrators: What is the purpose of all this efficiency and predictability? If the personnel specialists can only reply "Who knows?" or "Who cares?" or "That's the way Grover would have wanted it," then it would seem that they have lost any justification for interfering so heavily in our lives. If we begin asking questions, perhaps the word will seep through to personnel administrators, and they may begin to redeem themselves. They must if we are to survive.

THE PERSONNEL PROCESS

Personnel administration has come to include a variety of separate techniques, all held together by the single goal of efficiency. Even Charles Milton, in his not-so-critical "critical history of personnel philosophy" comes to the conclusion that, through personnel administration, humanity's highest ethical aspirations are nothing more than calculable items in the efficient management of "industry's human assets."[2] European students have been less taken in by the glittering goals which justify the personnel expert's work. Back in 1938, Zoltan Magyary, a Hungarian observer of the industrial state, remarked on the American invention of a "personnel program," the goal of whose principles and measures was the scientific attainment of both "individual efficiency" and "operating efficiency."[3] Later the Frenchman, Georges Langrod, pointed to personnel as the area in which "the most spectacular efforts towards rationalization are being made."[4] Rationalization, of course, is understood as the progressive integration of the individual into the organization.

In American public administration, the techniques of personnel administration are dressed up in terms of "merit." An item from a manual published by the Ohio Department of State Personnel will give an idea of what is meant by merit:

> The idea of a merit system is closely related to the principle of a democratic form of government. This basic idea is that the selection, placement, advancement, and retention of employes should be based entirely on individual merit. A citizen's personal beliefs, ancestry, or group membership should not be considered. The requirements of the merit system are fulfilled if the actual practices of hiring and promotion are based on the measured ability and performance of applicants and employes.

The article of faith that merit exists in measurable form and that personnel administration is merely the business of ensuring through scientific means that a worker's position within the organization depends upon the possession of a certain amount of merit still colors the operation of the civil service. The distinct steps in personnel administration must be seen as efforts at promoting merit, with that word defined as relating to the efficient functioning of the organization:

1 *Recruitment.* Some governments still perform the traditional function of discouraging anyone from entering government on the assumption that the applicant is likely to be the crony of some corrupt politician. Most, however, are committed to the positive enticement of qualified people into working for government. A major controversy has arisen here in the form of "equal opportunity" and "affirmative action" programs which resulted from claims by minorities and women that they had been systematically excluded from meaningful government employment. The issue is still unresolved, as is indicated by the hair-splitting arguments about the difference between "quotas," which are bad, and "goals," which are good.

2 *Examination.* This is the heart of the merit idea, and it also presents the stickiest problems. Does merit exist in measurable form and if so, can one go to any length to measure it? Again, the groups which have been excluded from participation in government employment argue that whatever civil service exams measure, it is not merit. Other critics claim that the public service is full of people whose only skill is taking exams or otherwise putting together an impressive set of credentials.

3 *Appointment.* Actually landing a government job is complicated by a number of legal requirements concerning appointments. This is another legacy from the era in which it was assumed that any official, if given half a chance, would open the doors to all sorts of unqualified political appointees.

4 *Promotion.* Promotion can be viewed as another way of filling a vacant position. Public personnel administration remains oblivious to the fact that promotion is the center of the basic power struggle within the organization, and instead it cheerfully insists that promotion can be done according to objective standards. This leads to, among other things, the principle described by Professor Peter: People are promoted because of what they *were* good at and go on to demonstrate their incompetence at higher levels.[5]

5 *Pay administration.* Personnel people strive to regularize the pay structure so that everyone doing the same job is receiving the same compensation. The structure may make more inflexible the methods by which good employees are rewarded.

6 *Position-classification.* The American way has been to break each mission down into its smallest components and find the individual to fill that single position. Our government employees are recruited because of an ability to do a specific job, and there has been little thought given to the effect of this encapsulation on the individual or the organization. Short-range efficiency has always been more important than the broader considerations.

7 *Training.* A major new area of personnel administration stems from the realization that many people are obsolete almost before they finish their formal education. A number of training programs have been instituted to enhance the value of the individual to the organization.

8 *Motivation.* In many organizations, the function of stimulating morale has been assigned to personnel. As we have seen, this leads to the unimaginative utilization of techniques designed to turn the worker into a more productive member.

9 *Evaluation.* If we are to retain and promote the meritorious, how do we identify them after they have entered the service? This is particularly difficult in government where the measurement of output is often impossible. But impossibility has not deterred personnel administrators from setting up a variety of forms and tests for evaluation, many of which have a distortive effect on employee performance.

10 *Conditions of work.* Aside from the motivational factors, such things as lighting, heating, workplace arrangements, and vacation policies will affect worker behavior. These things are under constant examination to identify the optimal level.

11 *Labor relations.* We will look at this latest addition to the personnel manager's job in more detail. From the very beginning, however, the unions have been viewed as the major threat to the future of the merit concept.

12 *Separation.* Contrary to popular belief, it is not impossible to fire a public employee, and they do die or retire. When a firing does occur, most jurisdictions demand that certain protections for the employee be exercised.

13 *Retirement.* This is the preferred way of getting rid of people—the old-timer who has devoted an entire life to the organization is gently put out to pasture. In an age characterized by a craving for security, the retirement system and the pension plan are often major inducements to join an organization.

From this survey of personnel administration, we can see that the work goes from portal to portal.[6] All contingencies in the working life of the employee should be taken into account so that efficient performance can be ensured. In each of the above-mentioned areas, personnel specialists have developed their tried-and-true techniques, so that their work is seldom a matter of high adventure or exciting ideas.

In fact, in its present form, personnel administration resembles a branch of animal husbandry. Whether dealing with cows or with people, the veterinarians will try to keep the beasts contented and productive. To provide a point for our increasingly pointless lives, they will convince us to accept the joys of the company bowling team or the agency picnic. Those maladjusted souls who refuse to fit into the new regimen can be shunted off into some sort of reservation such as making sandals or teaching in college.

As an alternative to this drab future, I suggest that personnel administrators might form the core of a new secular priesthood. They could become a selfless profession dedicated to the service of the inhabitants of the big organization—part nurse, part psychiatrist, part ombudsman, part fellow pilgrim. Most of all, they would be on "our side." There can be no doubt now about whose side the personnel apparatus is on; it is a wholly management-oriented proposition. From this orientation arises the critical difference between what Paul Goodman called "people or personnel."[7] As personnel, we are means for the accomplishment of organizational goals; as people, we must be taken as ends in our own right.

If and when such a reorientation occurs, personnel administrators can relax some of their dependence upon the creed of efficiency; they can concern themselves with the true welfare of the people involved. This does not seem such an outlandish proposal. It can be made simply in the name of common decency. Elting Morison, a leading historian of technology, felt that a central failure of our society is the way in which people are expected to perform within organizations; he suggested that we might arrange our organizations "so that men could take larger satisfaction, give fuller expression to themselves—even have fun—at making things with machinery, even if they made a few less things in slightly more time, at a little greater cost in money."[8]

"Even have fun!" What a strange phrase to use in connection with that large part of our lives we will spend at work. Personnel administrators, of course, have become adept at using the jargon of "job enrichment," "worker satisfaction," and "self-actualization," but only as a means for increasing production. One wonders if they could ever bring themselves to tolerate something so human, and therefore so unpredictable as "having fun." Certainly any relaxation, as Morison noted, would cost more, but who is to say the cost would be excessive? At the present time we are placing price tags on remedial action against external evidence of organizational pollution; perhaps it is just as urgent that we do something about the internal pollution of the hearts and minds of employees.

I do not advocate the demolition of the personnel process. The big organization is here to stay, and the personnel system is necessary if anything is to be accomplished. I am only criticizing the way in which essential practices have been pushed to self-defeating, sometimes nearly criminal, extremes, in a mindless search for greater efficiency. The emphasis must shift from "What can we do *to* people?" to "What can we do *for* people?" If that could be achieved, the personnel function might be salvaged as an important element in our complex organizational society.

A PERSPECTIVE ON PERSONNEL

So much for the diatribe. My point is that personnel administration, as now practiced, is not congenial to human nature. This is not to say that personnel experts are the cause of all the errors of the age; at the same time, it is not enough to suggest that these experts should be a little nicer. In order to be more specific, I will concentrate on two particularly potent sources of the modern feeling of angst.

First, there is what we can call the organized rat race. Are people satisfied with their present or prospective lot in the big organization? Anyone who has talked to college students will admit that the answer is an emphatic "No!" No student has ever expressed a deep sense of satisfaction about becoming a bureaucrat, despite the fact that there are fewer and fewer alternatives. The learned sociologist will tell us that work has become an alien part of our existence; the less sophisticated can rightly call work the curse of the drinking class. We abhor the idea of becoming preconditioned, prepackaged units for the use of the organization, although we know we are helpless from becoming so. We resign ourselves to our burden by gritting our teeth and picking up the material benefits which make the whole thing palatable; work, strain, and tolerate an oafish superior so you can buy a camper in order to find, with everyone else, a little respite over the weekends.

Second, there is the deep concern among all elements of society that democracy does not work as it should. There is an awareness that, as far as government action is concerned, the average citizen is out of the picture. We go through the democratic motions periodically, but there is still that suspicion that government is beyond the control of elected representatives. It is not a happy thought, considering the power government has for creating hell on earth.

Personnel administration has done quite a bit to make these unpleasant aspects of modern life come about. Individuality and democracy cannot be integrated with the modern personnel system, for in its perfected form there is no room for disagreement. The personnel system is concerned with the creation of interchangeable units of rational behavior. The individual and the politician represent the forces of irrationality and must be resisted. So American personnel administration has promoted intense specialization and bureaucratization as guards against the raw forces of life. Those two factors have done much to deflate our sense of individual competence and of democratic control of government. We will concentrate in the remainder of this chapter on the political impact of the public personnel administration process.

BUREAUCRACY AND DEMOCRACY

What is proper behavior for the personnel of a democracy? As I have been arguing, the distinguishing feature of democracy is the popular control of government decision makers. If a majority of voters do not like the decisions and the consequent acts of their governors, they can remove the officials and replace them with others. The great weakness of modern democracy is instantly revealed when we identify who are government decision makers. The fact is that almost everyone in government makes policy, at least if we define policy as the product of a nonroutine decision about the allocation of resources. This includes the decisions made by administrators and, for most of us, these are probably the most important ones. The activity of the President and Congress may make the headlines, but ordinary citizens are affected by more mundane actions. Will the highway department put the freeway through my backyard? Will the postmaster confiscate my plain, unmarked envelope from Denmark? Will the police officer arrest me for loitering when I am taking a nap in the park? Will the IRS agent question my contributions to the Powerhouse Church of What's Happening Now? In sum, every government employee, to the degree that the job is not purely routine, has the potential for acting like a governor. What does that mean for democracy? Obviously, we cannot elect the almost 15 million public employees in the United States.

The working fiction which preserves the peace of mind of Americans today seems to be that the elected politicians and their appointed administrators (or "team") will be able to move in at the top and assume control of the total operation. The fiction is becoming less believable, first, because the whole thrust of the civil service movement has been to reduce the size of the appointed team and, second, because the underlings in this arrangement are not infinitely malleable. They are bureaucrats and their very being resists the fluctuations of popular opinion. The question is then whether it is possible to find government employees who are professionally competent as well as responsive to political leadership.

Over 125 years ago, Honoré Balzac described the French bureaucrats:

> At sight of their strange faces, it is hard to decide whether these quill-bearing mammals became cretinous at their work, or whether, on the other hand, they would never have undertaken it if they had not been, to some extent, cretins from birth. Perhaps Nature and Government may divide the responsibility between them.[9]

To the extent that civil servants become "cretinous at their work," public personnel administration deserves censure. At the same time, one cannot say that the elimination of the personnel office would solve the bureaucracy problem since the two are really inseparable. In fact, one could take the elements of Weberian bureaucracy and refine them into chapters for a modern personnel manual. The division of labor into precise jurisdictions, the emphasis upon training, the concept of a career based on achieved merit are all instruments of the rationalization of work.

Have then the various techniques of personnel administration created a specialist-dominated bureaucracy which is impervious to outside control? It has happened elsewhere. The higher civil service in France—the so-called technocracy—has become a distinct class, and the elements of class consciousness are functions of the personnel system. Members are recruited from a common social background, receive a common training at prestigious institutions, and are organized into corps to produce a sense of exclusiveness. The result of the class mentality is a feeling of superiority over the political bunglers. A radically different style of personnel administration would undermine the sources of strength for the technocracy.[10]

The United States civil service is not so rigidly structured, but the personnel system has aimed at coupling the arrogance of high learning with the arrogance of high office. Job descriptions are narrowly fitted to a unique type; entrance requirements eliminate those without the right credentials; even the selection of very high officials is sometimes done according to test scores. All these practices tend to keep out the "intruders" from other fields of knowledge. Worst of all for democracy, personnel people have worked too eagerly to reserve parts of government for specific professions, leading in many cases to the marriage of public and private bureaucracies, both of which are beyond popular control.[11]

In addition to the substantive results of certain personnel practices, a civil service system may frustrate the politicians who are anxious for an energetic attack on society's problems just by its very complexity. Even if they did not face the raw power of the organized public employees, the political leaders who would try to rescue New York City from its ongoing crises would dissipate their strength in futile struggles with civil servants adept at using the personnel code for a defense of the status quo.[12] And it has not been too long since John Fischer issued his famous plea for a return to the spoils system. After his service in Washington during World War II, he concluded that we won the war in spite of the U.S. Civil Service Commission.[13] The recent investigation of the "Spoiled System" by the Nader group also found that personnel administration encouraged timidity and resistance to change while it offered little protection for the extraordinary public servant.[14] The public personnel fraternity keeps insisting that it is keeping pace with change and that things have improved. I doubt it.

THE CIVIL SERVICE MOVEMENT

If we are to make a valid assessment of American personnel administration, we need a historical perspective. We must be able to see that the cherished principles of the civil service movement are not absolutes but are rather the limited values of a particular time and place. In other words, the history of the reform movement will reveal the biases of the personnel specialists.

A shocking accusation, they would reply. Personnel people are neuters, the good, gray experts, happily putting themselves at the disposal of the chief executive. All they do is perform the mechanics involved in selecting the *best* people for government service. And there, of course, is the dead giveaway. Who are the best governors? That question has always been at the heart of political philosophy, and once you answer the question you have determined what sort of government there will be. The fact that another name for public personnel administration is the "merit principle" or "merit system" is a further clue. The concept of merit, though, is in direct opposition to the idea of free political choice; by promoting a specific image of merit, reformers have done much to discredit competing images. Down to the present day, the insistence upon the sanctity of a single definition of merit has had an impact upon the direction of our politics.

It is remarkable that the leaders of the civil service movement have been so confident about what is best since the general public has had a far more difficult time in deciding about the values to be manifested by government officials. Herbert Kaufman has done a lucid job of describing the divergent trends in American public administration; in his latest comments, he has argued that our attitudes toward administration and administrators change in a cyclical fashion, with the predominant value of one time always facing the challenge from opposing values.[15] Kaufman's version is in contrast to the reformer's insinuation that the merit system represents progress toward an absolutely good end and that the values it promotes are somehow preordained.

Kaufman claims that throughout the history of American public administration there have been three dominant values. The earliest value was that of representativeness, which gave rise to such phenomena as the supremacy of the legislature over the executive and a ballot which "grew in length until amost every public official from President down to dog catcher came to power via the electoral route." That value came to be opposed by the value of neutral competence. The essence of this value "was the ability to do the work of government expertly, and to do it according to explicit, objective standards rather than to personal or party of other obligations and loyalties." Around the turn of the century, a third major value, executive leadership, came to complement the idea of neutral competence. The exponents of this latest value felt that the chief executive should have the authority and responsibility for the direction of administration. Neutral competence and executive leadership were original parts of the "good government" reform package, but the alliance came close to purging the idea of representativeness from our political system.[16]

The three values obviously have a bearing on the nature of personnel administration. In terms of representativeness, should the public service be typical of the mass of citizens; does everyone have a right to public office, simply by virtue of membership in the polity? Or should those who have been trained to fill precise roles be the only ones with access to government jobs? Or, finally, should government employees, and especially those in policy-making positions, be totally dependent upon the will of the elected representatives? As a brief review of history will indicate, these basic questions have shaped the nature of the American public service.

The reformers have not seen themselves as part of a dialectical movement. In a unilinear fashion, they have taken as their inevitable historical role the job of telling the rest of us to "shape up or ship out." They played the role well and may have oversold their basic product. That product, of course, is efficiency. The quest for efficiency in government since the founding of the country can be seen as taking place in three phases. Better yet, there have been three distinct phases with the outside chance that a fourth is now emerging. Perhaps there is right now a growing resistance to the pursuit of the logic of efficiency to the bitter end. Or perhaps the idea of a fourth phase is only a delusion and the perfection of the personnel system of the third phase is unavoidable. Only time will tell.[17]

Phase One, 1789–1829: The Early Years Even though their party soon faded, the Federalists determined the early style of the American public service. The practice established by George Washington of appointing persons of honor and character was generally followed by his successors. The business of government remained the prerogative of the "notables," and this bias in favor of the aristocracy was reflected in the staffing of public offices. Of course, the early Presidents were still politicians, so they were capable of making partisan appointments and removals. Jefferson in particular was upset by some of John Adams's "midnight appointees." However, he did little more than complain of the Federalist holdovers that "none retire and few die." In spite of an occasional excitation, these were the stable years. The stability was in stark contrast to what was to follow.

Phase Two, 1829–1883: The Spoils System He was not one of its leading practitioners, but Andrew Jackson did give what little theoretical justification it had to what became known as the "spoils system." It was actually Senator William Marcy who summed up the idea most candidly when he said, "To the victors belong the spoils of the enemy." To Jackson, the idea was one of representativeness; and had it not been so widely abused, it might better have deserved the name of "rotation system." He believed that government should not become the monopoly of a small elite. Every citizen should be allowed to participate, and mass participation was possible because the duties of public administration "are, or at least admit of being made so, so plain and simple that men of intelligence may readily qualify themselves for their performance." Jackson was not so concerned with the partisanship of clerks; rather the great danger for him was the possibility that public office would become considered a form of private property by the incumbents.

Many writers have been struck by the similarity between Jackson's expression of faith in the simplicity of government work and Lenin's statement that "the great majority of functions of the old 'state power' have become so simplified and can be reduced to such simple operations . . . that they will be quite within the reach of every literate person."[18] For both men, this leap of faith was necessary if one were to advocate a truly representative administrative system. However, the idea was not even realistic in 1829. In the same address containing his intentions to open up the public service, Jackson went on to praise the U.S. Military Academy, our first attempt at professional education for public administrators. But if one does not at least posit the idea, even the most radical political change must be seen as only a movement at the top of the administrative machinery.

Whatever the philosophical merits of rotation in office, it almost immediately degenerated into what we know as the spoils system. Quite apart from the role it played in the general corruption of public morality during the latter half of the nineteenth century, it is clear that in terms of even moderately effective administration, spoils was hopelessly inadequate. In practice it meant:[19]

1 Public work was either neglected or required the efforts of more than one employee since officeholders were expected to spend much time in party activity.

2 Incompetent party hacks were employed because government work was more complex than Jackson thought.

3 There was a great incentive for officials to rip off what they could before the next election tossed them out.

4 Much time was spent on orientation, an especially difficult job when the whole office had just been purged of "rascals" from the other party.

5 The chief executive was constantly harassed, and even Lincoln complained that his hardest job was not the Civil War but rather the constant stream of office seekers.

In retrospect, we can see that the spoils system would have collapsed under its own weight once America had opted for the benefits of an industrial society. If reasonable and farsighted leaders had been in control of events during the late 1800s, a gradual transition to a more realistic system might have been carried out. But neither the friends nor the foes of spoils managed to keep a balanced perspective at the height of the struggle. To be sure, participants in the spoils system were the intransigent and selfish defenders of inexcusable abuses. On the other side, the reformers were inclined to turn their movement into something resembling a holy crusade. Spoils and its defenders were beyond the pale, were completely irredeemable, and had to be eliminated root and branch. For generations, "spoils" was to be the most obscene word in the American political vocabulary.

Through the haze of nostalgia, it is possible to regard spoils with some fondness. However, we should not go too far in glorifying the system and the characters it produced. Roscoe Conkling was colorful and George Washington Plunkitt was clever, but few of us would really welcome them back into our statehouses or city halls. No one today advocates the resurrection of Boss Tweed. The point here instead is that there were excesses involved in the reform movement. If the spoils system was democracy carried to an absurd extreme, was not then the reform movement, with its total antipathy toward spoils, something of a reaction against democracy? Undoubtedly, it was not so intended, but the end result is about the same. It can at least be argued that there might have been a more equitable compromise between representativeness and neutral competence before the reformers discredited all alternatives to their proposals.

Phase Three, 1883–????: The Triumph of Reform A madman named Charles Guiteau, soon to be immortalized in history books as a "disappointed office seeker," convinced himself that he had won the election of 1880 for James Garfield. In the grand spoils tradition, he requested the consulship at Paris and, when rejected, shot the President. The revulsion against this insane act provided the reformers with the popular support they needed to launch the modern civil service system. The Pendleton, or Civil Service, Act of 1883 marked the real beginning of personnel administration in the United States. As the first major legislation, it served as a model for enactments at the state and local levels. From the start, the act contained two major provisions for the removal of political influence over public offices. First, the administration of the act was vested in an independent, bipartisan commission; independence from the chief executive has remained the classic form for the personnel organization. Second, the act required that applicants for government jobs pass a "practical" competitive examination; it was now more important to know something than to know somebody. The Pendleton Act remains the major landmark in our efforts to take politics out of government.

POLITICS AND PERSONNEL

Since 1883, there has been a steady expansion of the merit principle; as a group of experts had recommended in 1937, it has been "extended upward, outward, and downward to include all positions in the Executive Branch of Government except those which are policy-determining in character."[20] In fact, it has made inroads into the policy-making strata. Estimates vary, but it is generally agreed that an incoming President can appoint between 1,500 and 2,000 people to significant government jobs. The rest are selected and protected under some sort of merit provision. The question is whether the President, the only person the public can hold responsible at the polls, can use this handful of appointments to control the 2.5 million civilian government employees.

The disastrous history of the Nixon administration indicates that it is difficult, if not impossible. Authors are now cranking out all manner of esoteric explanations about why Watergate happened. I feel that the definitive history will come up with the ultimate explanation in nothing more glamorous than personnel administration. Nixon came to power with an intense distrust of the Washington bureaucracy; the primeval "enemies list" was the civil service roll. Many of his domestic programs can be interpreted in terms of doing battle with the bureaucracy for the control of the federal government. Even the most constructive innovations of his administration were stimulated by the same impulse; the New Federalism, for example, can best be understood as a strategy to decrease the power of the bureaucracy by farming out its functions to state and local governments.[21]

Nixon was not fighting the boogeyman of an overworked conservative imagination. Empirical political science, as usual trailing events by a distance of several years, has recently confirmed that "the federal bureaucracy was not fertile soil in which to plant the most conservative of the Nixon administration's social policies."[22] Even a panel drawn from the public administration establishment was forced to admit that the unhealthy climate in Washington during the Nixon years was partially due to the aggressive efforts which "were made to use administrative machinery to carry out political and policy ends, and growing frustration and exasperation developed over alleged bureaucratic impediments." The tenor of their report, however, implies that some other means should have been found to control the bureaucracy. The civil service ideal is so enshrined in our thinking that we do not find it strange that elected leaders should face "frustration" and "exasperation" in the implementation of policy. Nixon's goal was impeccably democratic; the way he went about achieving it was something else.[23]

Anyone so Washington-wise as Nixon must have realized that a frontal assault on the bureaucracy would be futile, and therefore that more devious means were necessary. During his first term, when the dirty work of Watergate was initiated, the White House staff grew rapidly; largely because Nixon and his aides were doing on a grander scale what previous administrations had been forced to do—create a counterbureaucracy in the basement of the White House. Just as Kennedy and Johnson had given up on the career "cookie pushers" in the State Department and had developed a separate organ for foreign policy, so Nixon despaired of getting his domestic programs implemented through regular channels, especially since many of these policies called for the dismantling of the bureaucracy itself. Unfortunately, this sub rosa bureaucracy, staffed as it was with callow loyalists, developed that infamous "all's fair in love, war, and politics" mentality which was to cause so much grief. And being hidden, it remained unchecked by other political bodies until gross abuses had already taken place. Now Nixon and his would-be bureaucrat slayers are in disgrace, and business continues as usual in Washington. It is not an encouraging lesson for future Presidents.[24]

The bales of documents churned up by the Watergate investigations reveal some rather seedy aspects of this attack on the bureaucracy. That includes even the President's fulminations that "we have no discipline in this bureaucracy. We never fire anybody. We never reprimand anybody. We never demote anybody. We always promote the sons-of-bitches that kick us in the ass."[25] One must shiver when reading the "I.R.S. Talking Paper" concerning the lack of key Republican appointees which "precludes the initiation of policies which would be proper and politically advantageous."[26] But despite the questionable means it endorses, it is possible to appreciate the problems expressed in the so-called Malek manual (named for Fred Malek, one of the chief White House personnel advisers). Starting from the premise that there is a difference between ruling and reigning, the manual details the job to be done. For example, in the key department of HEW, only 47 positions out of 115,000 were found to be subject to presidential appointment. In view of such statistics, one can agree with the statement that "you cannot achieve management, policy, or program control unless you have established political control."[27]

The Civil Service Commission, as the personnel office, was of no help in the establishment of political control. It only stood by its established procedures which in turn had to be subverted by the politicians. The pertinent question is whether the Commission learned anything that can be applied to post-Watergate personnel administration. It would appear as if the only result was a confirmation that evil lurks forever in the hearts of politicians. In a recent panel discussion among senior civil servants, as reported in *The Bureaucrat,* the fear was expressed that a likely reaction would be further inflexible enforcement of the same regulations which led to the original abuses. As one of the participants put it:

> We are already planting the seeds for a later subversion of the system as bad if not worse than what happened under the Nixon administration, because we are rebuilding a rigidity which could go well beyond the rigidity we had before and the response to that, inevitably, is going to be a subversion of the system.[28]

The Bourbons learn nothing, and they forget nothing. So it seems that the personnel profession is incapable of offering a way to break what is coming to be a vicious cycle.

THE STATE AND LOCAL SCENE

State and local governments have been moving in the same direction as the federal system, although there are numerous variations. Mayor Daley, for example, conducted his classes in how to run a machine in spite of a merit system. California, which has been vigorously "good government" since the Progressive era, illustrates the basic problem. At the state level, 98 percent of California's public servants are protected by a merit system. In 1966, Ronald Reagan was elected Governor by a plurality of over a million votes. This was no Tweedledum-Tweedledee election, for Reagan, an outspoken conservative, defeated a liberal incumbent. Following democratic theory, one might have assumed that the electorate had made as clear-cut a decision as is possible. But the implementation of his program depended upon the cooperation of the 100,000 state employees. At the end of eight years, it was not clear that the Governor had established his authority over the bureaucracy.

Although Reagan continued to express surprise over the fact that the bureaucracy was sabotaging his major programs, I will cite only one small, but illuminating, example of what reform has come to mean. In the first months of the new administration, a department head distributed to his subordinates a brief summary of the Governor's platform; he tried to explain to the workers who were to carry out the programs exactly what it was that Reagan had told the electorate he would accomplish. Immediately the organization of state employees blasted the move as an outrage and "a blatant attempt at brainwashing." The administration quickly backed down. No one mentioned the basic rights of citizens to get the sort of government they had voted for; no one asserted the right of elected politicians to put into effect a distinctive program.

From the standpoint of democratic control, the situation is probably worse at the local level in California. The city of Los Angeles is inexplicable to anyone who does not understand that the government is run entirely by civil servants. Los Angeles mayors have been noted for having their own foreign policy, but what else is there for them to do? The structure of government is rigged in such a way that it is impossible for them to govern the city. They do not even hire and fire department heads, and so the real work goes on without them. It did look as if there might be a major change in 1971 when a charter revision commission recommended more flexibility for elected officials in the selection of policy-making subordinates. However, the ancient clichés carried the day. The proposed charter, it was charged, would be "opening the operation of the city to political manipulation." Even the politicians of Tinseltown took to the airwaves to warn the citizenry against, of all things, politicians. The charter was defeated by the forces of "good government." If California is the wave of the future, how long will it be before all our elected officials are entertaining but ineffectual politicians on the order of Sam Yorty?

Probably not too long. With the passage of the Intergovernmental Personnel Act of 1970, the civil service movement opened up the last frontier. This act is nothing less than the nationalization of the American civil service. Its purpose is "to assist State and local governments to strengthen their staffs by improving their personnel administration." Improvement is understood as the slavish duplication of the federal procedures. It is implemented through a variety of means: grants for management improvement, support for training programs, technical assistance, cooperative recruiting and training, and the promotion of interstate compacts to upgrade personnel administration. The act is commendable only if one is persuaded that existing personnel practices are the only ones worthy of duplication. The IPA, plus a 1976 Supreme Court decision which undermines the practice of patronage, guarantees that politicians will be even weaker when it comes to confronting the bureaucracy. There is now no alternative to the present apolitical personnel system.

Again, my alternative is not in any way a return to the spoils system. We are all too much a product of the late twentieth century to desire the conditions of 1876. Few of us would want the mayor's brother-in-law to perform open heart surgery on us; if one ever has a choice in such matters, it would probably be preferable to be busted by the Los Angeles Police Department than by Chicago's finest. But something is wrong if our only choice is the spoils system or total reform. Is there no way we can modify the existing system in order to ensure a little more in the way of democratic accountability? It would accomplish little to go back to appointing third-class postmasters on the basis of political affiliation. It might help, however, to reassess the decision-making capacity of important officials to see whether they should be selected through merit techniques or by political appointment. No blanket prescriptions will do for every jurisdiction, but it would be a generally healthy development if personnel administrators and civil service commissions would relax their vigilance against the ghosts of the spoils system and evaluate how specific appointments bear upon the capacity of the chief executive to represent the will of the public.

Such a change would reinvigorate the representatives for the nonrational. And it can be done. It is in fact the policy which has been pursued in this country since the beginning to control our most feared professional group. What else is implied in the hallowed concept of "civilian control of the military"? That policy has worked, in some cases perhaps too well. Can we not then safely ask for civilian control of the State Department, of the schools, of the police department or whatever agency? It does not seem to be such a heretical proposition. The concept only demands that a different way of thinking be represented at the top of the hierarchy.

WHO'S IN CHARGE HERE?

As I indicated in an earlier chapter, whether the elected officials can control department heads is an interesting question only if in turn the department heads can control their employees. Today that final link is in serious doubt, and so a new threat has arisen to make the viability of democratic institutions all the more problematic. I am alluding here to the growth of public service unions and the militancy of organized civil servants. In fairness to personnel specialists, it must be admitted that this is one development in public employment which cannot be attributed to the inherent weaknesses of their work, although their response to the challenge has been uninspiring—a retreat to petty techniques rather than a direct confrontation with the main issue.

In a way, there is a large measure of justice in the development of the unions. For almost 200 years, American public managers have been able to tell new employees: "Your rights are easily defined. You have none." Working for government was a privilege and not a right, so every sort of indignity could be—and often was—heaped upon the civil servants. Their right to participate in politics was curtailed, their privacy was violated on and off the job, they were subject to arbitrary dismissal if suspected of subversive behavior, and, most of all, they were forbidden from engaging in collective bargaining.[29]

The worm has turned, and in its turning the courts have been throwing out the rules and regulations which relegated civil servants to a second-class citizenship.[30] Now civil servants have much the same right to bargain collectively as their counterparts in private employment. The one issue which has not been fully resolved is whether the public servants can use the ultimate bargaining tool, namely, the right to strike.

A number of perfectly reasonable arguments can be advanced to prove conclusively that public employees should not have the right to strike, and most legislatures in the United States are committed to the perpetuation of antistrike legislation. Unfortunately, the theories and the laws are largely irrelevant. Public employees have taken the initiative, and after more than a decade of unionization, two obvious facts emerge. First of all, strikes cannot be prohibited by law. The only thing really prohibited is an unsuccessful strike. That is, if only a few people walk out, management can jump all over them. When an entire city closes down, the practice has been for the managers to capitulate as gracefully as possible. After all, when the police themselves are out on the picket line, who will enforce the law?

The second point concerns the role of the strike in modern society. We are obviously so intricately interrelated that there are some functions which must be performed on a regular basis if we are not to suffer social breakdown. It is highly unrealistic, however, to draw the line between those who may strike and those who may not on the basis of the employer. Many private employees—in the transportation or communications industries, for example—are far more indispensable than public employees such as filing clerks and librarians. We need a better formula for determining when strikes are a true threat to the general welfare. The dilemma is that if we try to identify such groups, we are waving a flag at them telling them that a strike would be particularly effective.

Civil servants have not been slow in learning these points and across the country they have marked up an impressive series of victories. Now no one doubts that they will strike, with or without legislative permission. And few have serious doubts about their ability to disrupt the smooth operation of an urban society. Various civil service organizations have jumped into the act, pushing demands and increasing the cost of government until today we have our largest city tottering on the brink of bankruptcy. One cynical power play after another has made some people suggest that the motto of the United States should be "Stick 'em up!" rather than "E Pluribus Unum."

Out of many, one—how far away that seems today, as government becomes more and more divided against itself. We are no longer citizens but instead the victims of the bureaucrats. Robert Theobald, an economist, is one who has deplored the ugly turn taken in labor-management relations. It boils down to the fact that the public (everyone outside the immediate bargaining group) is left holding the bag. In effect, we are made to suffer twice. First, the hurt is applied to an undifferentiated public. Management, especially public management, is not going out of business, and the manager is probably not suffering any personal financial loss. The public itself must be made to holler out of fear of the threatened or real anarchy. Second, the public bears the cost of the settlement as labor and management pass it on to the rest of us. So Theobald concludes, "much of the apparent union-management bargaining involves a tacit alliance against the public and the workers who are not unionized. . . ."[31]

Theobald also suggests that eventually we will have to demand a "right to service"—a right more sacred than management's right to hire and fire or labor's right to strike. How we establish that right is another matter and no one, least of all the experts in personnel administration, seem to have any good ideas. But the overall problem is one more function of the decline of politics, in this case with the larger interests conflicting with the privatized rationality of the individuals in government. No one is involved with the crucial question of what it means to be a public employee. Government, I still believe, is different, and working for it is not quite the same as working for General Motors or McDonald's. Public service is indeed a public trust. If that phrase means anything, it means that the citizens must be able to count on their survival needs being met without being subjected to periodic extortion. If there is a new meaning, perhaps we have wasted a considerable amount of time and money in celebrating the two-hundredth anniversary of a document which supposedly explains why "Governments are instituted among Men."

There is no easy way to attain peace in the public sector, but we will take the first step in the right direction when all members of the public organization realize that they are on the same side. There must be identified some transcendental organizational purpose which will permit all, from highest to lowest, to get along. This is not to say, as industrial psychologists have been preaching for years, that the workers should adjust to the benevolent despotism of the managers. Quite to the contrary, the major change will have to be on the part of the managers when they come to realize that their subordinates are not a pack of animals. Somebody—politician, manager, personnel specialist, union leader—will have to try to convince workers that there is some sacrifice attached to the position of public servant.[32] I wonder if the workers, having been corrupted by the taste of power, can change their minds.

Whether such a Golden Age will ever come about is highly doubtful. In the meantime, we can distract ourselves by contemplating an even greater threat posed by organized civil servants. So far, most of the strikes have been by workers interested in more material benefits, e.g., higher wages, better pensions, shorter hours. The absence of police officers, fire fighters, teachers, and sanitation workers can be very inconvenient—even dangerous—for the rest of us, and getting them back will certainly cost the taxpayers something. Yet these actions are not so different from the activity of private employees and do not necessarily endanger democracy. Such blue collar strikes, however, may become increasingly rare.

The union, as it becomes more white collar, will take on many of the attributes of the professional association; or, more likely, the professional association will be forced by competition to behave more like a union. In any event, if the theory of professionalization is correct, members will be less interested in monetary payoffs and more concerned with professional autonomy. They will claim the professional right to be the final judge of what is needed for the adequate performance in certain areas of government. I am suggesting, in other words, that there is a considerable difference between the American Federation of Teachers demanding more wages on the one hand and the right to determine the curriculum on the other. One is political only insofar as it takes money from one group of citizens and gives it to another; the other is political in the direct sense of making policy for the whole society.

In such a situation, government—to the extent that one can say that a government exists—will be the referee of disputes among a number of feudal domains. Each profession will be in a state of siege, ready to strike out from time to time in order to defend its perception of the One True Faith. The public will be a meaningless concept since there will be no way in which a public can enforce control, at least not as long as the group on the rampage has the power to bring society to a standstill through withholding its services. Then we will need no legislature, but only a clerk to receive demands and threats. The end result, however, will not be an apolitical world. Conflict over allocative decisions will be as hot as ever. It will be a matter of where we locate and how we arrange the political arena. If professionals are permitted to defy political control and to enforce their defiance through aggressive tactics, whatever political system we are left with cannot be a democracy.

I would regret it if my remarks are misconstrued as a recommendation that the Cossacks or the Pinkerton agents be called out to break up a meeting of typists. I will defend the right of public employees to organize and to bargain collectively; in fact, I have participated (unsuccessfully) in the unionization of professors at public universities. Joining with others is obviously the most effective way for individuals to defend themselves against attempts by management to control their behavior. More pragmatically, it is also a good way to increase one's material rewards. Despite all that, however, one cannot ignore the significant political questions raised by the role of the unions. How to resolve the dilemma I do not know. Perhaps it is best to hope that we are still in the formative stages of a resolution and that people of goodwill can avoid the dire consequences of a projection of present trends.[33]

CONCLUSION

The "official" doctrine of public personnel administration still exudes an air of supreme confidence about the manageability of people within government. It is nearly thirty years now since Wallace Sayre dismissed the collected wisdom of the field as representing the "triumph of technique over purpose." The charge still holds, and Chester Newland concludes that the aim is still the bureaucratization of models derived from the 1930s.[34] The imposition of techniques, based upon a crippling view of efficiency, upon a roiling vortex of political, moral, and individual values is positively harmful to society. With their presently limited concept of rationality, the personnel specialists cannot help us in our agony. If they are to be useful, they will have to reevaluate their techniques in light of the fact that the politicians and employees are also quite capable of being rational too. Such a concession would be the beginning of a more productive style of personnel administration.

REFERENCES

1 "The Port Huron Statement," in Robert Goldwin (ed.), *How Democratic Is America?* (Chicago: Rand McNally, 1971), p. 6.
2 Charles Milton, *Ethics and Expediency in Personnel Management* (Columbia: University of South Carolina Press, 1970), p. 1.
3 Zoltan Magyary, *The Industrial State* (New York: Thomas Nelson, 1938), p. 83.
4 Georges Langrod, "The Rationalization of Methods and Means of Action in Public Administration," *International Social Science Journal,* 12 (1960), p. 382.
5 Laurence Peter and Raymond Hull, *The Peter Principle* (New York: Morrow, 1969).
6 For all you will ever care to know about public personnel administration, see O. Glenn Stahl, *Public Personnel Administration,* 7th ed. (New York: Harper & Row, 1976).
7 Paul Goodman, *People or Personnel* (New York: Random House, 1965).
8 Elting Morison, *Men, Machines, and Modern Times* (Cambridge, Mass.: M.I.T., 1966), p. 121.
9 Honoré Balzac, *Bureaucracy* (New York: Harper and Brothers, n.d.), p. 427.
10 F. F. Ridley, "French Technocracy and Comparative Government," *Political Studies,* 14 (1966), pp. 34–52.
11 For a good discussion of the political environment of personnel administration, see Joseph Cayer, *Public Personnel Administration in the United States* (New York: St. Martin's, 1975).
12 Blanche Blank, "The Battle of Bureaucracy," *The Nation,* 203 (1966), pp. 633–637.
13 John Fischer, "Let's Go Back to the Spoils System," *Harper's,* 191 (1945), pp. 362–368.
14 Robert Vaughn, *The Spoiled System* (New York: Charterhouse, 1975).
15 Herbert Kaufman, "Administrative Decentralization and Political Power," *Public Administration Review,* 29 (1969), pp. 3–15.
16 Herbert Kaufman, "Emerging Conflicts in the Doctrines of Public Administration," *American Political Science Review,* 50 (1956), pp. 1057–1073.
17 For history, see Paul Van Riper, *History of the United States Civil Service* (New York: Harper & Row, 1958).

18 V. I. Lenin, *State and Revolution* (New York: International Publishers, 1932), p. 38.

19 See Herbert Kaufman, "The Growth of the Federal Personnel System," in Wallace Sayre (ed.), *The Federal Government Service* (Englewood Cliffs, N.J.: Prentice-Hall, 1965).

20 President's Committee on Administrative Management, *Administrative Management* (Washington: GPO, 1937), p. 7.

21 Richard Nathan, *The Plot That Failed* (New York: Wiley, 1975).

22 Joel Aberbach and Bert Rockman, "Clashing Beliefs within the Executive Branch: The Nixon Administration Bureaucracy," *American Political Science Review,* 70 (1976), p. 467.

23 Frederick Mosher et al., *Watergate: Implications for Responsible Government* (New York: Basic Books, 1974), p. 9.

24 Richard Nathan, "The 'Administrative Presidency,'" *Public Interest,* no. 44 (1976), pp. 40–54.

25 "Transcripts of April 19, 1971 Meeting," *Statement of Information,* Hearings before the Committee on the Judiciary, House of Representatives, Bk. V, Pt. 1 (Washington: GPO, 1974), pp. 330–331.

26 "SSC Exhibit No. 44, 4 SSC 1682-85," *Statement of Information,* Hearings before the Committee on the Judiciary, House of Representatives, Bk. VIII (Washington: GPO, 1975).

27 "Federal Political Personnel Manual: The 'Malek Manual,'" *The Bureaucrat,* 4 (1976), p. 430.

28 "Discussion of the Federal Personnel Crisis," *The Bureaucrat,* 4 (1976), p. 393.

29 Arch Dotson, "The Emerging Doctrine of Privilege in Public Employment," *Public Administration Review,* 15 (1955), pp. 77–88.

30 See David Rosenbloom, *Federal Service and the Constitution* (Ithaca, N.Y.: Cornell Unviersity Press, 1971).

31 Robert Theobald, "Strikes and the Public Welfare," *Los Angeles Times* (May 14, 1969).

32 See Robert Miewald, "Conflict and Harmony in the Public Service," *Public Personnel Management,* 3 (1974), pp. 531–535.

33 Things are in constant flux, but for one of the best discussions of the problem, see Sam Zagoria (ed.), *Public Workers and Public Unions* (Englewood Cliffs, N.J.: Prentice-Hall, 1972).

34 Chester Newland, "Public Personnel Administration: Legalistic Reforms vs. Effectiveness, Efficiency and Economy," *Public Administration Review,* 36 (1976), pp. 529–537.

Chapter 11

Responsibility

There is *a difference—most unfortunately—between acting rationally and acting rightly.*

Gwyn Griffin
An Operational Necessity

Throughout this book, I have been standing on my vantage point, screaming at you that the dam is about to break. The last barriers will collapse, and we will be swept away in a flood of administrative rationality. But from another view, the majority of students in the field will admit only that in some cases the added pressures of administration have caused some creaking and groaning of the structure; yet there is no need to panic. If we keep our heads, we can patch a little here and prop some there so that we can ensure a "responsible public service" which will not do terrible, inhuman things to us. I could be calmed down by these assurances if only I could understand how something so insubstantial as "responsibility" can be turned into concrete shorings.

In this chapter, we will look at specific means for the establishment of responsibility in public administration. The major problem is that although everyone is in favor of responsibility, it is a hard concept to pin down. One author found a number of values mixed up in the term: responsiveness, flexibility, consistency, stability, leadership, probity, candor, competence, efficacy, prudence, due process, and accountability.[1] How does such a list of nice things make the administrator behave responsibly or aid the citizens in their evaluation of public activity?

Discussions of responsibility in public administration usually begin with the classic debate between two political scientists in the early 1940s. Herman Finer took the traditional approach that responsibility of the civil service must be imposed through some sort of outside power, be it the legislature, executive, or courts. Carl Friedrich expressed a more modern view that "responsible conduct is never strictly enforceable, that even under the most tyrannical despot administrative officials will escape effective control." The answer as he saw it was the encouragement of a sense of responsibility in the mind of each bureaucrat; in the act, it would be up to each official to balance the requirements of the public interest with the necessities of his expertise.[2] An interesting colloquy perhaps, but still not too practical since neither author gave an operational definition of responsibility. Neither they nor any other writer have reconciled the fundamental dilemma, described in a recent review of the literature as "accountability and responsiveness on the one hand with effectiveness and expertise on the other."[3]

Assuming that there is no easy answer, the most effective way to approach the subject may be through a description of those things which most people would regard as irresponsibility on the part of public employees. By this means, we may more readily understand what it is we are trying to prevent. By now it should be clear that my personal concept of the worst type of irresponsibility involves administrators who submerge themselves so much in the limited rationality of the organization that they cannot see their larger responsibility as members of society. Persons who have assumed the administrative mentality so well that any other perspective is excluded violate whatever trust is extended to them by their fellow humans. If a significant number of public officials display such behavior, the elements of a free and open society are destroyed. There are, however, other specific bureaucratic sins:

1 *The arrogance of high office.* The officials are in control, and they know it. Their attitude resembles that of the Prussian officials who claimed that a private individual was not qualified to comment on the actions of the king and his officials.[4] John Q. Public is simply told to be quiet, because his best interests are already known by the state. This is the deadliest of bureaucratic sins against democracy since it makes impossible a dialogue between citizens and their government. It implies that the ends of government are firmly fixed and that administration is the inexorable movement toward those ends. Citizens are certainly not encouraged to mess with the operation.

2 *Political involvement.* Here I refer to the attempts of bureaucrats to influence the outcome of the political process in a way favorable to them. The sort of role which the Nixon administration planned for some agencies is one example. More insidious is the sincere feeling on the part of the bureaucrats, without pressure from outside, that certain politicians are good guys and therefore ought to be helped by, say, the judicious approval of government grants and contracts. Or perhaps embarrassing information about a troublesome politician might be leaked before an election.

3 *Corruption.* By this I mean acts which are in direct violation of the law and which are for the personal advantage of the official. The acceptance of bribes and acts tantamount to outright thievery—stealing anything from millions of dollars to government pencils—are the greatest dangers. I do not believe that American public officials are corrupt. This is not to say that they are all models of probity, but it is true that the major scandals in government have rarely been the work of career officials. I do believe, however, that they are as corruptible as any other human and therefore eternal vigilance is necessary.

4 *Unethical behavior.* This term covers those acts which are less precise in meaning than corruption. An act may be within the letter of the law but still be highly questionable conduct for anyone entrusted with public power. The Watergate episode was full of instances in which officials did things which were not quite indictable offenses. The problem exists at all levels of government. For example, should a city planner, a person who can influence land-use patterns in a community, be allowed to invest in a land development scheme? The whole controversial area of "conflict of interest" legislation is a cumbersome way of approaching this matter.

5 *Gross inefficiency.* I have admitted that I am willing to live with a certain degree of inefficiency, especially when the alternatives are so terrifying. However, there are some abuses which must make one sick at heart. The General Accounting Office is forever, or so it seems, coming up with cases in which one part of government sells surplus widgets for 15 cents to a private contractor who in turn sells them to another bureau for $15. The major blunders in public housing construction provide more examples to cause any taxpayer to wince.

6 *Failure to respect legislative intent.* This involves the deliberate refusal to do what the legislature has mandated in its laws. The military provided many examples during our Vietnam adventures. In fact, despite all the clear legislative prohibitions, do we know for sure that the fighting in Indochina has actually ended? The current attempts at controlling the CIA may prove futile since that agency has a long history of doing whatever it pleases.

7 *Ignoring procedures.* Government bulks so large in our everyday lives that it is possible that bureaucrats could easily deprive us of our life, liberty, and property through administrative decisions. We must accept this

possibility as the price we pay for living in a complex society, but it does not mean that we must suffer from completely arbitrary behavior. We expect officials to exercise extreme care in fooling around with our rights, but it is not always easy for harassed individuals, especially if ill-prepared to defend themselves, to enforce responsible actions on the bureaucrats. The officials must accept the rightness of due process of law, even when it makes their jobs all the more complicated.

8 *Manipulation of information.* This includes the problems discussed under secrecy and publicity. In a free society, the officials must resist the temptation to play games with the information they control. If too many of these self-styled "guardians" begin to believe in the "golden lie," the public will have no way of learning whether government is responsible.

9 *Abusing subordinates.* The individual member of the civil service is also a human being and deserves to enjoy the rights of citizenship. As we saw, for a long time, public employees were regarded as second-class citizens and could be subjected to all manner of nonsense just because they were drawing a public paycheck. An organization which regards its own members as a lower form of life cannot be expected to treat outsiders with utmost respect.

10 *Failure to show initiative.* Among some public employees, a slipshod piece of work is justified with the remark: "It's close enough for government work." Too often, the advice of the old-timer is don't make waves, do the minimum, and hope that you retire before the organization collapses. A stagnant government, immobile except for the strict requirements for action spelled out in the job specifications, is not a responsible one. We should receive from our public officials an extraordinary level of performance because the problems they face are extraordinary. The very fact that a matter has become an object of public policy should indicate that.

An individual or organization which exhibited any or all of the above sins would be irresponsible. I do not say that the American public service, as a whole, is guilty. But history has shown that even the noblest governments are not immune from such transgressions, and therefore a concerned public ought to be aware of methods of preventative maintenance. The following ideas are ones widely discussed as ways of preventing or remedying the problems of irresponsibility.

ADMINISTRATIVE LAW

As the name implies, administrative law refers to the legal processes involved in administrative decision making and execution. As a practical matter, any would-be administrator is well advised to know something about the field. Given the growing inclination of Americans to take everything to court, the life of even the lowliest bureaucrat can become very complicated. A good lawyer can make a constitutional issue out of something apparently so trivial as the enforcement of leash laws for pets. The opportunity for the violation of the law is so good because of the bewildering body of information. This information would include the following:

1 The constitution, statutes, compacts, ordinances, charters, contracts, and resolutions defining the powers and duties of the administrative agencies
2 The rules and decisions made by the agencies
3 The decisions and orders made by the agencies under the governing rules
4 The investigations and hearings before the agencies
5 The judicial decisions and precedents relating to all of the above

From this brief outline, one can see why many lawyers eat very well. Many of them can afford to specialize in the law of a single agency. Mastering the patent law or the IRS code might well be the lifetime accomplishment for a lawyer. Some organizations have full-time employees who do little more than read the *Federal Register,* the document which publicizes the actions of the federal agencies. There is a lot of busyness involved in administrative law, but our main question here is how effective it is in ensuring administrative responsibility.

Obviously for a people supposedly committed to the idea that we are a nation of laws and not of men, there are a number of serious legal problems surrounding administration. If we are not to be at the mercy of administrators, there must be some procedural safeguards. Administrators can deprive us of the chance to make a living by denying or revoking a license; they can modify our domestic behavior so that it does not offend public health, safety, welfare, or morals; they can hassle us indefinitely about our tax status. To take but one minor example, most municipalities have an ordinance concerning weed abatement. Suppose one goes on an extended vacation and returns to find that city crews have mutilated his carefully nurtured lawn with a huge mowing machine and, to add to the injury, have sent a bill charging him for this "service." In a world-historic sense, not an earthshaking event, nor is it the sort of thing to set a mob marching on city hall; but it is the kind of personal outrage which can get individuals steaming about the conduct of their government. Administrative law should provide the channels through which the aggrieved party can seek satisfaction.

A number of other examples come to mind. Our children should not be expelled from school simply because the teacher does not like them. No matter what one felt about the military or Vietnam, surely it could be agreed that those draft boards which took away a person's deferred status because of involvement in demonstrations were acting in a despotic manner. Any person of humane inclinations must have been revolted when it was revealed that bureaucrats were requiring welfare mothers to submit to sterilization as a condition for the receipt of relief. These are only a few instances of the types of abuse which a lawless administration can impose upon a defenseless citizenry.

If lawyers were in every case the heroic defenders of individual rights, riding off at a moment's notice to challenge the bureaucratic monster wherever it raises its ugly head, administrative law would be much easier to describe. However, it is far more than a matter of "doing justice," and the role of the lawyers in the bureaucracy has been for years a basically ideological debate about the nature of modern administration. The outcome of it all will not, I think, add much to the larger problem of the enforcement of responsibility. If anything, it may be that administrative law has been used to reinforce a certain style of irresponsibility.

The Anglo-Saxon legal tradition, with its innate distrust of executive discretion, pushed our administrative law along lines different from those countries in which administrative law is about the only game in town. Beginning in the late nineteenth century, British legal commentators such as A. V. Dicey warned about the invasion of a new version of the French pox. Administrators were usurping the traditional functions of judges. Without legal training or an appreciation of the methods of the law, these clerks were in effect making judicial decisions. The impact on American legal thought was even more severe. Nourished as they had been on the doctrine of the separation of powers, the minds of lawyers were boggled and have remained so ever since. When the modern welfare state emerged in the United States, the legal profession tried to cram the agencies within the traditional categories. But nothing seemed to fit anymore.

The horror of horrors was that administrative agencies, and especially the newly created regulatory agencies, were performing all three governmental functions at once. They were executing public policy as administrators were supposed to do. But they were also acting as a legislature in making that policy. And worst of all, they were acting as judges in the application of the very rules they had created. The bar came to the conclusion that we had here a new beast—a "quasi-legislative" and "quasi-judicial" unit of government. But the addition of that bit of Latin—meaning "sort of"—did not change the fact that it was all administration.

Therefore, anyone faintly acquainted with the complexity of the administrative process has to stand in awe of the colossal ignorance of the judges and lawyers when they began blundering into the field. Their frenzy was inspired by the fact that administrators enjoyed some discretion in making decisions. Since the bureaus were neither a congress nor a court, they must be outside the law and, to the legal mind, that which is outside the law is arbitrary, capricious, willful—all those unrestrained, irrational forms of behavior which threaten to plunge us back into the direst type of social disorder.

The major battles were fought out in a weird landscape, the contours of which are explicable only to the legal mind. The major issue was the doctrine of delegation. The principle stated that a legislative body could not delegate its legislative power to any other body. As the Supreme Court said in 1892, "That Congress cannot delegate legislative power . . . is a principle universally recognized as vital to the integrity and maintenance of the system of government ordained by the Constitution."[5] The principle would imply that the administrators have no discretionary power whatsoever, which if true, would negate all I have said about the involvement of the bureaucracy in the political process.

Of course, the courts were forced to articulate the principle at exactly that time when it was becoming ever more evident that delegation was a fact of life. Congress could not write detailed legislation to cover every contingency which might arise in the regulation of a complex area of the economy. The members only knew that they wanted certain problems solved and that some experts claimed they could provide solutions. The Supreme Court watched this development with some anguish and particularly during the New Deal handed down what is still the binding injunction against delegation to administrative agencies in the famous *Schechter* decision which threw out the National Industrial Recovery Act. We are now in such a theoretical bind that if the *Schechter* rule against delegation were applied, the entire United States government would go out of business.

To appease the legal mind that delegation is not really delegation, the courts have said that there must be some guidelines set by the legislature before the administrators can take charge of a policy area. The courts are satisfied if the guideline is nothing more than a plea for the bureaucracy to "go solve the problem." A leading example is the Federal Communications Commission where the FCC is urged to award radio and TV licenses on the basis of "public interest, convenience, or necessity." Such a broad grant, however, is not delegation. Ernest Gellhorn, a leading authority on administrative law, expresses the typical resignation of the bar; society is too complex for a demand that "Congress spell out meaningful standards to guide administrators in fulfilling their assigned tasks," and therefore "to force Congress to act otherwise is to ask it to perform an impossible task and . . . to invite chaos."[6] The legal mind is content with its fiction and because of that mind's pervasive influence on political thinking, so are the rest of us.

Theodore Lowi is one of the few modern writers to denounce the pernicious effect of the delegation doctrine on our political system. He sees it as a critical element of the pluralist model of decision making, helping to shift the locus of power from Congress to the closed arenas of interest-group conflict. He does not believe that the legislature is so helpless in the face of social complexity and does feel that a change in values is possible if we are seriously interested in resisting the erosion of public power. He concedes the practical difficulty in stemming the decline of law as an effective instrument of control, but he argues forcefully that to see the existing reality as unchangeable is "to doom the system to remaining always locked into the original causes and effects."[7]

This indictment is all the more valid because of the new attitude taken by the legal profession toward the administrative agencies. Today, most judges would break out in giggles if a lawyer dared to bring up the *Schechter* decision. But the lawyers are not likely to make such a drastic error. They have accepted the delegation doctrine and have turned their considerable energies toward thwarting the impact of government by bogging it down in procedures. For whatever reasons—and some ulterior motives have been attributed to conservative economic interests—the law has been committed to turning the administrative process into a judicial system. Through such triumphs as the Administrative Procedures Act of 1946, the American Bar Association and its allies have contributed mightily to making the agencies the arenas for the clash of the rich and powerful interests to the detriment of the general public and the unrepresented interests of society.

The lawyers now fight on three major fronts. The first concerns the rule-making power of the agencies. Rule making deals with the formulation or interpretation of a policy which will apply in the future to all persons engaged in the regulated activity. To cite one recent breakthrough, the Food and Drug Administration has finally put forth a rule about the definition of a potato chip and about how far the makers of reconstituted chips can go in advertising their fabricated goodies as the real thing. The rule imposed there will apply to anyone entering the potato chip game. According to legal terminology, this is the quasi-legislative function of the agency, although the prefix adds absolutely nothing to our understanding. The agency is making law, a law which in most cases is as authoritative for the individual as any solemn decision made by legislators in Congress assembled.

Lawyers have fought for a wide range of judicial safeguards to be imposed in rule making. Notice, a hearing before an impartial body, and a decision based on the record are the optimum. This is obviously impractical because legislation has to remain a special combination of expertise and value judgments. The expectation that the administrators are to remain uncommitted throughout the process, just as judges in a court of law, is particularly deleterious in effective policy making. If a policy is to be developed and executed in the most expeditious manner, we cannot rely upon impartiality from the administrators. In those areas where the rule-making process has been judicialized, we find considerable inaction. Goulden describes the great peanut butter decision of the FDA. After twelve years of dedicated endeavor by grown men and women, it was decided that for a product to be labeled peanut butter, it must be 90 percent rather than 87 percent peanuts.[8] If each policy were to be argued so thoroughly—and there is a legal establishment for hire to make the arguments—the wheels of government would come to a complete stop.

Secondly, the lawyers are more properly involved in the adjudicative function, in the application of a policy to a set of past actions or an order concerning a named party. This is the equivalent of a judicial case, and the lawyers have had much success in making this aspect of administration like a court. For example, shall the ICC approve the termination of rail service to Flatrock, Wyoming? Ideally, there would be notification to all concerned parties, the taking of testimony under the standards of the courtroom, a decision based only on the information submitted in the hearing, and the chance for all parties to appeal the decision. Is this a good way for government to attempt to implement a coherent policy? I suspect that it is not, but rather a long, slow process in which larger interests can wage a war of attrition against the less advantaged parties and, in the process, negate the creation of a national policy.

The third area of administrative law is a confession that the formal processes have become so awkward that most of the business can only be conducted through the so-called informal process. That is, the agency and the lawyers have it out as best they can beneath the surface. For example, no food processor wants to be hit with a formal "cease and desist" order from the FDA because of the suspicion that there is an inordinate amount of rat dung in the chow mein. No stockbroker, however innocent, wants it known that he is under investigation by the Securities and Exchange Commission. At a lower level, very few of us are ever going to try to wrestle the IRS to the mat. In such cases, the objects of administration will probably try to come to some sort of understanding short of the formal procedures.[9] It means that administrative law has, in effect, driven the whole thing underground, which is obviously an anomalous result for a system designed to ensure responsibility.

By my remarks I do not wish to disparage the noble profession of the law. Insofar as lawyers are experts in justice, they have my underlying respect. I have no evidence that they have made a conscious effort to undermine the effective operation of government, although it should be noted that administrative law is an extremely lucrative field of practice and that the "Nader phenomenon" of lawyers arguing *for* the public interest is a recent thing with an uncertain future. I rest my case, as it were, on the obvious point that legalism, as an ideology, is not far removed from the bureaucratic pattern of thought. In her discussion of legalism, Judith Shklar reiterates the basic fact: The unique cultural trait of Western civilization is that concept of rationality which can take form either in the law or in bureaucracy.[10] One can argue that the lawyers are just as rigid and conservative in their peculiar style of thought as any bureaucrat and that legal rationality has been as capable of gross injustice as any administrative process.

In practice, it is touch and go whether any group of bureaucrats will be able to rise above their natural inclinations to attack effectively the multiple problems of society. The judicialization of the administrative process only goes to sap what little vitality the organization may have started with. Bureaucrats and lawyers find a firm area of agreement—procedures are more important than substance. Lewis Mainzer points out that danger in mentioning those regulatory agencies which have "sought to model themselves on the courts, taking pride in the formal propriety of their hearings, but losing sight of program effectiveness and the purposes for which the program was established."[11] How much more comfortable to pick procedural nits instead of charging boldly into the world to do something. The degeneration of administration into the most formalistic bureaucracy has been documented often enough. See Emmette Redford's analysis of the Civil Aeronautics Board or Philippe Nonet's study of the California Industrial Accident Commission as examples of how an agency can be distracted from its goals by excessive judicialization.[12]

Martin Shapiro's investigation of the judicial review of administrative decisions comes to essentially the same point. Lawyers may like to believe that they bring something fresh to the administrative process, but in fact it is unrealistic to argue that courts add anything unique to bureaucratic decision making. Since the intense conflict of the 1930s, Shapiro finds, the courts and the agencies have come to share the same consensus. Therefore, "given these similarities it is more reasonable to assume that a basic harmony will exist between courts and agencies than that they will be in conflict."[13] Bureaucrats and judges are likely to think in the same way, which is according to a dry, bookish rationality that is out of touch with social reality. If the courts contribute anything, it is an air of generalism, but that is a generalism marked by the trained incapacity of the law school graduate.

Again, this is not an attack on the rule of law. I only argue that the law has very definite limitations when used as a means for the control of the tendencies of administration. One does not use law to confront the foundations of the administrative mentality. As Jim Hougan writes of those who sought to prevent the rational exploitation of the environment through the courts: "What's been surrendered is the irrational animus of the movement, its entire *raison d'etre*: conditioned to the sanctity of Progress, Due Process, efficiency and reason, ecologists were focused to jettison from their legal briefs such vague nouns as freedom, dignity, beauty, and tranquility."[14] I suggest then that responsibility will not be ensured when every bureaucrat is turned into a jailhouse lawyer. The law cannot effectively challenge the administrative mentality to reconsider the nature of social reality. As far as real control is concerned, administrative law comes down to a matter of one bureaucracy checking another. This strikes me as a weak defense and one which does not speak at all to the issue of the larger rationality. If we are to have an effective guardian over the bureaucracy, my candidate, as always, is the politician; but as Lowi has noted, the politician's role has evaporated. I would much prefer to see politicians reclaim their prerogatives—those same prerogatives they lost when they came to believe that they were in truth too dull to grasp the complexity of society.

Whether politicians can regain control of administration is doubtful given the existence of those enduring monuments to the judicialization of administration, namely, the independent regulatory commissions. At first glance, the longevity of these institutions, for which no one has a kind word, is remarkable. Representing the highest form of judicial administration, these agencies have compiled a sorry record of accomplishment. Yet they hang on, despite wave after wave of reform proposals. The answer to their durability is not hard to find. They constitute the apex of a bounded political subsystem, and they survive through the establishment of strong relations with the immediate set of regulated interests. They have worked so well in that respect that instead of inviting abolition, they encourage others to strive for their own little reservation. The guiding political philosophy is then: "Don't correct abuses. Go out and set up your own abuse!" Until we force politicians to think in terms larger than the parceling out of domains for tangible interests, we may expect to remain the victims of the coalition between the lawyers and the bureaucrats.

If Peter Woll is correct, the only movement we can expect in this area is toward a "substantive administrative law" in which the judges take a more active role in imposing decisions on administrators. We have seen examples of this direction already as courts demand that administrators, despite a lack of resources, solve overnight the problems of racial imbalance in the schools, fiscal inequity among welfare recipients, or the condition of state prisons. All these things may be splendid goals, but I do not regard their imposition by judges as being either wise politics or jurisprudence.[15] In effect, we may be moving toward the German ideal of the *Rechtsstaat* or constitutional state in which the courts played a disproportionate role in policy making. German statescraft, since the 1850s when the *Rechtsstaat* ideal gained supremacy, does not present the prettiest model. In his comparative study of German and American administrative law, Fritz Scharpf certainly gives us little incentive to make more Teutonic our approach. Scharpf argues that the low intensity of legal control in America, as compared with Germany, is more conducive to the political control of administration.[16] I am in agreement with him, and I would urge that the strengthening of the political means of control cannot be promoted if the courts are to become even more involved in the substantive aspects of administration.

THE OMBUDSMAN

The concept of the ombudsman was derived from Sweden. The word itself means "agent." In terms of administration, the ombudsman is the agent of the public in its relations with the bureaucracy, serving as a grievance person, the citizen's representative or advocate, our ally in Washington or in the state capitol or in city hall. The ombudsman is a friend who patrols the corridors of power and who intercedes on our behalf with the bureaucrat. If nothing else, the rapidity with which the term has caught on indicates that there is a need for such a person. In what inevitably came to be called "ombudsmania," everyone seemed for a time to be jumping on the bandwagon. Top-40 radio stations billed themselves as "your ombudsman station," department stores retitled their complaint offices, and universities created ombudsmen to ease the pressure from rebellious students.

At a more substantial level, many governments have borrowed from the Scandinavian models. In his 1973 survey, Kent Weeks found that the real article existed in Denmark, Fiji, Finland, Guyana, New Zealand, Norway, Sweden, the United Kingdom, and Tanzania. In the United States, several states and municipalities have experimented with the idea; Hawaii and Nebraska have been leaders in the establishment of the office. The title varies—parliamentary commissioner, public protector, commissioner for complaints, or public counsel, in addition to ombudsman.[17]

Calling someone an ombudsman, however, does not necessarily achieve the desired ends. To see the purest model, we must look at the Scandinavian experience, keeping in mind that other countries have introduced a number of mutations in the basic idea. William Gwyn summarized the elements of the office:[18]

1 Ombudsmen are the agents of the legislature. At any rate, they are to be independent of the executive chain of command that they are to oversee. Even in relations with the legislature, they are given as much independence as possible so that they will not become an instrument in the political conflict between the two branches.

2 They receive complaints from citizens about the activity of government officials. Anything seems to be acceptable—illegal behavior, inefficiency, sloth, simple bad manners. The range of complaints is far wider than those things which might become a matter for administrative law. One cannot take a postal clerk to court for being a miserable grouch, but one can complain about such surly behavior to the ombudsman.

3 Ombudsmen weed out those complaints which appear to be unjustified. At the same time, cranks and nuts are treated with a degree of dignity for, after all, loonies have rights too. A couple of examples from the report of the Iowa "citizen's aide" will illustrate some of the stranger complaints:

> A citizen called to complain that his new false teeth didn't fit. The citizen "didn't want to cause his dentist any trouble," and said he felt better after talking about the problem.

A citizen complained that a clinic was using electronic devices on the body. The citizen could not give details and was not completely rational. C.A. could not help.

4 With the legitimate complaints, ombudsmen quickly begin the investigation. They usually begin with a request for an explanation from the administrator in question, and most cases are resolved at that level as problems in communication are worked out. If they are unsatisfied with the bureaucrat's response, they can demand a look at the files and otherwise conduct an independent investigation.

5 Ombudsmen can also conduct investigations which have not been triggered by a citizen's complaint. They may also inspect the overall operation of the agencies.

6 If something is found to be wrong, they cannot order remedial action. They can only recommend that something be done. Their most powerful weapon is publicity, either before the legislature or the general public. It is usually effective since bureaucrats are not anxious to have outsiders too closely involved in their internal affairs.

7 They submit an annual report to the legislature, outlining needed legislation for the improvement of the public service. This helps the legislature in the performance of its oversight function.

From such an office, we are told, a number of good things result. Again according to Gwyn, these include the following:

1 The existence of such an official keeps the bureaucrats on their toes. They know now that they cannot violate the rights of the citizens. It induces in them a much needed sense of humility.

2 The legislature is better prepared to check the bureaucracy. The ombudsman's annual report provides lawmakers with the basis for a sensible reform of administration.

3 The civil servants are themselves protected from unjustified complaints. The ombudsman is not an adversary of the bureaucracy and is therefore also solicitous of the rights of the officials.

4 Individual grievances, most of which could not be made into court cases, are taken care of with dispatch. Citizens are able to cut through several layers of red tape at one stroke.

5 The citizens learn more about proper procedures. According to the Nebraska ombudsman, his major function is directing people to the correct agency for the solution of their problem. He is largely something of a traffic director, a role which is badly needed as government becomes larger and more complex.

6 Perhaps most of all, the ombudsman promotes domestic tranquility. People will have more faith in their bureaucracy just because of the existence of such an office, and their resentment about the apparent irresponsible activities of government will be lessened. They know that they are not completely helpless before the bureaucrats. Being less alienated, it is believed that they will take a more positive attitude toward public affairs.

All these benefits of the ombudsman may very well be realized in practice. At least there is no reason to believe that, under the right conditions, they could not be achieved. If the office did only half of what its advocates claim, it would still be a great boon to the art and science of government. So if the simple proposition is to ombuds or not ombuds, let us do it. However, as a solution to the basic problems of life in the administrative state, I would have to dismiss it as a classy palliative. It is government's version of the currently popular "action line" columns in the newspapers. It is part of the existing reality and not a means of transcending the bounded rationality of the bureaucracy.

Eventually, we get back to the argument that it is the fox guarding the welfare of the chickens against other foxes. We have placed one bureaucracy to check up on the operation of another. At its worst, the ombudsman idea could degenerate into something typical of the inspector-general racket in the military. "Tell it to the IG," the unhappy soldier is advised. But who does the IG depend upon to get to the bottom of the complaint? Why those very same officers against whom the complaint is lodged. Not unnaturally, the inspector finds a great deal of good sense in the explanation given by a fellow officer and gentleman. Both are members of a fraternity whose premises include the notion that private soldiers very seldom know what they are talking about anyway.

The point is that the ombudsman is expected to be a member in good standing of the bureaucracy. Most authorities insist that the persons appointed must be expert, nonpartisan, impartial officials, preferably with training in law. They are to approach their work as impersonally as any good bureaucrat, and Donald Rowat, a scholar who has done much to advance the study of the office, dismisses as "a lot of sentimental twaddle," the idea that the ombudsman should exhibit some sort of personal touch.[19] As Herbert Kaufman remarked, "apparently, it takes a bureaucrat to control a bureaucrat."[20] If so, what sort of real control do we achieve? We have people who will be inclined to appreciate the reasoning behind bureaucratic decisions. They will not be true outsiders with a radically different perspective. Therefore, it is unlikely that they will be able to sense the irrationality of bureaucratic rationality, or that they will be able to shake things up to a significant degree. Studies in New Zealand, the home of the oldest English-speaking ombudsman, show that the bureaucrats no longer feel threatened by the office, a fact which I take as an ominous sign.[21]

This brings us to the greatest argument against the ombudsman. Under the remnants of our democratic system, we do have the potential for a true outsider to enter the administrative process. This is the elected representative. If the ombudsman idea is implemented, what effect will it have on one of the most important jobs of the modern legislator? Gerald Ford, then a representative, put the legislative role well when he advised some freshman legislators: "We try to make our office the human link between a vast

Federal Government and the individual at home. If your office becomes this link I think you will render excellent service to your constituents."[22] Gellhorn agrees that members of Congress have been able to fill this role of "humanizers" very adequately.[23] But somehow that element of humaneness is not good enough for the advocates of ombudsmanship.

Through their intellectual acrobatics, the advocates are able to write off the legislators. They are too busy, it is said. Busy doing what I am not sure, since we have seen they are not making much law. Not all legislators do their "casework" with the same degree of skill. Following that line, we might conclude that since there are great variations in the ability of politicians in all areas, we should replace them with a uniform corps of technocrats. And most of all, the greatest failure of the legislator is the lack of impartiality. But who wants impartiality? Impartiality in the bureaucracy means going along with the system. If I have a gripe about the bureaucracy, I am not particularly interested in a sober analysis of the existing rules, especially if those rules have caused my anguish. I do not need an ombudsman to provide me with another explanation of Catch-22. I want some action.

I have in mind a grievance person along the lines of the late Senator Wayne Morse of Oregon. His political enemies insisted that a kick in the head by a horse had made him somewhat erratic, but for whatever reason, he had those qualities which would throw the fear of God into the officials in Washington. That is the sort of person I would place in opposition to the bureaucrats. We need people tuned into a different perception of reality if we poor citizens are to receive a break from government. Citizens and politicians, working together, may have some impact on the artificial reality. The ombudsmen, unless they are themselves certified zanies, will only reinforce that reality.

In the sterile, depoliticized world of administration, the control provided by politicians is not acceptable. It is too disruptive. In truth, it looks too much like democracy. So we must have a bland, nonoffensive invention like the ombudsman. As Victor Thompson notes, the ombudsman is the typical bureaucratic response to a perceived problem, in this case the bureaucracy itself.[24] Larry Hill implies that ombudsmen tend to exist in those societies where they are least needed, that is, where the "administrative civic culture" is so pervasive that questions about reality are never raised.[25] By accepting the ombudsman as a cure-all, we are denigrating the political function and therefore closing more tightly around us the administrative mentality.

INDIVIDUAL RESPONSIBILITY

My perception of the matter does not lead me to believe that bureaucratic responsibility can be ensured through formal means alone. History supports me in this view since even the most regimented peoples have commited enormous crimes through their administrative structures. Administrative law and complaint procedures cannot be regarded as solving any of the basic problems of responsibility in the administrative state. Other nostrums such as the occasional promulgation of a "code of ethics" for officials are likewise depressingly futile. When one recalls the sad history of the code chiseled on stone at Mount Sinai by the Lord God Jehovah, one cannot be too optimistic about the impact of a code mimeographed by some junior personnel clerk.

I hold that it is the individuals within the organization, as the ultimate repositories of human values, who have the painful job of enforcing responsibility through their own behavior. A nice idea, perhaps, but one which is increasingly difficult to put into operation. In his important study of authority and resistance, Herbert von Borch noted that, at a time when the technical power of the state is at its most advanced stage, the bureaucrats have an even greater responsibility to resist authority; as he put it, "bureaucrats are at their most dangerous as depoliticized tools."[26] The "resistance function" of the officials is the ultimate defense for the rest of us. As we have seen already, the elimination of that final line through the establishment of perfect compliance is the purpose of management science.

Uplifting banalities about doing the right thing are not enough, and the issue has recently been cast in a new light by Ralph Nader. After suffering frustration by attacking organizational malfunctions through external controls, Nader has concluded that only the individual members can offer a realistic source of resistance. He and his followers have therefore been emphasizing the social utility of "whistle blowing." The term itself is not particularly inspiring, but it is far better than what it replaces. Even today most people would be more likely to refer to the whistle blower as "fink," "traitor," "stoolie," "canary," "tattletale," "snitch," "squealer," or "informer." As the richness of the invective indicates, we have not tended to glorify persons who turn on their own group. The vilest epithets have been reserved for such people; the most stringent penalties have usually followed.

Nader makes a convincing case that when the individual feels that his or her organization is behaving in a way detrimental to the public interest, there is an obligation to inform those outside. The whistle blowers are to be led by their conscience to publicize the alleged case of wrongdoing in order to "let the public be the final jury as to whether its interests are jeopardized."[27] Some notable examples of whistle blowing included Ernest Fitzgerald, the man who disclosed the cost overruns of the C-5A; Jacqueline Verrett, who persevered in making public the danger of cyclamates; and John McGee, who informed us that the Navy was losing millions of gallons of gasoline through its sloppy methods of accounting. There are more cases of such simple heroics, but not nearly enough.

The stark fact is that whistle blowing is not a profitable course of action for anyone. Perhaps not all will suffer the dreadful consequences of a Frank Serpico, but most of the people honored by Nader and the *Washington Monthly* have had trouble in their jobs (including losing them despite civil service safeguards); and in many cases the superiors carry on much the same as before. Richard Nixon, who I feel qualifies as an expert witness on this point, said, "Either way, the informer is not one in our society. Either way, that is the one thing people can't survive. They say no (characterization deleted) informs."[28] Informers place in grave jeopardy their source of livelihood. It stands to reason that the organization is not going to look too kindly at being caught, and other organizations which might provide employment will look askance at someone who has already demonstrated a capacity for disloyalty. The informer should be independently wealthy or able to make it as a clerk in a candle boutique.

I regard with great sorrow the costs of whistle blowing, but I am not so sure that there is any way in which the process can be institutionalized into a painless thing. Even its advocates admit that their proposals do not "mean that whistle-blowing should become a riskless proposition or that the rules of loyalty and the sanctions behind them should be abolished."[29] I agree with O. Glenn Stahl that "loyalty and reasonable conformity are a sine qua non of any organized effort."

> When an organization is formed to achieve a certain end, there is nothing wrong in its leaders expecting that all who work in the organization (a) are sympathetic with those ends, (b) have a contribution to make in determining how they shall be achieved, (c) are willing to exert energy and even display a certain amount of enthusiasm to help achieve them, and (d) will not sabotage them.[30]

It is therefore not a manifestation of incipient fascism for managers to put on a plaque those old words of Elbert Hubbard: "If you work for a man, for heaven's sake work for him. Speak well of him and stand by the institution he represents." As I hope I have made clear, the organization must depend upon a reliable degree of cooperation from all its members.

Blowing the whistle, then, must remain a lonely act. And apparently for many it is an act too horrible to contemplate. Of course, the material loss is important, but there must be more to it than that, even in an acquisitive society such as our own. I believe that it is the suffocating pressure of the group which inhibits going outside. It takes a special type of person to buck the group. But it is not mere cowardice. Irving Janis makes a compelling case about the crippling disease called "groupthink." In his study of major foreign policy blunders from Pearl Harbor to Vietnam, he concludes that the nature of group decision making prevented individuals, many of whom suffered pangs of conscience, from protesting, either internally or externally. He theorizes that the development of a policy-making in-group results in regarding outsiders as something less than human.[31] Thus, in the councils of the mighty, no one has the capacity to notice that things have gotten out of hand. Who would dare to tell the "best and the brightest"—McNamara, Rusk, Bundy, Rostow—that they were making a disastrous mistake? Is it not natural that a John Dean might have believed that the President of the United States, the Attorney General, and a couple of the most important aides knew what they were doing and that their actions were reasonable?

In a profoundly disturbing report on the weaknesses of our higher public officials, Edward Weisband and Thomas Franck describe the lack of "ethical autonomy" in American government. They find that we are victims of a "political tradition that fosters conformity rather than conviction, group loyalty rather than individual accountability, that borrows its terminology from the language of corporate athletics—in which a man's willingness to 'play ball' is his true measure—rather than moral ethics."[32] Their dreary chronicle includes cases such as McNamara and John Gardner, who realized that something was sadly wrong yet withdrew meekly from government when the times called for the most vigorous denunciation of perceived evils. To go out shouting and screaming about the errors of one's erstwhile colleagues is not good sportsmanship; one is not being a team player, and as we saw in the Watergate hearings, that sort of accusation terrified the Magruders, Porters, and Sloans. In an age when our real athletes are not notoriously good sports, it is ironic that the old gentlemanly rules still apply to decisions which affect the destiny of us all.

What then shall we do? Sad to say, I cannot conjure up an answer to fit within the confines of a multiple choice quiz—A, B, C, or D, none of the above. For film buffs, perhaps the answer is easy. We have all thrilled at the sight of Jimmy Stewart flinging back the immoral orders into the face of his evil boss and skipping off with Doris Day to live happily ever after on a chicken ranch in Montana. Or if it is a war flick, the hero is led off to face gallantly the firing squad. That all may be fine cinema, but it strikes me as one hell of a way to run a society. Let us be frank and earnest with one another: most of us are not heroes. Most of us are weak enough to prefer anything to losing the house in Regency Estates, or the color TV, or the two cars. Moral victories, after all, do not pay the orthodontist bills.

But it is more than simple fear of losing the good life; moral issues within the organization seldom occur in the form of a dramatic clash between the forces of light and the forces of darkness. Morality tends, as always, to be an ambiguous mess, so ambiguous that one can easily worm out of making a commitment. Our desire not to get involved may stem from the fact that it is hard to tell what there is to get involved with. Take the Arnheiter affair of a few years ago. The crew of a Navy ship, after suffering for many months under the command of a captain who they felt was dangerously unstable, finally took steps to have him removed. Even after formal action was taken, it was not absolutely resolved to everyone's satisfaction that the proper course had been followed. No one could claim a clear-cut decision for either side.[33] The point is not surprising. After all, people in big organizations have left their visceral reactions at the door, and it is small wonder that their resolution is sicklied o'er with the pale cast of thought. The pale cast of thought is one of the tools of the trade.

If we wish to forgo the outright heroics, the other extreme solution is to work from within. If an evil order is given, why not take it upon ourselves to countermand it? And if that is to be the suggestion, I ask whether a Heinrich Himmler might not be preferable. Strutting around in his black uniform, he was at least an identifiable target for anyone who wanted to know who had decided what. If one is to claim the right to be the last best judge of organizational activity, then we in the public must demand that he make himself known. A democratic society is impossible without that degree of accountability. But as we know from experience, the argument that "I'm really doing society a favor by retaining my high-paying government job in a corrupt regime since I am able to do more on the inside" is the plea of a thoroughly coopted individual. The author of *MacBird!* captured the real reasoning here: "To quit the club! Be outside looking in!/This outsideness, this unfamiliar land,/From whom few travellers ever get back in. . . ."[34]

"ALL WE ARE SAYING . . ."

The development of a precise moral code for the age of administration is not something for which I wish to take responsibility. Near the end of a book in which I have tried to shake our grip on certainty is no place for a portentous disquisition on how you should behave. The only thing I know for sure is that each individual does after all have a choice to make. It may be a hard choice; the way things are today, it may well be a fatal choice. The realization that there is a choice between following orders and doing what one feels is right is the only antidote to the factors which promote the easy avoidance of moral decisions within and without the organization. The cop-out that "I was only following orders" is no alibi because one still has made the decision to follow orders. Having opted to follow orders, one must be reminded that there are costs attached.

Individual responsibility begins as resistance to the sanctimonious perpetration of rotten tricks, i.e., antihuman acts which are followed by some sincere explanation that there is no other possible course of action. Indeed we know that something else can always be done, and at the very least the bureaucrats must be forced to admit that they are pulling rotten tricks because they do not have the courage to do otherwise. We have all heard, we have all said, "I would like to help you, but . . ." or "I am really sorry, but. . . ." Perhaps we should take more time to examine the components of that "but." Where do the qualifiers come from? To what extent are they in the nature of things and to what degree are they the product of the limited calculations of individual bureaucrats?

Jonathan Winters, a notable observer of worlds that never were, once had a routine about a man whose downfall began when he "started believing his own stuff." We, as the administrators and as the administered, have tended to believe too much of our own stuff. But it is not worthy of our belief until it is demonstrated that it is the only credible stuff available. Up to that quite improbable time, each one of us is free to accept or reject as much of it as our personal values will permit. Organizational morality is ultimately for the individual to decide. The crucial question is at what point one will be induced to conform to the needs for cooperative human effort. More bluntly, when do we sell out? I leave it to each person who comes in contact with administration to determine the proper price. I am content just as long as everyone realizes that some price is involved.

But an awareness of individual responsibility is only a way station to social responsibility. Simply to suggest that responsibility is an individual matter is to invite fanatics, their brains "hopping like a toad," to launch their crazy crusades. Already we have learned that the self-righteousness of bureaucrats in their bounded rationality is more than matched by the attitudes of a number of psychotics whose motto is "We will not be held responsible." Guerilla warfare against the established powers pits two equally deluded forces against each other, with society serving as a ravaged battleground. That is sheer irresponsibility.

The conflict must be conducted, as civilly as possible, within the arena provided by the sweet art, the master science of politics. A people working out the dimensions of their shared public space through politics ought to be the end result of any resurrection of individuality. The noblest form of responsibility is participation in the attainment of true rationality for an entire society; it is the cooperative speculation which should always precede cooperative effort. The establishment of, and resistance to, lesser and false versions of the rational through force can never succeed, or so painful experience should have taught us.

"Their souls are God's, the rest is mine," is reported to have been the attitude of Frederick the Great of Prussia toward his officials. That is probably the best deal we can expect. As long as our souls are our own, there is the possibility that we can resist the inspired manipulation of our bodies by the agents of administration. If we can understand that our soul is yet free, we can continue to grope toward the establishment of true responsibility to our fellow human beings.

REFERENCES

1 Charles Gilbert, "The Framework of Administrative Responsibility," *Journal of Politics,* 21 (1959), pp. 373–407.
2 The dialogue between the two professors is reprinted in several places, including Francis Rourke (ed.), *Bureaucratic Power in National Politics,* 2d ed. (Boston: Little, Brown, 1972).
3 Mark Nadel and Francis Rourke, "Bureaucracies," in Fred Greenstein and Nelson Polsby (eds.), *Handbook of Political Science,* vol. 5 (Reading, Mass.: Addison-Wesley, 1975), p. 428.
4 Henry Jacoby, *The Bureaucratization of the World* (Berkeley: University of California Press, 1973), p. 35.
5 *Field v. Clark,* 143 U.S. 649 (1892).
6 Ernest Gellhorn, *Administrative Law and Process in a Nutshell* (St. Paul, Minn.: West, 1972), p. 26.
7 Theodore Lowi, *The End of Liberalism* (New York: Norton, 1969), p. 155.
8 James Goulden, *The Superlawyers* (New York: Weybright and Talley, 1971), pp. 185–189.
9 Peter Woll, *Administrative Law* (Berkeley: University of California Press, 1963).
10 Judith Shklar, *Legalism* (Cambridge, Mass.: Harvard University Press, 1964).
11 Lewis Mainzer, *Political Bureaucracy* (Glenview, Ill.: Scott, Foresman, 1973), p. 45.
12 Emmette Redford, *The Regulatory Process* (Austin: University of Texas Press, 1969); Philippe Nonet, *Administrative Justice* (New York: Russell Sage, 1969).
13 Martin Shapiro, *The Supreme Court and Administrative Agencies* (New York: Free Press, 1968), p. 93.
14 Jim Hougan, *Decadence* (New York: Morrow, 1975), p. 69.
15 Peter Woll, "Administrative Law in the Seventies," *Public Administration Review,* 32 (1972), pp. 557–564; Roger Cramton, "Judicial Law Making and Administration," *Public Administration Review,* 36 (1976) pp. 551–555.
16 Fritz Scharpf, *Die politischen Kosten des Rechtsstaats* (Tübingen: J. C. B. Mohr, 1970).
17 Kent Weeks, *Ombudsmen around the World* (Berkeley, Calif.: Institute of Governmental Studies, 1973).
18 William Gwyn, "Transferring the Ombudsman," in Stanley Anderson (ed.), *Ombudsman for American Government?* (Englewood Cliffs, N.J.: Prentice-Hall, 1968).
19 Donald Rowat, "The Parliamentary Ombudsman: Should the Scandinavian Scheme Be Transplanted?" *International Review of Administrative Sciences,* 28 (1962), p. 405.
20 Herbert Kaufman, "Administrative Decentralization and Political Power," *Public Administration Review,* 29 (1969), p. 6.
21 Kent Weeks, "Public Servants in the New Zealand Ombudsman System," *Public Administration Review,* 29 (1969), pp. 633–638.
22 Quoted in Kenneth Olson, "The Service Function in the United States Congress," in A. de Grazia (ed.), *Congress* (Garden City, N.Y.: Anchor Books, 1967), p. 328.

23 Walter Gellhorn, *When Americans Complain* (Cambridge, Mass.: Harvard University Press, 1966), p. 80.
24 Victor Thompson, *Without Sympathy or Enthusiasm* (University: University of Alabama Press, 1975), pp. 62–64.
25 Larry Hill, "Institutionalization, the Ombudsman, and Bureaucracy," *American Political Science Review,* 68 (1974), p. 1085.
26 Herbert von Borch, *Obrigkeit und Widerstand* (Tübingen: J. C. B. Mohr, 1954), p. 6.
27 Ralph Nader, Peter Petkas, and Kate Blackwell (eds.), *Whistle Blowing* (New York: Bantam, 1972).
28 New York Times, *The White House Transcripts* (New York: Bantam, 1974), p. 83.
29 Charles Peters and Taylor Branch, *Blowing the Whistle* (New York: Praeger, 1972), p. 298.
30 O. Glenn Stahl, "Loyalty, Dissent, and Organizational Health," *The Bureaucrat,* 3 (1974), p. 165.
31 Irving Janis, *Victims of Groupthink* (Boston: Houghton Mifflin, 1972).
32 Edward Weisband and Thomas Franck, *Resignation in Protest* (New York: Grossman, 1975), p. 1.
33 Neil Sheehan, *The Arnheiter Affair* (New York: Dell, 1973).
34 Barbara Garson, *MacBird!* (New York: Grassy Knoll, 1966), p. 23.

Epilogue

This book has no ending—at least not in the sense of a dynamite summation of all that has been said. The entire book is itself a conclusion about and summary of a large number of ideas concerning public administration. The whole effort, then, is intended as a beginning for those eager to learn how the modern world works.

But after the beginning, what is the next step? One innocent of the realities of academia might assume that the Yellow Brick Road leads directly to a department of political science or a school of public administration. Wrong! The wizards to be found there seem a particularly inept bunch when it comes to grappling with the central dilemma of this book. In fact, the academic disciplines of political science and public administration are more valuable as proof of the deterioration of knowledge in modern society than they are as a source of assurance that humanity shall prevail.

It is ironic that, at about the time the dichotomy between politics and administration was seen as too artificial, there began the estrangement of public administration from political science. Whether public administration, the child, was thrown out of the house of its parent or left of its own accord is of interest only to those anxious to carry on ancient feuds. The main point is that neither has done very well on its own. That is, neither has done much to advance our understanding of the administrative society. Political science, in its desire to be a "real science," has turned itself into the world's oldest floating trivia game. As an aggressively "practical" discipline, public administration has helped to reinforce the bureaucratic reality. Both are destined to become dead sciences, for without an appreciation of politics, administrative questions are, at best, technical problems. And without an appreciation of administration, political questions are sterile exercises.

Not that public administration, as an academic field, has had a rough time of it. Since the split, it has come upon fat and happy times. Schools of public administration, some housed in gaudy new tabernacles, have sprung up on several campuses. The National Association of Schools of Public Affairs and Administration (NASPAA) is rapidly growing in size and influence. Government grants and contracts for research are increasingly available. Most important, because of a renewed interest in vocational opportunities, students are deserting political science and the other social sciences and are turning to areas which appear to provide some sort of job license upon graduation. They mean new faculty, new courses, new power within the academic community at a time when higher education in general is facing retrenchment. The danger, of course, is that public administration might be content with its role of cranking out minor-league mandarins and thus lose sight of its true educational function—that of teaching people about the larger implications of administration. Schools of public administration may wind up being as intellectually creative as manual arts high schools.

If public administration were both wise and magnanimous, it would welcome back into its house the wayward parent. The continued separation of the two fields is a foolish waste of effort. Each discipline will have to reinvent the other if it is not to become completely irrelevant. Already there are signs that a reconciliation is slowly emerging. Political science has had its fling with the development of quantitative tools, but it lost touch with the reality which one might presume justified its existence, namely, the reality of politics. Political scientists are now rediscovering the world of administration as the study of "public policy" becomes a major focal point for the discipline. The investigation of the formation, articulation, and implementation of public policy cannot proceed without an awareness of the administrative component. The common ground for a reunion of the two disciplines is now clearly visible.

However, the coming reunion of politics and administration could turn out to be bad news indeed for society. Given that both disciplines are still infected by scientism, it is quite possible that public policy will become a form of massive social engineering of the type described in previous chapters. That is, the scholars may very well commit treason to speculation by concentrating on narrow research topics in order to develop the "New,

Improved" welfare, transportation, energy, resources, or educational policy. The improvements, naturally, will be in terms of refinements in the existing administrative reality.

It is up to the confused, perplexed, and afraid (including, it is hoped, the readers of this book) to keep the reunited discipline intellectually honest. It will be easy for the new superdiscipline of public policy to become complacent in its work of rationalizing further the present system. As a citizen or as an administrator, it will be up to you to keep things in turmoil by use of the one sure universal solvent of academic cant—the asking of the question "So what?" Unless the answer to that question concedes the existence of a world outside the boundary of administrative rationality, we will know it is not an answer at all.

Name Index

Page numbers followed by *r* indicate superior-numbered text citations corresponding to end-of-chapter references.

Subject Index